Reading like an Australian writer

BELINDA CASTLES is the author of four novels: *Bluebottle*, *Hannah and Emil*, *The River Baptists* and *Falling Woman*, and winner of the *Australian*/Vogel's and Asher literary awards. She teaches writing at the University of Sydney.

What a generous and necessary anthology this is. Enriching and illuminating, it offers layer upon layer of interest. In unravelling their own passions as readers, the writers in this collection reveal, too, their own writerly processes. Individually, the essays here offer tools for the writer and for the reader. Together, they form a communal praise song to Australian literature in its many guises. I'll be returning to these pages repeatedly – for reading lists, for writerly wisdom, and for sheer pleasure.

KATHRYN HEYMAN

Belinda Castles has produced – through canny, insightful curating – an invaluable new resource for studious writers and devoted readers alike. The essays collected within these pages not only serve to document contemporary Australian literature, they actively work to sustain its future.

SAM TWYFORD-MOORE

This is a timely book, bringing fine and inventive reading strategies to so much significant and personally cherished writing.

BRENDA WALKER

Reading like an Australian writer

Edited by Belinda Castles

NEWSOUTH

A NewSouth book

Published by
NewSouth Publishing
University of New South Wales Press Ltd
University of New South Wales
Sydney NSW 2052
AUSTRALIA
newsouthpublishing.com

 A catalogue record for this
book is available from the
National Library of Australia

ISBN   9781742236704 (paperback)
        9781742245294 (ebook)
        9781742249858 (ePDF)

Internal design Josephine Pajor-Markus
Cover design Madeleine Kane
Cover iIllustration Michelle Pereira

This project is supported by the Copyright Agency's Cultural Fund and
The University of Sydney School of Literature, Art and Media.

Contents

Introduction   1

Kinship in fiction and the genre blur of *Swallow the Air* as novel in stories   Ellen van Neerven   7

Rhythm and play in *That Deadman Dance* by Kim Scott Julienne van Loon   13

A big sunny shack: *Cosmo Cosmolino* by Helen Garner Tegan Bennett Daylight   26

Short stories ... but linked: Steven Amsterdam's *Things We Didn't See Coming*   Ryan O'Neill   42

Reading crises, writing crisis   Rose Michael and Jane Rawson   56

The sad old flesh: How we use non-human characters to interrogate humanity   Anna Spargo-Ryan   75

Starting from place: An introduction to a different way of thinking   Felicity Castagna   88

Read to find yourself Peter Polites   100

Postcards to Charlotte Wood: Revisiting *The Natural Way of Things*   Ashley Hay   112

Fearless: On Christos Tsiolkas   Nigel Featherstone   125

Caught in the rip: The first seven pages of Tim Winton's *Breath* Cate Kennedy   137

Ending, unfurling: *The Life to Come* by Michelle de Kretser Roanna Gonsalves   152

An uneasy anticipation: Tension in MJ Hyland's novels Angela Meyer   167

Structure in Nam Le's 'Love and honour and pity and pride and compassion and sacrifice'   Fiona McFarlane   184

If you see the Buddha in suburbia kill him: *Anguli Ma:*
  A gothic tale by Chi Vu Hoa Pham 193

Sabotage and repair: Intertextuality in Carrie Tiffany's
  Exploded View Maria Takolander 207

Structure, serpents and Serena McGarry: Kate Jennings' *Snake*
  Debra Adelaide 219

'Not crying now, but brilliant-eyed': Epiphany in Harrower's
  'The fun of the fair' Emily Maguire 233

How to build a glass church: Peter Carey's *Oscar and Lucinda*
  Belinda Castles 244

A metaphysical meeting place: *Sixty Lights* by Gail Jones
  Irini Savvides 259

Lines of sight: Living images in the short fiction of
  Gerald Murnane Stephanie Bishop 272

An obsidian mirror: David Malouf's *Ransom* A.S. Patrić 286

Ten thoughts on fiction that slays: Reading Julie Koh's
  satire in a post-truth pandemic' Beth Yahp 297

A manual for writers: *Elizabeth Costello* Nicholas Jose 314

Everywhen in everything: Reading *Carpentaria* like an
  Aboriginal writer Mykaela Saunders 325

References 344

Contributors 353

Acknowledgments 359

Index 360

Introduction

'Like most – maybe all – writers, I learned to write by writing and by example, by reading books.' – Francine Prose, *Reading Like a Writer*

'*Monkey Grip* changed reading for me. It was more than just the feeling of recognition ... For the first time I was consciously learning about *writing*.' – Tegan Bennett Daylight, 'A phone call to Helen Garner' in Debra Adelaide (ed.), *The Simple Act of Reading*

All writers begin as readers. And one day, as for musicians, dancers and painters, a connection sparks: the magic we absorb wants to emerge in a new form, shaped by our own minds and bodies. We respond, touching the pencil to the page to begin our story. As we go on this alchemy becomes purposeful, intended – we search out the elemental mixture and process that will conjure gold. Reading takes on a particular attentiveness as we develop an interest, a stake: in method and effect. How, we ask the writing, are you making me think the things I am thinking; feel the things I am feeling?

I call myself an Australian novelist, though I was not born here. More than one place made me – a common story for our writers. The voices in this book often have complex relationships to the country from which they write. Australian writing speaks in its many accents of the diversity and unique history of this country: its thefts, losses and struggles, its distinctive sensory experiences, its imagined futures.

When we read Australian stories we see what it is possible to say, and perhaps what still needs to be said.

The array of contributors and stories in these essays gives us an insight into the kinds of conversations taking place in Australia between writers and particular kinds of readers – those who themselves make things out of words. It begins to show the skeins of voices and experience in Australian stories and is a record, at a point in time and in the midst of various contingencies, of a particular editor making connections. As a picture of Australian fiction, it is energetically incomplete, part of a conversation that is always moving forwards. Nicholas Jose has called Australian literature a 'body in time': that is, 'a connective body of material, an entity that moves beyond the individual to a community of writers and readers linked through history and geography and culture ... a set of relationships' (104). This book is one such set of relationships, made through reading and writing in the context of Australia. To repurpose a term that Roanna Gonsalves applies to the fiction of Michelle de Kretser, it is a conversation that is not closed, or finished, but 'unfurling'.

The writers of these essays are distinguished writers of fiction, and also teach and mentor others writing their own stories. They show us how they read and in doing so give us two gifts: models for attentive reading – for 'reading as a writer' – and the fascinating results of their attentions. They offer us insights into their own ways of processing experience at the same time as illuminating the 'close-up magic' of stories (as Cate Kennedy has it in her essay on Tim Winton). Most students of creative writing will recognise this mode. They too are asked to write reflectively, exploring the texts that have meaning for them as they work towards their own writerly ambitions. When they do this, they also give this double reading, showing what is important in their own work by where they place their attention in the writing of others.

There is an electric hum in this meeting place of reader–writer. We witness the reading mind at work, its thoughts laid out on the page.

We enlarge our sense of what it is to be a reader and a thinking person alive in this world. We encounter different minds, different approaches to sometimes familiar stories, and our reading attention is renewed.

It has been a difficult year in which to write, and the traces of this difficulty are threaded through the collection. The pieces grapple not only with matters of craft but with method more broadly, and existentially. How does one write in such times? As always, we look to our reading for help.

Julienne van Loon, writing on Kim Scott's *That Deadman Dance*, tells us that stories 'become blueprints for methods of thinking' and we see this enacted not only in her writerly appreciation for this novel, but in several of the essays here. (This phrase could be said to articulate a philosophy for the collection.) Rose Michael and Jane Rawson explore the fiction of viral and climate catastrophe to think through our possible futures. A.S. Patrić approaches David Malouf's *Ransom* as an 'obsidian mirror' in which we might see our own times reflected through myths of Ancient Greece. And Beth Yahp reads satire as a way to process this post-truth world in Julie Koh's 'fiction that slays'.

A revelatory consideration of time, and its handling as a base material of story, emerges in several of the readings. Fiona McFarlane considers, with the insight of years of teaching Nam Le's 'Love and honour and pity and pride and compassion and sacrifice', his expert orchestration of the 'disorderly time' of diasporic experience. Hoa Pham reads Chi Vu's *Anguli Ma* through the lens of Buddhist dimensions of time and 'interbeing'. Roanna Gonsalves considers how the experience of time, the anticipation of finale, works in Michelle de Kretser's *The Life to Come*, with its unfurling sense of an ending. And Mykaela Saunders reads for us her favourite novel, Alexis Wright's *Carpentaria*, 'a text that centres our ways of knowing, being and doing', illustrating the Aboriginal concept of 'everywhen'.

Two of the essays here ask us to consider the limits of identification and empathy. Ashley Hay writes postcards to Charlotte Wood in an act of writerly gratitude, and yet one of this essay's most profound lessons is in its appreciation for Wood's resistance to 'relatability', her encouragement to: 'Put yourself in the space where you're uncomfortable, where you have nothing in common with whoever else is there, and find a means of being there'. Anna Spargo-Ryan, writing on animals in contemporary Australian stories, shows us that: 'In literature, we have an opportunity to see what we are when written in the context of the Other'. Discomfortingly, as we blunder through history in our deeply flawed manner, what these animal characters and narrators offer us is the feeling that 'we have been *seen*'.

In several of these essays the contributor's role as a particular kind of literary critic comes to the fore. The pleasures and interests of the text are narrated with a gentle patience that feels like a way of being in the world, and which must surely infuse their own writing of fiction. These golden threads are found everywhere in the collection but here are some examples. In Stephanie Bishop's lucid accompaniment to the meanderings of Gerald Murnane she engages in a 'kind of attention that can tolerate a maximum of uncertainty and instability' – an attention that is 'both loose and sharp'. Nicholas Jose considers JM Coetzee's *Elizabeth Costello* as 'its author's work of arrival' as an Australian novelist, after a long and distinguished career in South Africa, and offers the highest form of appeciation: 'As a manual for writers it teaches us that the novel can be anything'. And Maria Takolander begins her sensitive reading of Carrie Tiffany's *Exploded View* by placing intertextuality and influence at the forefront of the writer's craft, reminding us that the Ancient Greeks experienced '*communitas* through repeated engagement with a communal repository of stories'. These essays (all the essays) remind me of the distinctive pleasures of reading, this quiet communion we return to all our lives.

Fiction takes many forms and some essays illuminate the house in which the story lives. Debra Adelaide's loving memoir of reading the novella *Snake*, by Kate Jennings, shows just how expansive short forms can be, how their detonations can echo through a reader's life. In his immaculate dissection of Steven Amsterdam's *Things We Didn't See Coming*, Ryan O'Neill shows how it is possible to build a world and a character gracefully through glimpses and gaps in these 'short stories ... but linked'. Tegan Bennett Daylight invites us irresistibly to wander through the 'big sunny shack' of Helen Garner's *Cosmo Cosmolino* (as Tim Winton called it) to end with the eternal question of what makes a novel a novel.

There is a deep, geeky pleasure for me in discussions of the inner workings of stories, of what Margot Livesy calls the 'hidden machinery'. Machinery is an apt metaphor: imagine a beautifully designed car winding along a magnificent clifftop road, clinging hair-raisingly to the tarmac, leaving an aura of dangerous glamour behind it along with a trailing scarf. Under the hood is its concealed magic, and here we are, after its thrilling journey, standing around it, rags over our shoulders, a secret society of nodding mechanics.

Several of these essays reveal the gorgeous engineering to us. In Angela Meyer's meticulous detailing of tension in the novels of MJ Hyland; in Emily Maguire's stunningly clear charting of epiphany in Elizabeth Harrower's 'The fun of the fair'; in Felicity Castagna's fascinating account of place in Alexis Wright and Luke Carman, and in Cate Kennedy's exhilarating reading of the opening pages of Tim Winton's *Breath*, we are invited to share the hard-won knowledge of expert commentators. I, in my own ways, have tried to look inside the lovely machine of Peter Carey's *Oscar and Lucinda*. Perhaps though, for all our tinkering, stories retain a core of mystery, whose effects, happily, we only partly understand.

Another kind of reading has emerged in these essays too, the experience of writing as a light, passed on. I have noticed it more now than I would at other times. Ellen van Neerven writes about kinship in fiction and in the reading of it, recalling her discovery of Tara June Winch's *Swallow the Air* with another Aboriginal student at university

– the revelation of 'finding voices that spoke to us'. Peter Polites, as a gay Greek-Australian writer, tells us of the secret attraction of reading books in the library that he didn't want on his lending record, and that 'one of the reasons I read is to find myself in Australian writing'. Nigel Featherstone writes of the way Christos Tsiolkas inspires us 'to invest all of ourselves, including our bodies' in our writing, to give it everything, fearlessly. Irini Savvides writes of her professor at university, the novelist Gail Jones, and her novel *Sixty Lights*. In the darkness of lockdown, at the time of Greek Easter, she recalls the communality of past celebrations, invoking the lights of Jones's novel. 'In its flickering and sparks', she writes, 'we transfer light to light and the shadows disperse, if momentarily'.

I did not know, when I began to commission these essays, that what I was embarking upon was an act of literary community, that its meaning would be in its collectivity. We write alone, and we read alone, but we do not remain alone. Community is made, shaped and deepened by shared enthusiasms, enacted and ritualised into a form of love. I thank the writers of these essays, and of the stories they write about. I welcome you, the reader, to extend the network of stories that make sense of our lives. In our reading and our writing, we make our own *communitas*. It is for you to enrich our storehouse, to keep our writing alive.

Belinda Castles
Sydney, 2020

Kinship in fiction and the genre blur of *Swallow the Air* as novel in stories

Ellen van Neerven

I grew up just out of Brisbane in the late 1990s. In the outer north-western suburbs, top of the agenda was sport. My currency was my football ability, which got me places in representative teams, and I caught my first flight to Mackay for the state championships when I was thirteen. Most of my time was spent going to training or practising in the backyard. I spent a lot of time outdoors.

There was no real incentive to be engaged in the arts. I would only enter Meanjin/Brisbane's art quarter (named after London's West End, but with the Jagera and Turrbal name of Kurilpa – place of the water rat), at the age of sixteen, when Mum worked at State Library of Queensland. It was there I saw coffee shops for the first time – outside of the Queensland chain cafe *The Coffee Club*, where me and my friends would go for hot chocolates after our church group on a Friday evening because it was the only place open at eight o'clock at night. In West End there were artisan bakeries too, beyond the *Bakers Delight* chain available in my suburb, and Greek, Italian, Middle Eastern and

South-East Asian food. West End was only a thirty-minute drive but it might as well have been Greece compared to where I grew up. Here cafes were open to midnight, and there were bookshops and theatres. I did not know then the significance of Kurilpa/West End to Aboriginal people. But I soon would.

I liked writing from an early age thanks to Mum bringing us books back from the library. Due to her work, we grew up believing in libraries as places where our imaginations could thrive. When I read, I also imagined my own worlds. As I've said in other places, I read no Indigenous-authored books at school. None at university either. And as far as I was aware, neither Mum nor any of my numerous extended family members (I come from a large Mununjali Yugambeh family – we are all descendants of Bilin Bilin, who survived the invasion by negotiating the safety of his people with the settler-invaders) read Indigenous-authored books, so I have concluded that these works were deliberately made elusive to young Australian students. There are alarmingly few people who know who the Ngarrindjeri man on our fifty-dollar note is – David Unaipon – and if they do know, very few know he is considered our first published Aboriginal writer. His work was not first attributed to him, but to anthropologist William Ramsay Smith in 1930. It would be seventy years later that his writing would be repatriated and its author correctly acknowledged.

As a young mixed-race Aboriginal queer person growing up in Queensland I felt a deep psychological shadow on my being. I did not see anyone who represented me on television, in movies, or in books. I didn't understand the strange alienation I felt as one of very few Indigenous students at my school, even though I was part of such a strong culture and lineage to south-east Queensland, my Country, my ancestral home.

All this is backdrop to the transformative moment of reading *Swallow the Air* by Tara June Winch for the first time.

I was with Yasmin, a talented first-year student from Rocky, who I was tutoring in a computer room with no windows. I was in my second year. Yasmin is now one of my most longstanding friends but at the time, we were just two First Nations womxn from Queensland studying creative writing. Yasmin and I were slowly discovering the rich canon of Aboriginal and Torres Strait Islander writing together. We were finding voices that spoke to us. We both loved *Swallow the Air* and used it as inspiration for our own fiction. This young voice spoke to us more than any had previously.

Swallow the Air (2006) is broken up into twenty chapters, some of them slight, just a few pages long. It follows the character of May from the ages of ten to seventeen, starting with the death of her mother in the self-titled opening chapter, 'Swallow the air'. The novel-in-stories flows from family members, using kinship as a guiding thread.

May and her brother Billy grow up in Wollongong, as did the author. The language Tara uses to describe the coastal setting is beautiful and lyrical and often tinged with metaphor. Billy, older by a few years, disappears after a fight with Aunty's violent boyfriend, leaving May alone. In the chapter 'Cocoon', May remembers nights by the fire with Billy and her mother, and the catching and cooking of fish. The emotive language and the young voice is consistent throughout the story as May moves from place to place, searching both for her white father and her Wiradjuri mother's belonging. She stays with mob in 'The Block' in Redfern before going out to western New South Wales in search of her Wiradjuri family. She hasn't had any contact with her extended family before, and she doesn't know how to find them. She goes on a winding journey and ends up in an unexpected place. In the chapter 'Country', the relative she meets tells her, 'There is a big missing hole between this place and the place you're looking for' (181–2). This also plays into the reader's romanticised expectations that a return to Country will bring the story a happy resolution. A relative of May's continues, 'It's gone. It was taken away. We weren't told, love; we weren't allowed to be Aboriginal' (182). This statement signals the damage past policies and institutionalisation have inflicted on the present. But it also offers a chance for a younger generation to understand the past. *Swallow the Air* ends with May's realisation that Country lives within her and her brother, mother and aunt, allowing her to feel strong in her identity without the shame of not living or growing up on Country. We end the novel where it began, on the coast, with May, Billy and Aunty.

The book has won so many awards it is difficult to list them all, but it began by winning the 2004 Queensland Literary Awards – the David Unaipon Unpublished Indigenous Writers Award – in manuscript form, with the original title *Dust on the Waterglass*. Tara was in her early twenties at the time. The UQP editor Tara worked with, Sue Abbey, a white American-Australian, would coincidentally be my mentor shortly after I graduated from university, giving me the tools to become an editor of Indigenous-authored work. After *Swallow the Air* was published, it went on to win the Nita May Dobbie Award, the New South Wales Premier's Literary Award (UTS Award for New Writing), and the 2006 Victorian Premier's Literary Awards (Prize for Indigenous Writing). From the review quotes I've selected you can see the profound effect it had on critical readers: 'Winch's prose is gloriously idiosyncratic ... it works triumphantly' (*The Advertiser*); 'Sometimes in life you are lucky enough to stumble upon a book that irrevocably changes you and profoundly changes how you experience the world. Tara June Winch's *Swallow the Air* is one of those rare books' (*Courier-Mail*), and: 'Extraordinary, too, is her economy of language and her ability to take the reader to the heart of a matter swiftly on the wing of simple words – I was weeping by page nine' (the *Sunday Telegraph*).

Recently, while speaking about a very First Nations practice of writing relational novels-in-stories (see Aunty Jeanine Leane's *Purple Threads* and Aunty Gayle Kennedy's *Me, Antman and Fleabag* as further examples), I introduced a piece: 'Cloud busting' from *Swallow the Air* to university students at RMIT. The tutor told me it was hard to hold back tears when reading this work. I can't overstate how emotion lives within these pages.

Swallow the Air is a breath of fresh air from an author who lists her influences as the *Charcoal Lane* album by Uncle Archie Roach and Uncle Tony Birch's body of work. Like these two Elders, Tara writes about fracture and repair with beautiful sensitivity. The child's voice is brought to life in Tara's characterisation of May, who is willing to see the best in people. She is warmly embraced and cared for by community Elder Aunty Joyce in Redfern, and they immediately share a strong intergenerational bond.

I wrote in my *Australian Book Review* review of Tara's Miles Franklin-winning novel, *The Yield*, which is partly written in reclaimed Wiradjuri language, that she is not afraid to play with the form and shape of fiction. I wrote this about *The Yield* but I could easily have been writing about *Swallow the Air*: 'Australian rural novels are often humourless sketches with characters more like caricatures, grimly serious or full of despair. Refreshingly, the characters in *The Yield* are capable of communion, humour, and dignity despite tragedy, sexual violence, and substance abuse. In this deft novel of slow-moving water, they are borne by love, not pity'.

At the time of writing, *Swallow the Air* is fifteen years old. I have no doubt it has a lot more power to give its future readers and writers. When I touch its pages, I'm reminded of Yasmin; reading this book with her, and Yasmin's own lyrical and poignant prose, inspired by Tara's, but undoubtedly her own. I remember a beautiful line in one of Yasmin's micro fictions, poetically tracing the moon and the saltwater of her Country. I hope my thought of her finds her writing and creating. Another one of my kinship sisters, and another saltwater woman, Frej, is reading the book currently for the first time. I'm on my way to see her in Kurilpa for a cuppa, following the river, where thick dense rainforest used to grow, walking down Boundary Street, which Samuel Wagan Watson describes as 'the line ... the limit/where the dark-skin were told—/DO NOT CROSS!', history tinged with violence but also pride, past Whynot Street, the title of an Oodgeroo Noonuccal poem against gentrification, feeling the protest in the soil beyond the bitumen many generations strong. I'm almost at my saltwater sister's house. I can't wait to hear what she has found in the tide of the stories.

Rhythm and play in
That Deadman Dance
by Kim Scott

Julienne van Loon

This essay was written on the land of the Woi wurrung, and Boon wurrung language groups of the Eastern Kulin nations – land never ceded – and I wish to pay my respects to their elders, past and present, as well as to acknowledge and pay my respects to the Traditional Custodians of lands and waters across Australia, particularly the Noongar, whose language and stories are depicted in *That Deadman Dance* and discussed here.

The pleasure of reading

As writers, language is our medium. We can talk about 'painting' with words, or 'shaping' sentences or 'composing' scenes, but these are metaphors carried across from other forms of arts practice. While writing novels has a lot in common with other expressive art forms, reading Kim Scott's *That Deadman Dance* reminds me that what we are working with as novelists is language in its written form: letters joined together to make words, words joined together to make sentences,

sentences joined together to make paragraphs, then chapters, then whole novels.

The experience of reading, of course, is never exclusively about language. Sometimes we achieve the pleasure of reading with such gusto that we forget all about the words; we forget altogether about the artifice of language, we are thinking instead about the relationship between one character and another, or about the dramatic event that hasn't happened yet but we're pretty sure will happen before the next chapter ends, or sometimes we're just caught up in the sheer pleasure of forgetting all about ourselves for a while by seeming to dwell inside someone else's head. I love all those kinds of reading pleasures, too.

But the pleasure of reading as a writer is often very much to do with language and its usage. We look into one another's books and see how the strangeness of words on paper intrigues other writers too, in a way that reminds us artfully of the very thing we're playing with in writing: not clay but words. No matter which language we speak or read or write, it is always a language introduced to us by others, and even though we may sometimes think of a language as something to which we belong, few of us would ever claim to belong completely, that is, to have mastered the language(s) we use. It is also an odd quest to seek to find a home inside of language, though plenty of us go looking for one there. Perhaps that is in part what we do – foolheartedly, endearingly – as readers of novels.

Kim Scott's novel *That Deadman Dance* is an example of the kind of book I take pleasure in reading because of the way the author plays with and investigates language and its usage. The first word on the first page of this book is *Kaya*. It is a very old word in the Noongar oral tradition, but it is still pretty new to the art form we know as the novel written in English. In Noongar, *Kaya* means something between 'hello' and welcome, and sometimes it simply means 'yes'.

Importantly, on the first page of Scott's novel, it's not just *anyone* writing that word – *Kaya* – with a piece of damp chalk on a thin wedge of slate. It's the protagonist of *That Deadman Dance* – Bobby Wabalanginy – and he's thinking as he does it about phonetics, about writing, about the power of this thing we call language:

Kaya.

Writing such a word, Bobby Wabalanginy couldn't help but smile. Nobody ever done writ that before, he thought. Nobody ever writ *hello* or *yes* that way!

Roze a wail ...

Bobby Wabalanginy wrote with damp chalk, brittle as weak bone. Bobby wrote on a thin piece of slate. Moving between languages, Bobby wrote on stone. (1)

Those of us not all that familiar with Noongar language would probably stumble (twice) in those first few lines of the novel to articulate the word Wabalanginy. *Kaya* is easy, but *Wabalanginy* ... how would you say it? The English-speaking characters in the novel can't pronounce Wabalanginy either, nor easily remember it. They usually drop it off the end, and just call the protagonist by his English name. Bobby is a moniker they've given the boy themselves, and it doesn't require them to register a worldview different to their own. One of Bobby's elders, Menak, confides to Bobby the meaning of the name given him by his own people: 'Wabalanginy, Menak had recently said to him, means all of us playing together' (350).

That Deadman Dance describes early encounters between the Noongar and colonial settlers in Kinjarling, or the area now known as Albany, Western Australia, during the 1800s, but those first encounters are not just physical, they are also first encounters with different forms of knowledge, including language, and for a Noongar boy like Bobby, with the peculiar technology of writing. And once readers are fully away with the reading, and we're inside Bobby's head as protagonist, we're looking into all this with an Indigenous inflection, that is, we are looking through a Noongar lens. Questions we are prompted to consider expand beyond the practice of writing in English to include the performative aspects of Noongar storytelling traditions, including enactments, re-enactments, and parodies of first contact rendered through dance and song. Can writing something down make it happen, the way singing a particular song about whales, in the Noongar tradition, can help to bring forth the seasonal arrival of these animals in the bay? Bobby plays with these knowledge encounters through the written and spoken word, and Scott, as novelist, is also engaged in and driven by a form of play with words.

On the first page of the novel, Bobby is 'trying out the potential of writing' while Kim Scott commences trying out the potential of the novel for carrying us into thinking about first contact in Western Australia in the 1800s through the eyes of early Indigenous peoples. Scott is also asking us to imagine a question of another sort: how might it have all gone very differently? The area in which the novel is set has been said to be a 'friendly frontier'. What might it have looked like, this friendliness? What kinds of conditions, what kinds of people, sparked that friendliness at first contact, and then witnessed its decline over time?

The pleasure and necessity of play

The thing I most admire about *That Deadman Dance* is its playfulness. This playfulness is a characteristic both of the narration and the central character Bobby Wabalanginy. It's also stylistically what we have come to expect of Scott, even in the midst of what can be some pretty sobering subject matter: his treatment of eugenics in his earlier novel *Benang* is a case in point. At the beginning of *That Deadman*

Dance, Bobby Wabalanginy is often described as 'a child, a boy' and we accept his playfulness as arising, like child's play, out of a pliable and adventurous mind, but it also arises out of 'a most intelligent curiosity' (an observation of the Noongar employed by the friendly colonist Dr Cross and later parodied by Bobby in his own writing) (39). Bobby has a particular talent for improvisation. He is 'laughing and loved' and is described as knowing nothing of fear until he is a much older man (67). As 'a light-hearted laughing fellow' but also someone who observes and can remember stories very well, and can carry them off in dance with a 'concentrated power' well recognised by his elders, Bobby Wabalanginy takes on a bit of a magical quality too, because it sometimes seems like he's everywhere in those early contact stories, witnessing every key event, riding on the shoulders of whales and humans alike (59): 'Was it really Bobby? No matter who, it was a very young, barely formed consciousness, and watching from some safe place, somewhere else' (72).

Scott is playing with Bobby being more than one consciousness for several reasons. The name 'Bobby' appears in the colonial archives so many times to refer to male Noongar subjects – just another whitefella name given to every second Noongar boy. It is probably drawn from the English slang name for policeman and applied comically, a long way from London, for representatives of a people whose power in their own landscape is being progressively denied. Scott is reclaiming all those so-called Bobbies from the archives and giving them back their power, their dignity, their skill. He is engaging in what Australian literature specialist Philip Mead calls a 'a kind of alternating documentary current ... always resisting and probing the imperialisms embedded in ... explorers' journals, settler diaries and letters ... for their bias and prejudice' (149). But there is something else going on too. For Bobby's pluralism belongs to a cultural understanding radically different to the European Enlightenment notion of contained selfhood and the imperialist fantasy of the self-made man who is in charge of his own future. Bobby's selfhood is porous: he is a character imaginatively capable of 'knowing' and 'being' well beyond his own skin.

As a reader I am porous, too. When I read myself into Bobby, I am the proud dancer, the skilful singer, the gifted whaler. I am the bringer together of black and white, I am his naïve confidence in sharing, his enthusiasm for learning new things. I want Bobby's faith in friendship, I want his faith in joy and belonging to Country, and his interest in the ways of the 'horizon' people. As a reader, I too am playing. In the Author's Note provided at the end of the novel, Scott outlines some of his intentions with *That Deadman Dance*, and in particular his aims in depicting the early-contact Noongar community:

> I wanted to build a story from their confidence, their inclusiveness and sense of play, and their readiness to appropriate new cultural forms – language and songs, guns and boats – as soon as they became available. Believing themselves manifestations of a spirit of place impossible to conquer, they appreciated reciprocity and the nuances of cross-cultural exchange. (398)

Scott has also spoken about this playfulness and humour in his fiction writing as a method that 'defuses some of the hurtfulness' that exists in the difficult history of Indigenous dispossession. 'It also seems gutsy to *play* in that context', he told the novelist Charlotte Wood, not only because it is difficult to do, but also because it seems 'very necessary' (quoted in Wood, 348). He acknowledges the idea that playing with difficult material might seem inappropriate to some, because the harshest aspects of history can be such a source of hurt, but he finds himself compelled to do so. I find this leaning into playfulness courageous, yes, but also remarkable. For in the space it creates for us as readers – a space of humour and fluency – we are more than a little disarmed.

Play is widely acknowledged in scholarly literatures including psychology, biology, ludology and education as being a deeply necessary aspect of the human experience. The neurologist Stuart Brown has observed, for example, that the opposite of play is not work, it is depression (126). The biologist Robert Fagen has posited that play in animals of all ages is a key enabler of species survival; it makes risk both possible and palatable (quoted in Sutton-Smith, 2). Further, it is a source of joy. Imaginative writing, such as fiction, is also an inherently playful art form, and as a reader I respond positively to work that plays with my own expectations not just about 'what happens next' but about form, being and meaning.

What *That Deadman Dance* can teach us about writing

That Deadman Dance is a book about literacy. As Australian Studies scholar Maggie Nolan has noted, it's about literacy in the broadest sense, that is, 'the ability to use and interpret language, images, performance and other means to understand symbolic systems of a culture', as well as in the narrower sense, to do with mechanics of writing, spelling, phonetics and syntax ('Shedding', 126). Like me, and many other writers I know, Bobby is fascinated by the alphabet and its potential to capture and carry meaning. He moves between the languages of Noongar and English mostly with ease, and he is at home with technologies of writing in a way not shared by some of the settlers he befriends, several of whom are illiterate whaling labourers and ex-convicts. 'The alphabet may be tracks, trails and traces of what we said', he ponders, at one point, always deeply interested in the relation between the written word and material forms (Scott, 165). He ponders, too, the capacity of writing to bring things into being. The entrepreneurial 'pioneer' Geordie Chaine, for example, is constantly making lists of 'THINGS TO DO' – 'Choose land, school children (?), lease island for rabbits (?)' (41) – and over time the 'settlement' the man has in mind does indeed take shape.

Is it because he wrote it down? Sometimes, Bobby Wabalanginy ('Even his name: Wabarlungiyn? Warbarlung-in-y? Bobby.') seems positively intoxicated by the possibilities of putting pen to paper (156). During school lessons with Mrs Chaine:

> He ran ink over the pages of that journal; made lines, prints, laid traces of what was happening. It was like he was moving, following, making tracks of time so that later – further along – they'd tell him, if not where he was, then what he'd been doing. (289)

Later, Bobby will experiment with the prophetic power of writing himself, making the whales come to the bay by writing about them, and reinforcing that relation by making it 'happen again and again in seasons to come' (5). Elsewhere he posits that in learning to read and write alongside the newcomers, both adults and children, they are 'all learning the play of putting their thoughts and sounds on paper together' (167). This understanding of writing as a form of wishful, imaginative, playful and communal thinking is very familiar to writers of fiction – world-makers with words – and causes me to ponder, usefully, the question of what fiction (or the novel) is for, and further, what it can do or become for readers and writers who engage with it.

The musicality of words and sentences

I have also found instructive lessons in *That Deadman Dance* to do with rhythm and the musicality of prose. There is a beauty to the writing that is concerned not just with precision about word choice drawn from careful observation, but also with the sounds of words and phrases as they join together to form sentences, and the patterning of different kinds of sentences, of differing lengths, in order to create poetic rhythm across paragraphs. Consider the following passage, which describes the coming of the whale season:

> Bobby saw the whale spouts sunlit on the grey sea, showing like blossoms, and flowers were appearing too, all across the dunes behind him, the undulating land beyond. Whales came, and creeks rushed to sea to meet them; kangaroos put their backs to the wind and their heads inland, toward sunrise; frogs rose from the ground, pulses calling.
>
> Diving into the ocean today, Bobby heard the whales singing. They sang for him. (274)

The care taken to get the rhythm right here, to make the prose itself sing, is born of a careful attention to poetics, and it is an attention that lessens, to some degree, the emphasis on plot and character we see in other kinds of novels. Reading group members have sometimes described *That Deadman Dance* as 'a difficult read' and Scott seems aware of perceptions among some readers that his writing is not always easy to engage with (Nolan, 'Reading', 6). He acknowledges that it is not a plot-driven narrative. 'If there is a plot, it's strategic thinking versus something like creativity', he told Anne Brewster in an interview (234). Later, in conversation with Charlotte Wood, Scott said that the 'savouring of rhythm' in his prose is 'a sensual sort of thing' closely related to singing and to dance (quoted in Wood, 349). The poetics of the prose alongside and as a companion to the often 'difficult' subject matter works to remarkable effect in *That Deadman Dance*. Consider this description of the careless exposure of an important Noongar character's gravesite, some years beyond his death:

> The original, still raw grave was hastily filled. A dog ran away with something in its jaws; a cat hunching its back and showing its teeth,

would not be moved. Small bones were left to grey in the sun, be trodden in horseshit and piss and vomit as the town grew and bright moons waxed and waned. (354)

In a discussion about musicality, Kim Scott has said:

> I think about the rhythm of reading, about where I want people to slow down, where I wouldn't mind if – this must be what people dislike about my stuff I think – where I wouldn't mind if they *reread* it. [laughs] Where I want the reader to just step back for a minute, have a bit of a think about what's going on. Or where I want them to just go through a few pages and not realise ... I think about things like that, and I think that's something to do with rhythm. (quoted in Wood, 350)

A novel as an instrument for thinking

For me, the aesthetic dimension of prose fiction is related to the question of what fiction can do. I recognise myself as the kind of reader Scott addresses directly in the novel when he writes, 'you can dive into a book and not know just how deep until you return gasping to the surface and are surprised at yourself, your new and so very sensitive skin' (86). Scott has spoken about the process of writing as a form of absorption and I think it's worth acknowledging that reading – when it's going splendidly – is a form of absorption too. Further, Scott is unafraid of complexity, a characteristic of literature he sees as being ultimately supportive of 'the intimacy of the collaboration between reader and writer' (quoted in Wood, 355).

'In fiction you sort of half-apprehend things, start to shape them a little bit, which leads to thinking more about those things in other areas', he told Charlotte Wood (345). Stories, then, become blueprints for methods of thinking, and a novel can be thought of as an instrument gently prompting both writers and readers, each in their own way, to 'try out' new and different ways of being or doing.

Resisting and probing the imperialisms embedded in writing

But writing can also be completely inadequate to the task of expression, and this too is an idea canvassed in *That Deadman Dance*. For Bobby, at key moments in the novel, literacy in the narrower sense of that term is capable of completely losing its shine. The 'deadman dance' from which the novel draws its title is a cultural memory that belongs to Noongar oral and performative heritage and, as Philip Mead has noted, Bobby enacts a 'creative curatorship of that heritage' through performance, song and dance at regular intervals in the novel. It is this broad and sophisticated literacy across cultures that enables him to act as intermediary, often with great success, between Indigenous and settler cultures. Bobby's dual literacy – and at the meta level Scott's playful approach to the form of the novel – reclaims such heritage from the text-based anthropological and colonial histories of Matthew Flinders and Daisy Bates (150). For Bobby, writing is only one form of cultural power. But as the novel (and the history of dispossession) moves forward in time, Bobby's capacity to win over his audience members through performance weakens. For the Noongar, the new world is increasingly violent and edged with anxiety as their early generosity in sharing knowledge is betrayed. In the end, Bobby's carefully choreographed performance before the governor and other powerful figures in the fledgling colony, an attempt to teach them something of the Noongar worldview, including their sense of having been betrayed, has 'no meaning for his white audience whatsoever. Outside he hears gunshots' (350).

Philip Mead sees *That Deadman Dance* as 'an explicit correction' to the archives, especially a particular passage in Flinders' journal, in which he observes, in 1801, an old man at the end of a column of marines performing a kind of parody of the European soldiers' drill in dance, and posits that the old man did not know what he was doing. In correcting the record, Kim Scott's novel wakes us up to the imperialisms embedded in writing in a postcolonial context. Thinking this over, Philip Mead asks, 'Can moments in history that appear to be concluded, past, in fact start up again?' Coming back to this question of what fiction can do, it is instructive to think about the possibilities *That Deadman Dance* might prompt for today's Noongar community. Whatever else this novel might be capable of doing as fiction, it is also a community resource (Mead, 151).

The story is not over yet

I suppose one of the reasons I have been drawn to read *That Deadman Dance* on more than one occasion is because as a white reader the book forces me to consider (over and again) that my own relation to Indigenous Australia, and the history we all share as contemporary Australian citizens, is ongoing and worthy of regular reflection. Understanding can deepen with re-reading. For Kim Scott, the project of Indigenous language revival, to name just one aspect of the novel, is also ongoing. Even though the story of Bobby ends in a form of defeat, 'Scott has repeatedly stressed in interviews subsequent to the novel's publication that the story told in the novel is not over yet' (Nolan, 'Shedding', 141). Speaking with his publisher of his intentions with the book, Scott has acknowledged the pressure of political imperatives on Indigenous writers to 'do a resistance polemical thing and to assert identity' but says that he suspects:

those early Noongar would probably [have been] really interested
in how you could use the novel form to just be expressive and
where you could get with telling a story like that particularly
using the point of view of non-Indigenous characters. So the
idea of a novel ... being inclusive, generous [and enabling you to
incorporate] other people ... in your own sense of the world.
(Scott quoted in Pan Macmillan, 2010)

Thus, a driving question for Scott was how the early Noongar might
'do' a novel about early encounters, and one way we can read *That
Deadman Dance* is as an instrument or tool for thinking through
that question. Maggie Nolan has observed that another, and perhaps
related, way of reading Scott's novel is to see it as an 'audacious, risky
performance' ('Shedding', 141). This, too, is a revealing approach. As a
historical novel, there is nothing else like this book in Australia. As an
exercise in writerly playfulness, again, it seems singular in its boldness
and cheek. I think any writer – whether aspiring or accomplished –
can learn something from considering the genuine complexity of
Scott's experiment and, indeed, his lasting achievements with *That
Deadman Dance*.

A big sunny shack:
Cosmo Cosmolino
by Helen Garner

Tegan Bennett Daylight

Last week – two weeks ago – several weeks ago – it's April 2020 and I can't remember how long it's been since I stood in front of a class – I taught a creative writing class online, to a group of students who had never heard of the writer Helen Garner. I designed this particular subject, called Australian Writers' Workshop, partly because of university demand, partly as a corrective to this situation. Every week the students have to read three extracts from something Australian: fiction, non-fiction, poetry, drama, screenwriting. Every week they have to write something. Every week I remind them that what they will be writing is Australian literature.

Many writers will find themselves teaching creative writing at some point in their careers, because few of us can earn our living simply from our writing. We all grow our methods from our own practice and our own personalities, but I'd say there's a general consensus among us, and it's this: simply, that less is more. Too many instructions, too many fussy little exercises about point of view and tense and conflict and character are likely to break the heart of the real writer, who is writing from an urge she can't quite name, a place she can't quite locate. When real writing begins, decisions are not made about point of view and tense. These things are for the writer to notice later.

But a teacher must set exercises – you can't leave your students alone in the landscape with no bearings, no destination. So I always start with an exercise that I'm currently calling 'People'. It's embarrassingly simple. I say to my students: I want you to introduce me to a character by showing them in motion – on the way somewhere, doing something, active. It's the classic fiction teacher's gambit; I say: you're not allowed to *tell* me about them. You have to *show* them to me. And then I read them this:

Suppose there were a woman once, not long ago or far from here, whose husband came home one night and stood at the door to make a simple statement. Voices were raised. Kitchen utensils struck walls and spewed their contents. So quick! Janet lay on the sofa. What was the point of weeping? He was already gone.

The euphoria which followed lasted, oh, a month. All her senses had perfect pitch. Crowds parted at her approach, old men and boys and babies smiled at her in the street, waitresses spoke to her with a tender address. Milky clouds covered the sky. A warm dry wind blew all day, and the leaves changed colour.

This is not so hard, thought Janet. I can do this. Why do people make a fuss?

For years she had made herself so flexible that she hardly felt a thing. Forgetting was her greatest skill. But now she noticed that the passing of time began to hurt her. Wherever she looked she saw the fleetingness of things. Mend as she might, clothes wore out. Things broke. Paper came briefly into her possession, was scanned or scribbled on, then screwed up and thrown away. Even the black mist that her fingers left on a café counter evaporated before the cup could reach her lips. It was painful to watch an old woman – and Janet was only forty-five – stumble unshepherded down the back steps of a bus while an energetic young one, admired by all the passengers, bounded aboard through the front, holding out her money. To see a couple of any age lean towards each other across a restaurant table caused Janet's stomach to fracture like an egg.

She looked at herself in a shop's long mirror and saw that she had grown crooked. Her right hip was higher than her left, and the opposite side of her top lip had developed, as it were in compensation, a bitter upward twist. If she placed two fingers against the outer point of each cheekbone and gently raised the skin, her jaw-line smoothed out, her upper lip lost its tense and radiating lines, and she saw a version of the girl she had once been; but the only thing that could take the years out of her face now was surgery, and the vanity of that she scorned.

She scorned many things. All she believed in was the physical, the practical, the stoical. Bite the bullet, she said. Plug on, one foot in front of the other and keep going. She had no children. Her family was scattered. She was too proud to take advice or sympathy: to a woman like Janet, nothing is more enfeebling than pity: and so she fell out with all her friends.

It was already years since she had severed herself, with rough strokes, from the demanding work she had been trained for and had arranged her life so that she could earn a living without needing to leave the house more than two or three times a week. She could turn her hand to most things an old-fashioned typewriter was used for. She could review, she could edit, she could sling words around grammatically into sharp little pieces for fashion magazines, weekend colour supplements, and the glossy publications found in the seat pockets of domestic airlines. She was known for keeping a deadline; and if anyone asked, she called herself a journalist.

So she lay on her bed and read. She sat at the table in her upstairs room and tapped the keys. At night she would open the blind and lean out when the pub on the corner of the avenue was closing, and watch the real people going home with gaiety, some singing as they slung their legs over saddles and pedalled away, their fitful dynamo lamps blossoming on the dark surface of the road. And sometimes, now, in the empty house, she heard her own footsteps hurry past on the other side of a wall, her own voice, more girlish, laughing in a closed room. Unwelcome memories of happiness rustled behind her or pounced from doorways. She remembered being the youngest person present, being a student with a job; how it was to tie on an apron and slap together sandwiches in a shop, taking orders, chiacking with the customers; to have sore feet from standing up all day to serve; and later, the surprised pride of being on a payroll and a promotions list, of belonging to a union and knowing where she fitted into her society. She remembered the pleasure of being driven to work on sunny mornings by a bunch of older colleagues from the staffroom, married men with shaven cheeks, viyella shirts, maroon ties: the tonic, laundered smell of the car when she climbed in with her newspaper at the pick-up point near the start of the freeway. (51–3)

This is a long extract for an essay, but its length feels necessary to me. It's necessary in order for the reader to see just what it is the writer does; what she *shows* us in this two and a half pages that begin the third, longest section of *Cosmo Cosmolino*, Helen Garner's least loved, least praised novel, published in 1992. It was David Malouf who described Garner as 'a natural sprinter'. The sheer careering speed of this passage, our original third-person meeting with the protagonist Janet, is phenomenal. This book is full of trams, chattering and chiming their ways down avenues; and the book itself is like a tram. It chatters and chimes and rocks but never quite leaves the tracks.

After reading this to my students I simply say – see how much life you can fit into a couple of pages? See how Janet is on the move; look, also, for the physical description, so hard to include in a limited perspective scene, but solved so quickly when Janet 'looks at herself in a shop's long mirror'. Notice how active it is, see all the Garneresque verbs: striking, spewing, bounding, slinging, slapping, laughing, blossoming. Severing, scorning, plugging on, singing, editing, chiacking. And hear that amazing opening 'Suppose there were a woman'. I love this device of Garner's, though it seems mean to call it a device – this voice, this shout of confidence. I unconsciously imitated this in my own early work, and just recently I found myself beginning a short story with the words, *Consider this*. This is a classic Garner opening. It says, I'm here, and I'm the one telling you this story. *Consider this*. It reaches all the way back to Jane Austen, who had the same lively, endless energy, who could not just tell you a story. She had always to knock a hole in the walls of her novels, to step out and say, here I am. I am speaking to you. In other words, *I am in charge*.

Some readers will know that the long passage I've just quoted is not the true beginning of *Cosmo Cosmolino*. The book begins with two shorter pieces, stories that are narratively connected to the larger body of the novel. What are they? Are they calved icebergs? They feel like things originally part of the whole, but things that had to break off. Things that had to break off but not float entirely away.

In her excellent literary biography *A Writing Life: Helen Garner and her work*, Bernadette Brennan notes that the original version of *Cosmo Cosmolino*, even up to a year before publication, was a collection of seven short stories, which included 'Cosmo Cosmolino', 'Recording angel' and 'A vigil', which make up the entirety of the published version. The book was marketed as a novel with two stories, related to the novel's material, attached. The other stories floated off, to be published in journals or other collections, or not at all.

I want to step in here for a moment, as reader, as writer, as teacher. I want to say that if I had been Garner's publisher – if I had been Garner – I would have published *Cosmo Cosmolino* as that original collection. I might have cut the title story into shorter stories – as with all her fiction, the novel contains many breaks, natural pauses. I would have seen the book as a whole as telling the central story through a kaleidoscope of scenes, points of view, small (and large) narratives. I am thinking particularly of Alice Munro's early short story collections *Lives of Girls and Women* (1971) and *The Beggar Maid* (1977), in which Munro builds a long narrative about her protagonist like you might a model train, adding stories like carriages until the narrative winds into the distance. The result, to my mind, can be more satisfying than the novel, whose every scene is roped to a single, central idea.

I also want to say (aware of, and perfectly happy to acknowledge the contradiction) that one of the things that charmed me about *Cosmo Cosmolino* – and the reason it has always been my favourite of Garner's fiction – is the very thing I have just criticised. Tim Winton puts it best when he says, '*The Children's Bach* was like a perfectly built cottage, all squared away, a lovely thing and an achievement to envy, but *Cosmo* was like a big sunny shack with all the windows and doors open to the light and breeze ... I love its raggedness, its waywardness, its openness' (Brennan, 119–20). In a sense, *Cosmo Cosmolino* is a book the reader can move around in. Its shape invites readerly freedom. But this shape drew criticism from many reviewers. I want to use this essay to agree and disagree with those reviewers who said that *Cosmo Cosmolino*, and other fictions of Garners, are not 'novels'.

To return to the book as it was published: 'Recording Angels' introduces us, though in the first person, to Janet, the larger novel's protagonist. This story is about the past, and memory. Janet's oldest friend Patrick is about to undergo surgery for a brain tumour. If his brain is changed by this, will she be free of him and his version of her? He is a conservative, loving soul. She is not sure she wants to be the person he is convinced she is. Garner makes couplets – irrepressibly male, like Pope's or Bacon's – out of his fixed opinions:

> Only *Dissatisfied Women* become feminists. Lesbians are *Heavy Drinkers*. Some women *Lack the Quality* to make a man *A Good Wife*. Ursula, for example, *Became an Alcoholic and a Prostitute*.

Janet, the I in this story, continues:

> Hostile, I objected: 'She was drinking, for God's sake. She got a job in a massage parlour.'

> 'I think you'd be hard put,' said Patrick, squaring himself and whitening his nostrils, 'to draw a distinction between drinking and getting a job in a massage parlour and what I just said.' (6)

This story tells us that the book to come will be about people and their pasts: the terrible struggle it is to both accept your past, and dismiss it. To insist that your past leaves you alone. The novel proper will return to this idea.

The second story, 'A vigil', has the same theme. But I confess to less familiarity with it. This is not because of its quality or length, but because of its subject matter. It is the grimmest story I've ever read, and I have taught Chekhov's *Ward 6*. It's about Ray, the useless ageing boyfriend of Kim, the daughter of Ursula who was drinking and got a job in a massage parlour. Ray ignores the fact that Kim is killing herself with a mixture of depression and downers – he uses her solely for sex and to have a bed to sleep in. One day he comes to find her where she usually is, under the covers. Feeling 'a surge of meanness' (31) he opens the curtains to let light fall on her unprotected face. He bends down to see her better. 'The smell hit him. Her mouth, half open, was clogged with vomit and alive with a busy-ness of insects' (31). She's dead. And it gets worse, as we move into the detail of her funeral, and Ray being forced by two dark angels – crooks, or simply crematorium workers – to watch the destruction of her burnt body in the flames of the crematorium. It's unreadably bleak. It offers no hope. It is pure punishment, biblical in its awfulness. Bernadette Brennan records Tim Winton as saying it was both unclear and too violent, too awful to be good (113).

It's an important story, though, because we meet Ray again in the novel itself. *Cosmo Cosmolino* begins as the story of Janet, who lives alone in her big house, which was once a house of friends, of children, a collective place, a place of communards who 'departed at the end of the seventies with armloads of collectively purchased kitchenware' (56). After this it was a house for herself and her husband; since he left, she has been alone. I'll let Garner take up the story and introduce the second character:

> Now consider Maxine, who lived in a shed and called herself a carpenter. Although she had little training and no worldly ambition, she was in the grip of such a powerful urge *to make* that she barely slept. Ideas came swarming through her, and like many people who labour in the obsession of solitude she lacked the detachment to challenge them; yet when pressed in company she never lost her temper but argued round and round with a serene unshakable courtesy. She expected good of everything, she thought the best of the world and against all evidence was full of trust. Auras, star charts, chakras, the directing of energy and rays, the power of crystals, the moral values of colours: these phenomena were her delight: they guided her. (57–8)

Let's pause a moment to think about Garner's sentences. Those colons in the last part of that last sentence don't function like other writers' do, as the precursor to a list. They're pauses – deeper than a comma, deeper again than a semi-colon. Again, I find myself under an influence – I am addicted in my own writing to the deep pause of the semi-colon and the deeper pause of the colon. There's a poetry, a chanting rhythm in all of Garner's work – but most particularly in *Cosmo Cosmolino*. She's championed for her sparseness – I'd like to champion her for her rhythm. Listen to Garner's reply to an enquiry of mine about her style, about the cadences of her prose – hear the verbs but also the balance, the airy balance of the punctuation: 'If you knew how hard I work on that. Reading everything out loud again and again. Flipping and hauling and wheeling the clauses this way and that ... and always bearing in mind what Fred Astaire said: "If it doesn't look easy, you're not working hard enough"' (author's correspondence).

Can I ask you, too, to notice how many verbs Garner uses to describe her method? Flipping, hauling, wheeling?

Ray is our third character. Here he is, some years after Kim's death, now saved – a Christian, but still down on his luck. He's been sent – not, as Maxine thinks on meeting him, by God – but by Alby, his older brother, a one-time lover of Janet's. Alby yearns for the cheerful, homely past of Janet's house, Sweetpea Mansions, and he's sent Ray ahead of him to re-establish that world, or so they both hope. When Ray arrives at Sweetpea Mansions he is greeted by Maxine, who has just started work as Janet's cleaner. Maxine has been looking for a sign; Ray must be it. He has a certain inevitability about him, for someone who is looking for inevitability. Ray, of course, thinks she is Janet – and is hoping to ask her if he can stay.

[He] followed, sniffing her wake with dread, but it was untainted by perfume: it smelt like wood or glue and he wondered why. He wondered too whether this was a car-stripping neighbourhood,

whether he should offer to go round the corner to the shop for a
couple of pasties, whether he could take a quick look round upstairs
by asking to use the toilet, and whether she was the modern angry
type of woman – whether he should time his announcement with
care, or just open his mouth and blurt it out. (65)

When Janet comes home she's unable to resist the neediness of both
these people; she lets them move in, rent-free, and the three form a kind
of household, Maxine moving into the shed with her carpentry and
Ray upstairs to one of the empty rooms near Janet's. And their story
is pretty simple – it's about belief, or faith. Maxine is suffering from an
excess of it. Neither Janet nor Ray have enough of it. Ray has Jesus but
no love, no happiness, no connection – Maxine, of course, is drowning
in connections. Janet has her intellect but nothing else, it seems: no
Jesus, no love, no connection; only work, cleverness and stoicism to
support her.

There are two things I want to address now, and they're related.
It's true that Garner has many thousands of readers who simply love
everything she writes: devoted readers. But it's also true that she provokes
other readers to all sorts of anger, disdain, outright antagonism. I'd like to
look at this, with *Cosmo Cosmolino* as our frame, and directly addressing
the contested notion that Helen Garner has not been writing novels all
this time. This came up when *Monkey Grip* was published in 1977, with
the late Peter Corris's famous review that suggested that all Garner had
done was publish her 'private journals'. I sometimes feel for Peter Corris,
quoted so often. Most latterly we heard this from Robert Dessaix, in
his 2008 review of *The Spare Room* in the *Monthly*. Famously, and yet
again, Dessaix declared that *The Spare Room* was not a novel. He went
on to say that none of her works of fiction were novels, adding,

They are all of them fine works of art and innovative explorations
of literary approaches to non-fiction, every one of them an

outstanding example of stylish reportage, but none of them is a novel ... Perhaps [Garner] still (quite understandably) feels a need to cock a snook at those early critics of her work, such as Peter Corris ... A real writer, it was implied, writes novels, and a novel is something more sustained, more imagined, more intricately patterned, more whole than the sort of thing Garner writes, however much she trims and transcribes ... However, Helen Garner is indubitably not just a writer, but one of our most gifted. Whatever sort of writer she is – tribal storyteller, memoirist, reporter, diarist, essayist – nobody's words on the page command attention quite like hers. (58)

I think many of us will agree with this last sentence.

In Dessaix's definition, a novel 'is primarily a work of fiction with an architectonic quality to it that transcribed diaries simply don't have'. He says, 'Just throwing in a bit of "purple prose", as she does in *Cosmo Cosmolino*, won't do the trick, either' (58). Architecture – we hear a lot about it when we hear about novels, and we get taught it in novel-writing classes too. And while I mostly share Dessaix's point of view – and would love to hear him unpack it at greater length – I don't think it applies to *Cosmo Cosmolino*. If it's architecture you want, look at its many-windowed points of view, its framing narratives of arrival and departure. Its outhouses, never knocked down, somehow still supporting the larger structure.

I realise here that I have changed my mind about how I would have published *Cosmo Cosmolino*, had I been Helen Garner or her publisher Hilary McPhee. I'm going to renounce the idea of the Alice Munro collection, and choose the novel. Perhaps, to make a more 'complete' novel, Garner needed to take longer over the editing of this book. Perhaps the outhouses of 'Recording angel' and 'A vigil' needed to be knocked down, and the remaining space used to extend the main building. Or perhaps they needed to be brought to join the main building, to make sense of its sprawl. Could they have been edited into the novel proper?

Let's return to the idea of the novel qua novel, and what it might actually be. Here's what I think: what makes a novel a novel is metaphor. Metaphor, central metaphor, when deployed in a novel, is as though life looked in the mirror and saw, not just its reflection, but something behind it. Just as Janet is shadowed by her shimmering pillar of darkness – the thing that Tim Winton suggested to Garner was The Holy Spirit – the novel is a collection of words shadowed by a larger meaning. Metaphor, just like faith or belief, is the sense of something larger underneath – a whale shouldering or bumping under the ship of story. If we commit to metaphor, we commit to a deeper meaning. We become believers.

And this is why *Cosmo Cosmolino* is a novel. I do cleave to Robert Dessaix's point of view of Garner's fiction, especially in the case of *The Spare Room* – a book I loved and have read many times. It lightly engages with a metaphor here and there – most obviously, the mirror that shatters in Helen's house before Nicola comes to visit. But its concern is reportage, and I say this with the deepest respect, because none report more clearly, more vividly, more engagingly than Helen Garner.

But could it be true that in *Cosmo Cosmolino* we see Garner surrendering to metaphor as her characters do, or try to, to God? Could it be possible that this is a book in which her vaunted and almost miraculous powers of observation gave way to something larger? Is it possible that in God, in belief or faith, Garner found the kind of metaphor her previous books had lacked?

Garner and I are friendly, and although I was careful not to ask her too many questions about *Cosmo* when writing this piece – very aware that each reader writes her own book, that my reading must be mine alone, as yours must be – we did have a couple of exchanges. And the thing she said most bluntly was this:

... when [*Cosmo Cosmolino*] came out I was stupid enough to agree to an interview with that hard-nosed leftie rationalist Craig McGregor and even stupider to blurt out my strange experience with the shadowy presence. After I'd spoken to him I panicked and called him, naively asked him to cut that part. He says oh don't worry I hardly even mentioned it. The piece comes out and my mysterious visitor is the backbone of the story. People who hadn't read the book ran round saying Garner's got religion etc. One neighbour said with a sort of patronising laugh 'what you needed was a big hug'. ... None of this matters to me now. But it taught me that in Australia you can't write about experiences of 'the numinous' without opening yourself to sneering and cynical laughter. Back then, anyway. (author's correspondence)

It seems a terrible shame to me that critics, in their rush to disavow something so tasteless, so unfashionable as belief, missed something so rich and deep in Garner's work. By becoming helpless before God she also became helpless before metaphor. We are the richer for it. We don't condemn Toni Morrison or Marilynne Robinson or even Herman Melville for their use of biblical metaphor. Could we perhaps banish the sneering and cynical laughter for long enough to read this book as it deserves to be read?

Let's return now to the narrative. Ray and Maxine have moved in. In her shed, Maxine is busily, even frantically, making: furniture, a cradle, and waiting, waiting for the thing to happen that will change her. She dreams of a baby; in her dream she calls it *cosmo, cosmolino*; world, little world. She 'discovers' that her great change, her great need, is for a baby. Ray gets a job on a building site and refuses all comfort other than his Bible; Janet continues to work and keep herself sealed off from Ray and Maxine. It's winter, the house is cold, no one eats together. Ray is a failure, Maxine is drifting, Janet is hiding. But one night Janet decides to cook. Everyone knows that the urge to cook for others comes only when we are close to happiness, or actually happy – there's something in appetite that speaks of openness to others, and to kindness.

> In the bowels of the corner cupboard [Janet] found an old-fashioned oval oven-proof dish, still with a lid, but chipped, stained and encrusted along its edges with nameless scum. She pulled it out and stared at it, tickled by a strange and distant sensation, an almost childish pleasure in its chunky shape and unusual depth. It radiated meaning, like an object from a forgotten dream. She set it on the bench, and with painful slowness, biting on the pen which upstairs in her room flew so readily across the pages, she began to make a list. (120–1)

> *[Later]* ... the dish was slid into the oven and at seven o'clock, when the rain had settled in for the long haul and Janet had run out the front to empty the wet letterbox of junk mail and then upstairs to position saucepans under all the best-known leaks, she wiped down the white table with an Ajaxed rag and set about making it beautiful: an ironed cloth, proper cutlery and crockery for three, glasses with stems, two candle stubs in silver holders, and even the serviettes that the household children, echoing their parents, had called 'serve-you-rights', pink linen ones with drawn-thread borders, dragged like the tablecloth from the utter bottom of the ironing basket.

> She uncorked the bottle of wine, laid the baguette at an attractive angle across the middle of the cloth, and stood back satisfied. (123)

The result is – nothing. Maxine is late home; she has been at a meeting of a group of people engaged in a pyramid scheme. Soon, she will steal – there's no other word for it – Ray's stashed pay, put it into the pyramid scheme and lose the lot. But Maxine doesn't believe in this future. She believes in the baby she is sure she will have, and the wealth that is sure to come out of the Golden Aeroplane.

No matter. She's late, the dinner is ruined, she goes to bed, and Janet has given up.

Ray is later still. He's been to the movies on his own. Janet is lying defeated on the couch. Ray has bought himself a kebab, and meanly she listens to him eat, believing he is alone, and waits until he has finished, and belched, to remind him that he isn't.

There follows a scene in which two sets of desires compete; Janet's for some kind of help, some kindness, some redemption; and Ray's for company – in fact, for the same thing. He works to convert her to Christianity, to drive the devil out of her. He quotes from his book. He demands that she join him in being saved. He pretends that she is the needy one. But all the while, what he really wants, so privately that he can hardly bear to admit it to himself, is love. Sex – but really, just kindness, and forgiveness, and love. At the end of the long scene, in the room that still shows the scars of Janet's last fight with her husband, neither is redeemed, neither is saved, nor loved; they leave each other desolate and empty.

But this is not the end. The book ends with the arrival of Alby, Janet's ex-lover and Ray's older brother, a striding, crackling version of Ray, full of wicked charm and bullshit. By now Maxine is pregnant, having dreamily made love to Ray while he is asleep; she has lost his money; but she is unrepentant, believing, full of faith and so glad to meet Alby, who she believes has been sent for some unfathomable cosmic reason. Something, whatever it is in Alby, fires the house up again.

Finally this book offers, as Garner's books don't always, redemption. Uncharacteristically, Garner gives the novel's triumphal moment to its silliest character, the one most open to uncritical faith or belief. Maxine transforms into an angel and flies over the house, strewing jonquils joyfully on Ray, Janet and Alby where they stand on the street. Flowers scattered around them, the three turn back to the house, and Janet asks the men to choose themselves a room.

So: belief. Let's return one last time to the discomfort many readers feel with Garner's writing, in general for the unsettling effect it has; in particular to *Cosmo Cosmolino* and its metaphor of belief. Religion or belief is the attempt to impose order where there is none – and surely, fiction is the same thing. In fact, from where I'm standing it's exactly the same thing. I don't believe in a god or gods, but I do believe in the power of fiction, the power of narrative, the power of metaphor to restore order. A great novel unsettles, then settles – it causes disorder, and then order. Order is restored in *Cosmo Cosmolino*; the metaphor that effects this restoration is a metaphor of belief.

Perhaps the reason Robert Dessaix said that Garner is not writing novels, perhaps the reason critics are often made uncomfortable by Garner's fiction is this: her work is often too much like life, and not enough like fiction. Perhaps what lies at the bottom of all this is an uneasiness with material that has been transformed into sentences we all wish we could have written; but not transformed into metaphor. Perhaps, in her other books, Garner has not soothed us, comforted us with metaphor in the way we would like. But perhaps *Cosmo Cosmolino* is the book in which Garner has allowed herself and her readers redemption: deliverance by metaphor.

I'm conscious that *Cosmo Cosmolino* itself has influenced my writing of this essay. It isn't the shape I intended it to be. I wanted a shorter, more tightly argued piece of writing, Tim Winton's perfectly built cottage rather than the shack with all its windows open. But instead I have surrendered to the shape and shapelessness of this great, strange book. I want to finish by telling you that it is a book whose doors and windows will be forever open to the breeze. Wander in it at will.

Short stories ... but linked:
Steven Amsterdam's
Things We Didn't See Coming

Ryan O'Neill

There is a wonderful scene in the 2007 film *2 Days in Paris* where Marion (Julie Delpy) meets Manu, an ex-boyfriend. When Marion asks Manu what he has been doing, he says proudly, 'Well, my book's just come out', and Marion replies, 'Great! A novel?' 'No. Short stories', Manu says. 'But ...' and he hesitates for a moment, searching for the right word, '... linked'. 'Great', Marion says, with far less enthusiasm. I have always loved this exchange for the way it comments on a number of aspects of writing and publishing. First, the idea that a short story collection is somehow less impressive than a novel. Second, the insecurity of the writer as he attempts to justify his work with that one word: 'linked'. Third, Manu's hesitation in describing his collection, which indicates the nebulous nature of linked collections versus story cycles versus novel-in-stories and so on, and finally, Marion's offhand dismissal of the whole enterprise. Despite Marion's lukewarm reaction, the linked short story collection is a form with a long pedigree, especially in Australia, and when it is done well, as in Steven Amsterdam's *Things We Didn't See Coming*, it can indeed be great.

Things We Didn't See Coming (*TWDSC*) is a work of fiction depicting a series of escalating political, social and environmental crises through the experiences of an unnamed narrator in nine stories. The events of the book occur over the course of more than three decades, from New Year's Eve 1999 to sometime in the 2030s. Two of the nine stories were published as short stories in anthologies before the book was released in 2009 by Sleepers Publishing. *TWDSC* went on to win the *Age* Book of the Year, as well as being shortlisted for a number of other literary awards. It was later published in the UK and the US, before being republished in Australia in 2016 by Hachette.

The book's well-deserved critical success is unusual in Australia in that it is essentially speculative fiction, a genre that is often ignored or worse, derided, by mainstream literary critics. The reception of *TWDSC* in some ways echoed that of Cormac McCarthy's *The Road*, which had appeared two years earlier, and was treated by reviewers as literary fiction first, and speculative fiction a very distant second, if at all. Critical reaction to both *TWDSC* and *The Road* demonstrates that historian and poet Robert Conquest's 1962 couplet about the attitude of literary critics to science fiction still holds true today:

'SF's no good', they bellow till we're deaf.
'But this looks good.' – 'Well then, it's not SF.'
(Amis & Conquest, introduction)

TWDSC was marketed as a novel in Australia and the UK, but as a short story collection in the US. Some reviews referred to it as being made up of 'chapters' while others mention 'stories' or 'episodes' or even 'vignettes'. It could be argued that it doesn't really matter what *TWDSC* is, novel, short story collection, or linked collection, as all that matters is that it does what it does extremely well. However, in order to fully understand and appreciate how *TWDSC* does what it does, it is first necessary to establish exactly what it is: a novel and a linked collection differ significantly in a number of important ways including how they deal with structure, plot, character and setting, so the question is more than an academic one.

Any discussion of definitions of a literary form, no matter how apparently straightforward, can quickly become an exercise in tedious hair-splitting. For instance, you might think a short story can be defined simply as a story that is short. But then you have to define what short means: 500 words? 3000? 20 000? And what is a story? How does it differ from an anecdote or a vignette? Defining a linked short story collection is made even more complicated by the numerous other terms used by scholars for the form, sometimes interchangeably and sometimes not: short story sequence, short story cycle, novel-in-stories, composite novel, fragmentary novel, discontinuous narrative and others. To confuse matters even further, some of these terms may or may not be used to indicate a greater or lesser unity or 'novelness' among the stories. Perhaps the clearest definition comes from the poet Forrest Ingram, who argued that the linked collection (or short story cycle, as he termed it) was 'a set of stories so linked to one another that the reader's experience of each one is modified by the experience of others' (105). As literary scholars Ann Morris and Maggie Dunn (1995) have noted, such collections can be linked through five ways: setting, narrator, shared characters, shared theme and shared style. If a novel sits at one end of the spectrum of unity in its style, setting, narration, theme and characters, and a collection of unlinked stories at the other, a linked collection such as *TWDSC* lies somewhere in between, being connected by four of Morris and Dunn's criteria: the narrator, shared characters, a shared theme and shared style. While each of the narrative units in the book could be read as a self-contained short story (and indeed two were published as such), others (especially in the middle section) depend more on the context of previous stories to be best understood and enjoyed.

In a sense, *TWDSC* is located in the same state of flux and instability regarding its narrative form as its genre: it is a linked short story collection that has been viewed as a novel, and speculative fiction that has been viewed as purely literary fiction. This tension between the unity of the novel and the discreteness of the short story collection poses a series of challenges in the writing of a linked short story collection, in the setting, characters, themes, point of view and structure of the book. Amsterdam's response to these challenges is a masterclass in how to write a collection of short stories ' ... but linked'.

The structure of *TWDSC* is complex, as each story is carefully constructed so as to function more or less independently, with its own beginning, middle and end, while also being part of the larger structure of the book as a whole, which has its own beginning, middle and end. Therefore, each story in the book does double duty: as a single episode in the narrator's life, but also as a way into the next story, and the next, leading to a picture of a much larger whole. For instance, the opening piece, 'What we know now' has the tight construction of a short story: the inciting incident is the narrator's father's panicked response to the Y2K bug, and a satisfying, if open-ended, resolution to the situation is explored. This story also functions as the inciting incident of the book as a whole, as the Y2K bug is the first of a series of disasters that the narrator has to negotiate throughout the next eight stories. The idea of cause and effect is still present, but whereas in a novel cause and effect are presented as a series of dominoes, with the first causing the fall of the second, third and so on to the book's end, in *TWDSC* many of the dominoes are invisible to the reader, their fall occurring in the ellipses between stories. As the narrator says at one point, they 'Wait for the next event to push us along' (93) and it is these underlying events that form the backbone of the novel's structure: floods, wildfires, plagues, riots, changes in government. Each story is a glimpse into a disintegrating world, seen through the eyes of the increasingly debilitated narrator. In the book's second story, the narrator's grandmother makes an observation that could almost be a description of the book's structure: 'A glimpse? Maybe that's what life turns out to be. Curtains open.

Curtains close. Ta-da'. *TWDSC* offers nine such glimpses of a life, and a world.

The book can also be broken down into three narrative units, each consisting of three stories. The first of these triptychs outlines the beginnings of the narrator's life: his childhood, teenage years and early twenties, and his learning the compromises he must make to survive in a rapidly changing world. The middle triptych, forming the central part of the book's structure, charts the narrator's relationship with Margo, a fellow thief and survivor who is better equipped than he is to deal with a world in seemingly endless crisis. By the end of this trio of stories, the narrator has aged and matured and appears to have found his place in the world, both physically and emotionally; mirroring this, society appears to have reached a fragile state of equilibrium, with the promise of political and social reformation at hand. The final three stories show the narrator's decline into illness and old age, which in the deadly world of *TWDSC* is forty years old. The narrator's physical decline goes hand in hand with yet another period of environmental and political upheaval. In the end, the structure of the book proves to be circular. The first story ended with the narrator, a child, sitting by his father, doing his best to heal him; the final story ends with the narrator's now elderly father trying to heal his ailing son.

The episodic structure of *TWDSC* allows for a wide variety of settings, in both place and time, from a city on New Year's Eve at the turn of the century, to a flooding forest decades later. The use of the indefinite article – 'a city', 'a forest', 'a country' – is evidence of the decision not to specifically set the book in Australia. In fact, the book was originally set in the US, but Amsterdam's editors encouraged the author to remove any concrete references to America. This decision was a smart one, and imbues the settings with a universal quality: as the unnamed narrator assumes the status of an Everyman, the unnamed setting assumes the status of an Everywhere. There is nothing to say that the locations are in Australia (apart from the use of 'Mum' rather than 'Mom') but there is also nothing to say that they aren't. Each of the stories is set in a different time and a different place, with much of what happened to the narrator in the years between stories, and how he left one place and came to another, left in the ellipses between them. The gaps between the stories are central to how Amsterdam uses worldbuilding; *TWDSC* is a masterclass in creating a world by the suggestion of small details, not the accumulation of endless exposition. Many SF novels rely on the 'infodump' to provide the reader with the necessary exposition about the world of the story. This can be done well, but all too often it can lead to long paragraphs resembling a Wikipedia article for an imaginary place. If the story is narrated in the first person, the infodump threatens to become even clumsier, leading the reader to question why the narrator would spend three pages describing a political system or a technological device that should be entirely familiar to them, and therefore beneath their notice. It's as if the narrator in a contemporary literary fiction novel spent three pages explaining what a car was and how the internal combustion engine worked, before they got in it and drove away.

Amsterdam's solution to this is to give credit to his readers, expecting that they should do some of the work in puzzling out the setting, and not simply be spoon-fed indigestible lumps of exposition. He also eases the reader into the book by beginning it not in a strange, broken future, but in the entirely recognisable past. The opening story is set in a deliberately specific time during the narrator's childhood (New Year's Eve, 1999) and a deliberately non-specific place. The narrator's father whisks his wife and child to the countryside, fearing the consequences of the Y2K bug. (Since *TWDSC* was published in 2008, this raises the fascinating idea that it might be an alternate history book as well as a dystopia: the remaining eight stories are set in a world in which the Y2K bug apparently did actually cause the first in a chain of global catastrophes.) The setting in the first story is familiar and realistic, but the second story is set several years into the twenty-first century, one that is quite different from our own. There are references by the narrator to the 'alternate economy' (26) and mention of rationing and allotment coupons. The reader gathers that the population has been divided into urban and rural zones but the exact cause of this societal and political collapse is left outside the margins of the story: perhaps it was the Y2K bug that caused the chaos, perhaps something else.

With each story, the reader is given another glimpse into the world, which taken together form a mosaic of catastrophes. In 'Dry land' a long rainy season and floods hint at the beginnings of environmental collapse; in 'Cakewalk' a pandemic has spread from birds to humans and the nation is under quarantine; in 'Uses for vinegar' people flee wildfires caused by oil drilling; in 'The forest for the trees' the forests have been destroyed by drought and male infertility has become an issue, and by the final story, the world is attempting to adjust to the disastrous effects of global warming. As well as environmental collapse, each story presents a small puzzle regarding the political and social breakdown of the global order. Some kind of government is always present in the background of each story attempting, usually inadequately, to deal with the bedlam. Sometimes the narrator is employed by the government. Cities wither and small rural communities rise; politicians appear to offer solutions; things seem to get better, but then become worse. Amsterdam very rarely spells anything out, and almost never resorts to the infodump. The evocations of the setting arise naturally from the story, and the situation the narrator finds himself in. The setting of each story is sketched in with the economy of a short story writer; but over the course of the book this adds up to a novel's worth of details. In one story, the narrator mentions he hasn't seen an apple in years; in the next, he matter of factly catches, fries and eats a rat. Those two details are worth more than twenty pages of description about the deteriorating economic and political situation which might be found in a more traditional SF novel. The world of *TWDSC* is in the background, not in the foreground. Miraculous medical technologies are not miraculous to the narrator; he has no idea how they work and doesn't attempt to explain them. Amsterdam leaves readers to do the bulk of the worldbuilding themselves. It is up to the reader to imagine what happens in the lacunae between the stories. In 'The forest and the trees' the narrator is living in a 'desperately healing country' (116), which appears to have achieved some level of sexual and social liberation, but by 'The profit motive', set only a few years later, government officials are being lynched and 'old style hatred is back' (142). What causes this regression is never explained: it's up to the reader to decide.

In *TWDSC*, Amsterdam's use of the same first-person narrator across all the stories in the book ensures a strong sense of continuity, even as time and place are rendered discontinuous. No matter how much time has passed between stories, no matter how much distance the narrator has travelled, the point of view remains stable; this proves essential in orientating the reader. The narrator recounts his experience using the present simple tense, a choice that has become something of a default in much contemporary fiction, with little justification for its use other than a vague claim to somehow 'make things more immediate'. As with other overused tropes and devices in literary fiction (child narrators, minimalism, mistaking a painstaking recording of mundanity for realism), the more often present simple narration is used, the less often it is used well. However, Amsterdam's use of the first person present simple point of view is expertly done. In almost all of the stories, the narrator is focused on issues of his own survival. He lives in the present because the future is uncertain, and the past is useless to him. It makes narrative sense that the narrator should use the present simple tense, and it also ensures that the stories do not get bogged down in exposition: what happened in the past is not important and is rarely referred to. What is important is what is happening *now*.

In a conventional novel, the reader can sometimes trace the growth and development of the protagonist from childhood to death (as in many three-volume nineteenth-century novels); or more frequently in contemporary fiction the protagonist is followed over a shorter but still continuous period of time: a few years, a few months, even a day. Due to the structure of *TWDSC*, there is no such detailed continuity in the development of the narrator; in order for there to be so, every story would have to be crammed with flashbacks explaining what had happened since the last story: how did he lose that job? What happened after he was shot in the leg? This would essentially transform the book into a much more conventional, and probably far less successful, novel. This is not to say that the narrator in *TWDSC* does not grow or develop; rather that instead of seeing this development in the form of a character arc, the reader sees it more as specific points along the arc, with the reader joining these points together to determine the shape of the arc themselves.

It is extremely difficult to create an internally consistent character that shows growth and change over the course of three decades by focusing on only a few days in that time with no reference, or only passing references, to the parts of the story within the narrative ellipses. One way Amsterdam resolves this problem is by emphasising the narrator as, above all, a compassionate person, and then charting how he struggles to balance this aspect of his character with the self-interest needed to survive in a hostile world. This compassion is established in the opening story, where the eight-year-old narrator leaves the warmth and safety of his bedroom to go out into the woods and sit with his father, a man burdened with the knowledge that the world as he knows it is ending. The narrator tells his father, 'I will take care of you when you get old' (22). In the next story, the now teenage narrator has learned something of the selfishness he will need to survive; he is a small-time thief not above pilfering pills from his grandparents in order to get high. Yet he also wants to be a 'good grandson', going so far as to take his ailing grandparents out into the country on a minor crime spree, one last fling before they take their own lives. In each story that follows, the narrator is generally faced with a choice between compassion and selfishness in an increasingly perilous landscape, often trying to find ways to reconcile these two apparently disparate choices. In 'Dry land' he has learned to monetise his compassion by taking on a government job in which he uses his empathy to persuade people to evacuate their homes; at the same time he steals from the homes once they are emptied. By the time of 'Cakewalk', the narrator has become an opportunistic thief and scavenger, living off the grid. During the pandemic, an infected man invades the narrator's camp, stealing and contaminating his things, leading the narrator to a kind of epiphany: 'I am done with stealing. It's the way I've been living for as long as I can remember, always on the lookout for every unwatched package and every unlocked lock – it all suddenly seems barbaric' (75). As good as his word, in the next story the narrator has joined a government organisation called 'Rescue', dispensing resettlement grants to displaced persons. However, living in a deeply compromised world taints the narrator's good intentions, as he plans to cheat the organisation of money. Such compromises recur throughout the book, tipping the scales back and forth between compassion and selfishness; the narrator finds work as a reforming senator's aide, but attempts to exploit the senator's goodwill; as head of security at a commune he uses his guardianship of a teenage boy to cure his terminal diseases. The choice is presented most starkly late in the book at an interview for yet another government position in yet another new regime where the narrator is asked to report whether his interviewer had done anything untoward:

> I could enforce compassion or I could enforce conduct, but
> whatever it's going to be I can't think too long. I have only instinct.
>
> 'No.' Compassion wins. (158)

The narrator's instinct, demonstrated throughout the novel, is always for compassion. However tainted by self-interest, this remains a constant. By the final story the narrator has become a tour guide for the dying, essentially a 'salaried embezzler for the state' (162), and the book ends with his body ravaged and prematurely aged by a life of hardship, receiving compassion from others, including his father. In the end, the son's promise to his father is fulfilled by the father: he looks after his son when he gets old.

The narrator is the only character to appear in every story. Milo, the narrator's father, appears in only the first and last stories, set decades apart, and is only mentioned once or twice in between. His mother Cate features in the opening story, and in a brief flashback in a later story. The narrator's grandparents appear as supporting characters in the first story and as main characters in the second, where they take their own lives, and are never mentioned again. Several other significant characters, including Liz and Jenna ('Dry land'), Juliet ('The forest for the trees') and Jeph ('Predisposed') appear in only one story and then disappear out of the narrator's life and the book, forever, their final fates unknown. Here, Amsterdam uses the episodic structure of the book to his advantage. If *TWDSC* were further towards the novel end of the spectrum of unity, such appearances and disappearances would be unsatisfying. If the first chapter of a novel featured the parents of the narrator as major figures, the reader would expect to see them continue to be featured throughout the book, in a major or minor way. But after the first story in *TWDSC*, the narrator's parents disappear almost entirely from the narrator's life and thoughts: from a narrative point of view, they are simply not needed, and so they live their lives in the absences between the stories. The same applies to Liz, Jenna, Juliet and Jeph: when their usefulness to the narrator finishes, their usefulness to the narrative finishes, and they are left behind by the narrator and the narrative.

By far the most important supporting character in *TWDSC* is Margo, a fellow survivor, thief and pragmatist with whom the narrator is in love. Margo appears in the suite of three stories which occupy the middle section of the book: 'Cakewalk', 'Uses for vinegar' and 'The forest for the trees'. These three stories form a sort of mini linked collection within the larger linked collection, tracing the beginning, middle and end of the narrator's relationship with Margo. This relationship roughly follows the classic formula of 'boy meets girl, boy loses girl, boy gets girl back, they live happily ever after'. In 'Cakewalk' the narrator and Margo have been scavenging together for a while, with the narrator unhappily aware that he needs Margo more than she needs him (boy meets girl). 'Uses for vinegar' is set after Margo has left the narrator for someone else, only to reappear and upend his life once more (boy loses girl, boy gets girl back). Finally, in 'The forest for the trees', Margo and the narrator are working for, and sexually involved with, Juliet, a powerful political figure in the new government. They have more wealth and security than they have ever known, and their relationship seems strong. Although their scheme to bring Juliet into their marriage union does not succeed, the story ends with a dead forest being set on fire to celebrate their recommitment, with the narrator realising in the story's final line: 'I no longer want anything at all' (they live happily ever after).

And then Margo disappears from the last third of the book. This is a strikingly unusual choice; it's as if in *My Brilliant Career*, Harry Beecham was introduced, fell in love with Sybylla Melvyn, then vanished without trace halfway through, with no explanation. Of all the ellipses in *TWDSC*, this is the most significant. In the story which follows, three years have passed, and the narrator is in charge of security in a rural commune. What happened to his working for Juliet? What happened to Juliet? What happened to Margo? These questions are never answered, all existing in the gaps between stories. If there is no definitive answer, however, Amsterdam has left several hints that the attentive reader might use to reconstruct the answers with some degree of certainty: the political situation in the book is in constant flux; Juliet's rapid rise in politics may have preceded an equally rapid fall; the fault lines in Margo and the narrator's relationship have been present from its beginning, and led to the end of their relationship once, so it would be no great surprise if they did so again. The disappearance of Margo is emblematic of the radically unstable nature of the world of *TWDSC*. Nothing can be relied on. There are no constants. Everything changes. There is no happy ever after.

Any form of writing, whether it be a linked short story collection or otherwise, poses a unique series of problems for the writer to solve. In *TWDSC*, Amsterdam's decision to follow the life of one character over more than three decades posed a number of problems in structure, characterisation, theme and point of view, all of which were inter-related and inter-dependent in countless overt and subtle ways. Through the writing of the book, Amsterdam solved all of these problems brilliantly. It is perhaps no surprise therefore that he returned to the linked short story collection for his next book, *What the Family Needed*. Though the form of this book was similar to *TWDSC*, the problems it posed were entirely different, as it followed the lives of several characters in one family, in a contemporary setting, over a much shorter period of time, and in a different genre (fantasy, rather than SF). It might have been a more difficult book to write, or it might have been an easier one; certainly, it was a book that required an entirely different approach to the eternal problems of structure, character, theme, plot and setting, and it is a fascinating experience to read and compare the two books, alike in form but utterly different in execution. A lot can be learned from how Steven Amsterdam approached *TWDSC*, and there are more lessons to be drawn from *What the Family Needed*, but it is important to remember that no writer ever learns to write a book: they learn to write the book they are working on, as they write it. That's the most wonderful and terrifying thing about writing.

Further reading: Some Australian linked short story collections

On Our Selection (1899) by Steele Rudd

Joe Wilson and His Mates (1901) by Henry Lawson

An Anzac Muster (1921) by William Baylebridge

Futility and Other Animals (1969); *The Americans, Baby:*
    A discontinuous narrative of stories and fragments (1972);
      The Electrical Experience: A discontinuous narrative (1974);
      Tales of Mystery and Romance (1977); and *The Everlasting*
    Secret Family (1980) by Frank Moorhouse

Hunting the Wild Pineapple (1979) by Thea Astley

The Bodysurfers (1983) by Robert Drewe

Postcards from Surfers (1985) by Helen Garner

It's Raining in Mango (1987) by Thea Astley

Ride a Cock Horse (1988) and *Fineflour* (1990) by Gillian Mears

Minimum of Two (1987) and *The Turning* (2004) by Tim Winton

Fifteen Kinds of Desire (2001) by Mandy Sayer

Mahjar (2003) by Eva Sallis

Shadowboxing (2006) by Tony Birch

What Came Between (2009) by Patrick Cullen

Having Cried Wolf (2010) by Gretchen Schirm

The Last Thread (2012) by Michael Sala

An Elegant Young Man (2013) by Luke Carman

Heat and Light (2014) by Ellen van Neerven

We. Are. Family. (2016) by Paul Mitchell

Leaving Elvis: And other stories (2016) by Michelle Michau-Crawford

Their Brilliant Careers (2016) by Ryan O'Neill

Barking Dogs (2017) by Rebekah Clarkson

Plane Tree Drive (2017) by Lynette Washington

You Belong Here (2018) by Laurie Steed

Reading crises, writing crisis

Rose Michael and Jane Rawson

As we write this the world is living through two crises we cannot see the end of: climate change and COVID-19. These global catastrophes are upheavals on a scale no-one living has experienced before. They are frequently described as 'unprecedented', even 'unforeseeable'. Medical and environmental scientists are providing guidance on what we can do to mitigate the impacts, but the social and political contexts are so complex we are largely travelling blind. Can fiction help? Can reading and writing stories enable us to transcend the limitations of our own time and minds in the radical act of adopting different points of view?

What about speculative fiction? As readers and writers of this genre we are both deeply invested in how it works – how to make it work – but we do not think, feel, or see, 'eye to eye'; this essay is a collaboration incorporating different, distinct perspectives: of 'one of us' and 'the other of us'. Writers have been imagining disasters for as long as fiction has existed. There are thousands of novels about people threatened by or emerging from plagues, and of societies riven by floods, fire, drought and extinction. There are far fewer about communities that have solved these problems, but even those exist.

Australian literature is not short of examples. Many have been published in the past five years, often in response to the worsening climate cataclysm. As that crisis bites deeper – the bushfire smoke that shrouded Canberra and Sydney for weeks made many more Australians realise climate change can kill – how do these dystopias strike us? And now we are at the mercy of COVID-19. As readers, and writers, of speculative fiction, how do these crises affect the way we feel about future writing?

This chapter is primarily about two recent Australian novels – Laura Jean McKay's *The Animals in That Country* (2020) and Lucy Treloar's *Wolfe Island* (2019) – though it also draws on others to ask: what can dystopian fiction teach us about living in a crisis, or writing through one?

In *The Animals in That Country*, Jean is a middle-aged woman, keen on a drink, divorced, and working as a guide in a wildlife park run by her son's ex-partner. As the novel opens, Australians are falling victim to a flu that lets them hear animals 'talking' to one another, and about us. Many who catch it are driven mad by the voices. Others are beguiled, becoming increasingly more animal themselves. When Jean catches the 'zooflu' she forms a strange, intimate, but adversarial relationship with one of the park's dingoes, Sue. The two of them take off in search of Jean's missing son and granddaughter.

In *Wolfe Island*, Kitty (who has some parallels with McKay's Jean) has spent almost her entire life on an island in the Chesapeake Bay. She speaks a local dialect, creates strange art, and has a wolf dog, Girl, for company. She is estranged from her husband, daughter and grandchildren. The island, once part of a chain populated by holidaymakers and scattered year-rounders, is now deserted. Rising water has made it almost uninhabitable, but for Kitty this is still her safest place, where she can control her own destiny. Everything is upended when her granddaughter and a group of undocumented immigrants arrive looking to escape an increasingly racist US.

Why read, or write, dystopian fiction?

For ten years or more one of us has been reading and writing speculative fiction (and speculative non-fiction) about climate change. Her mind and, to some extent, her life, have been preparing for the shocks of climate upheaval. Her reading has been about resisting and combating that threat – the threat of denial and avoidance, as well as the physical threat of the catastrophe itself. Now that we face a plague dystopia, she finds herself singularly unprepared.

The other one of us has been working on climate fiction that moves through seasons of fire and flood towards a sensed but unseen pandemic. Despite having spent the summer writing about an alien plague, she never saw this one coming.

It makes us wonder: what is dystopian fiction *for*? Some see it as a workshop, a way of authors individually – or collectively – working through possible futures: figuring out strategies to overcome fearful scenarios or bring about hoped-for alternatives. From this point of view dystopias act as survival handbooks, whether that is the author's intention or whether they are even aware of that possible interpretation. They can be read as preparatory texts, practical, literal and transactional, which prompt us to ask: how well would I cope in a crisis?

Others see speculative fiction working on readers as an act of 'cognitive estrangement', inviting them to re-view their own worlds from a new perspective. This more metaphorical or allegorical reading also, similarly, encourages us to appreciate what we have, or advocate for change – in politics, in our relationship with the natural world, in our social and economic structures.

The argument that speculative fiction is escapist has always been rubbish – these books engage with and consider our society and humanity more than most realist novels – but it is now more ridiculous than ever. As our world grows ever weirder, will we turn away from non-realist fiction, 'escaping' these un-real times by reading 'realist' fiction? Or will we, as readers and writers, be more drawn than ever to dystopic, topical speculations – whether in search of metaphorical meaning or literal truth and practical guidance?

Where do the recent, local examples we've been reading fit in this schema? *The Animals in That Country* and *Wolfe Island* are brutally realist in their literary styles. We've both written elsewhere about the pressure to publish one-plot anti-fantasies, but in these examples we see the advantages of a distinctly Australian style of literary realism when applied to 'invisible' climate and virus crises. We can imagine them: as rising tides and 'zooflu'. McKay and Treloar's novels take place in settings that feel real, and among people who are entirely relatable.

If books are identified as speculative fiction – as escapist, futuristic fiction – in the moment of reader reception (so a genre classic such as Margaret Atwood's 1985 *The Handmaid's Tale* can be re-categorised, later, as a literary work), then our changed world changes the way we read these books about changing worlds. We decide how generic they are, in the COVID-19 era – and anything we write about them, now, reveals as much about this world as theirs. This is particularly pertinent in the case of books about plague: while climate change has concerned some of us since the 1980s, and most of us for the past few years – so that any book about weather carries some freight of climate disaster and reference to a real crisis – few of us have lived through a pandemic before now.

Would one of us have read *The Animals in That Country* as so realistic if she weren't self-isolating to prevent the spread of a zoonotic virus?

Would the other one of us have read *Wolfe Island* the same way if she didn't live on a remote island?

How do dystopias work?

In recent Australian releases about epidemics – which include *The Second Cure* by Margaret Morgan (2018) and *The Trespassers* by Meg Mundell (2019) – the virus separates people. Most obviously the well from the sick, but other inequalities are also manifest (those who have care, who can afford care, and those who don't; those who are more vulnerable, for reasons of age, health, financial or family circumstance, from those who are more secure; those who know something, or have access to some kind of knowledge, and those who do not). Written before our pandemic struck, these novels use disease as a metaphor to reveal things about contemporary society: for example, our treatment of migrants and refugees. As Laura Jean McKay says in an interview with Booktopia, '*The Animals in That Country* is a novel that features a strange new flu, but it's mostly about connection – especially between species – and how we might find it in the strangest of times'.

McKay uses a virus that jumps across species to collapse the idea that there is any difference between human and animal: Jean's mother is 'so old she's gone reptile – like a snake' (44); her ex-daughter-in-law Ange is a 'bird woman. If she could strap Kim on her back she'd be up there too' (46). *The Second Cure* is also about 'the interrelatedness of life and the interaction between species' (54) – as well as more fantastic aspects of 'host behavioural manipulation' (57) (which were enough to make us wonder if COVID-19 had more surprises in store, as articles emerged about possible neurological consequences and atypical strains while we were awaiting the second wave).

In *The Trespassers*, Mundell uses a shipload of low-paid migrant workers coming to Australia to highlight the plight of 'boat people' today and our shameful immigration detention policy. Her tale references White Australia's heinous history of invasion and dispossession: the title refers at once to 'illegal' immigrants, the colonisers of First Settlement, and the virus the characters think they have escaped but which has been brought aboard – 'a deadly trespasser, crossing cell boundaries, seeking out new hosts' (112). This is a book about contagion and is at its best when it teases out the thoughts many of us are having today, in situations of surprisingly similar lockdown: 'who coughed in my vicinity, used the wash cube before me? Who leant too close, whose stale air did I inhale? How clean was that doorknob, the breakfast cutlery, my own hand?' (79). The treatment of infected passengers on the *Steadfast* has echoes throughout history but also today, where we may all be in the same storm but not the same boat, as migrant workers, bushfire survivors, the homeless and other marginalised people are confined in close quarters and don't have the privilege of self-isolating.

What does it mean for the way we read these novels that inequality, connection, surveillance and separation are now issues we're grappling with in the real world, in response to an actual virus? We challenge any reader in the current climate to read a virus as only metaphorical.

Even the most outrageous ideas in Morgan's *The Second Cure* – such as Queensland's becoming a breakaway country – might not be that unrealistic. As we write, that state's borders remain closed. Indeed, Western Australia claims it has become 'an island within an island', a surrealist take on geography. By referencing current politics and drawing on recent Australian history, Morgan creates an all-too-plausible alternative world where Sir Joh's inheritor remakes his banana republic. But the aspect of the novel that now seems most prescient is, of course, the way the central pathogen spreads between species: from animal to human. At the time of its release this was the aspect many reviews described as 'speculative'. Speculative, perhaps, but, it turns out, not just possible but probable.

When is speculative fiction realist?

In correspondence published by *The Victorian Writer* as 'Re Dear Extinction', McKay agrees that 'yes, animals can be metaphors (and so can objects, landscapes and human characters) but they can also represent animals. A dog can be a dog ...' But how does that change when a virus enables the reader to understand what that 'dog' – the dingo, Sue – is saying? McKay describes the animals' cacophony as an all-over, all-in bodily experience of language, which humans only tune in to once they're infected. (Unless, of course, this 'animal apocalypse' (107) is a mass hallucination and actually, 'we think they're saying things but it's just us, imagining it' (134) and – as it is for us now, and Jean at the end – 'The animals around us squawk their mysteries and we're none the wiser' (52).)

As mammals', birds' and insects' 'talk' becomes discernible, affected humans lose their ability to speak in proper sentences: 'I'm starting to talk like her' (166). The result of this 'Talking. Animal. Disease.' (35) is an even-more-truncated, laconic style – on both sides of the human/animal divide. The way Sue speaks, when her words finally emerge into print, is nothing like the twee 'voices' Jean 'does' early on in the book – or where the story starts, with Jean sensing Sue saying, 'Hey, *hey*. There's something coming' (1). It owes as much to Aussie slang as it does to poetry or song, in keeping with McKay's brilliant recreation of our 'titty-fuck' vernacular (158): 'Hell, fire, guts and blood. Fuck the police. A bird looking like that can't be saying anything nice' (20). McKay has been diligent in her effort to create animal dialects that cleave to the realities of non-human communication and reflect our scientific understanding. The resultant dialogue is difficult, slippery, and otherworldly – just as it would be if we could hear, but never quite understand, what the animals in our country are saying.

'Hey. Hey Sue? You wouldn't ... you're alright with me, aren't you, girl?' Her hair shifts. Body ripples with messages that join like drops of water in the sea.

> **Milk shine. (Leave it for**
>
> > **the pack.) Its**
> >
> > **door**
> >
> > **is barking.**

> I touch her gingerly. 'You wouldn't bite me again, would you, Sue?'

> > **Its anus**
> >
> > **is**
> >
> > **my north.**

> 'Jesus. I'm just asking you this one thing.'

> > **Mother**
> >
> > **can bite its**
> >
> > **pink. (144–5)**

McKay's dystopia pushes readers to think past generic animal rights to more specific practices, such as cross-breeding native species in wildlife parks and factory farming to feed pets as well as people. Her use of a thoroughly researched, imaginative, yet realist language reminds us that animals are complex, thoughtful, and in some ways unknowable – they are not symbols or projections, but individual beings in their own right. Her point is clear: 'people who anthropomorphise tend not to read cues, and people who don't read cues are dangerous. Dangerous to themselves, dangerous to the animals' (11). As our protagonist, the tough-as-nails alcoholic Aussie grandmother whose story this ostensibly is, would say: 'Woof'.

While the crisis in *The Animals in That Country* might be read metaphorically, *Wolfe Island*'s realism is never in doubt. In its contemporariness Treloar's novel acknowledges that dystopia and apocalypse are already part of many people's lives. This reveals a seam in the thinking of the literary establishment – generally Western, White, middle-class – of dystopias as something that happens in the future, and to other people; which won't matter until it happens to 'us' – which, before COVID-19, wasn't yet. By saying dystopian fiction is futuristic, by designating it as speculative, the literary establishment has refused to acknowledge many people's present realities. *Wolfe Island* contradicts that.

Treloar's work – intentionally or not – echoes earlier classics of realist ecological catastrophe, such as John Steinbeck's *The Grapes of Wrath*. Hers is a tale of a slowly encroaching environmental collapse that first reaches those who are most precarious but eventually laps at the doorsteps of even those better off. Once touched, everyone is turned into members of the underclass.

'Is this now?' the reader asks herself. 'Is this real? Is this happening today?' We look for clues in the text that tell us whether we can safely assign these stories to a distant future or whether, in fact, the end has started to come for people like us. 'It's a dystopia', we think, 'so it must be the future; it must be made up. It's science fiction, so I don't need to take it seriously'. But the language, the settings, the relationships all point to here and now, and we begin to remember that yes, child immigrants in the US are kept in cages; parts of America, and Australia, are being made uninhabitable by flood and fire and drought. We think uncomfortably about Indigenous people in both countries, who have been driven off their land by a different kind of apocalypse, who have seen their populations winnowed by disease, massacre, environmental collapse and despair.

We try to remember whether the island we have shored up for ourselves is a safe place or not.

It's easy to find reviews of all these crisis fictions that describe them as being set in the 'near future' – it says it on the cover of *The Trespassers* – but the near futures of these writers is our reading present. We see little that is speculative here, from their minimal, realist styles through to their ideas, which are not only not that far-fetched, but not far off. The 'real' world has caught up with these 'non-realist' titles; there is no need for the complex worldbuilding traditionally associated with science fiction. These literary experiments are literal. Could these examples of climate fiction and epidemic thrillers – which are not *only* metaphorical, which benefit from the distinctive realism that contemporary Australian writing is famous for – be read as a new kind of less-speculative, not-that-fictional field guide to crises?

Can we tell if we are in a dystopia?

Before COVID-19 we had a harrowing Black Summer. Do you remember? Rolling infernos of 'unimaginable' ferocity. It reminded one of us of Jennifer Mills' *Dyschronia* (2018): Sam, the main character – another solitary woman, though considerably younger than Jean and Kitty – occupies multiple times simultaneously. She is beset by visions that are inexorably, inexplicably, bound up with the fate and history of a quintessentially Australian country town. The devastated, devastating, atmosphere surrounding the abandoned community seemed to describe the smoky days we were experiencing: 'It's a hot morning, strange for the season. There's a smell in the air we don't recognise, and it wakes us in our beds' (11).

In Sam's claustrophobic confusion our own solastalgia was reflected; in Mills' anger we recognised rage at a ravaged landscape – and the destructive role played by governments and corporate greed. To describe Mills' book as science fiction, to read it as an intellectual time-travel puzzle, is to miss the bigger point: speculative novels are designed to evoke the mess and contradiction of lived experience in ways minimal modernist narratives may not. 'Here's a prediction: the future never turns out the way we think it will. Simple enough, but that's not the end of it. The past isn't what we thought it was either' (237). This read, and still reads, true to us.

As Mills wrote on Twitter on 21 May 2020: 'Australia as a vast island of fracking camps run on the labour of precarious workers exiled from trashed universities and a broken arts sector. Easily as dystopian as anything I've come up with'.

Critic and author James Bradley describes Mills, in the *Australian Book Review*, as having left behind 'the niceties of literary realism', but we read her as bringing literary realism with her into this eco-crisis the same way that the other Australian writers described here do. Bradley himself writes 'non-realist' fiction with a robust realism, tackling topics as wide-ranging as the multi-generational impact of our climate catastrophe in *Clade* (2015), or the wild idea of Neanderthal de-extinction in *Ghost Species* (2020). We agree with him that the literary novel is mutating – has already mutated – 'its boundaries and subject matter evolving in sometimes surprising directions as it attempts to accommodate the increasing weirdness of the world we inhabit' (*Australian Book Review*). This increasing weirdness demands that writing also evolve in unprecedented ways. As Australian realism takes in the reality of now, we see crisis novels offering a way to write, and write through, the current crises, none of which will end any time soon.

Often the presence of technology (the 'science' of science fiction) alerts readers that a story is set in the future. Contemporary realist literature frequently sidelines the technology of our times – even the most ubiquitous tech, like smart phones and surveillance cameras, are elided, as though to mention them would risk making the text dated, somehow un-literary in its temporal specificity. Treloar plays with this, letting the reader see a speculative setting: 'I turned. Luis's head was skywards, checking behind. "Looking for trackers?" I asked' (15); 'A walk around the house discovered the solar system panel at the back door. I turned it on and a green light lit up. With any luck it would still work' (27). The initial impression may be futuristic, but it only takes a moment for us to realise these are everyday technologies – drones, solar panels – present everywhere around the world.

It isn't only the technology that at first suggests Treloar's tale takes place in a different time: Kitty tells her story in the first person, in an old-timey language that makes the setting seem distant and hard to place – is this the nineteenth century? Is it a far future? 'The islands were worlds and you didn't move lightly from one to the other, and people's way of speaking wasn't quite the same from one island to the next' (4). But by the beginning of the second chapter we realise that while Kitty may not be of our time and place, she does live in it: ' ... town made me edgy (all those people in their bright clothes looking at me, their faces saying, My God, who does she think she is?)' (8). She is here. And so are we.

Wolfe Island reminds us how fleeting our focus on any crisis is: 'TV people used to do reports on "the situation". They'd put some folk in a room ... and some pretty young girl would say, "How do you feel about your world disappearing?" ... They'd act like something might come of it but nothing ever did. We were "the island that time forgot" then they'd go right ahead and forget us again' (51). Treloar reminds us that the media cared, for a moment, about a heatwave that swept Europe in 2004; about a drought that threatened metropolitan water supplies in our capital cities in 2007; about Brisbane and the Lockyer Valley flooding in 2010; about bushfires across Australia last summer.

Once upon a time the world – *we* – cared about SARS, and bird flu, and Ebola, and eventually we will have once cared about COVID-19. And then the next thing comes along, and takes us by surprise, before being forgotten again.

It is the style of Treloar's writing that keeps bringing us back to our own world, to this present and these crises. *Wolfe Island* is not escapist; *Wolfe Island* offers no escape. This book makes us ask, repeatedly: is this my dystopia? Am I living in a dystopia now? Kitty's sinking island is not in our future, but in our past, and our present (echoing Briohny Doyle's more hardcore science fiction novel *The Island Will Sink*, from 2017, with its complicated projections of Pitcairn Island). This is our dystopia: rising tides and salinated soil and climate refugees.

'How can we see what we can't imagine?' asks Mills (12). This has always been the purpose of speculative fiction: to speculate, to imagine. To write the future. But how might we imagine dystopias differently if we accept we are living in one now? How can we tell a dystopia? Who will do it? These are, and always were, someone's end times.

In the face of COVID-19 we find ourselves without words, asking questions that for all our speculative prepping (admittedly for a different crisis) we cannot answer. What does this pandemic mean? When will we know? What will the COVID-19 crisis we are living through – separately – reveal? The issues of aged care, casualised work, the cost of child care, the possibilities and limitations of online communication, have never been so much in the news. The advantage of work that can be done from home, the disadvantage to those who provide services deemed non-essential, has never been so stark. Those who don't have access to technology are completely cut off from any community beyond their immediate circle while those who have a garden, a bigger house, a block of land, are obviously privileged. How, and when, will we know the meaning of COVID-19?

Where do we go from here?

How will we return to 'real' life once we close the pages on these fantastic tales of global, and more local, crises? This pandemic has taught us that this is the question that preoccupies most people: when does this end and things go back to 'normal'? When can I restart all the parts of my life that are on hold?

This is not the way fiction usually works. Unless you're reading *Dyschronia* (or one of our own time-slip, time-trip works), novels don't generally go back to where they started – let alone further back, to before that. Narratives usually move the reader forward through time: a conflict or inciting incident occurs, which is then resolved to create a new reality. Australian environmental dystopias often follow this pattern. In Daniel Findlay's *The Year of the Orphan* (2017), Australia, hundreds of years from now, is a destroyed society with small groups of people living scattered in the desert. The Orphan seeks knowledge about how things got to be like this, and – to our point – how a better future can emerge. In Sally Abbott's *Closing Down* (2017), droughts and food shortages have forced Australia to sell off rural and regional towns; their inhabitants have become refugees. Will kindness to strangers forge a new society from this broken one? The hero of Alice Robinson's *The Glad Shout* (2019) has been forced by flooding to live in a make-do camp in central Melbourne, where she dreams of escaping to a better world in Tasmania.

Dystopias pick over dusty clues and buried secrets to reveal the traumatic breakdown – similar to something the author sees in our very, very near future – which led to the terrible state of affairs the characters now find themselves in. But here we are, in our very own dystopia, and for most of us the pressing questions are not: what went wrong? How did we get here? But: where can we go from here? And how quickly will we get 'back on track'?

Climate change may match the conventional arc of dystopian fiction – and that form might be the ideal way to encourage us to think more about how we got here, what we might have done differently or where the tipping point was (where we began to 'see' the deep time of this slow – and still-growing – catastrophe). But COVID-19 is an acute crisis, and its acuteness might be what enables us to think differently: about activism and consequence; the importance of cultural speculations; the malleability of a seemingly unchangeable way of living. How else would we be able to act collectively to 'flatten the curve'?

The Second Cure and *The Animals in That Country* toy with the idea of positive aspects, or not wholly negative side-effects, of dystopic infections. In *The Second Cure* it's the idea of synaesthesia, sensory cross-wiring that enables the infected person to see sounds or hear colours, which leads to new art and new experiences. 'Happenstance in other words', its protagonist Charlie acknowledges, 'like all evolution. A genetic mutation that found itself in the right place at the right time' (9). These slight benefits do not outweigh the overall devastating impact of the viruses; all the main characters end up taking clear sides against the aberration, but the point is made that for some people life would be better, different. As a passing character in *The Animals in that Country* puts it: 'Personally, I don't think they're after a cure at all' (132).

We have all made the connection between the images of silent cities in lockdown and science fiction. Monkeys, moose, moving in. Could this be our extinction, we wonder? Probably not. The doors will reopen but COVID-19 has shown us what the world can do, based on scientific advice, to bring about a delayed effect that benefits not only an immediate us, but others, and future generations. Did you see – or, rather, not-see – Wuhan, from space, once the lights went out? 'Without electricity', McKay writes, 'the whole world has been returned to its proper darkness' (52). Venetian canals run clear. People hear birds. Moles wander parks, fearless. Famous landmarks are finally free of pollution. Could something good come of this?

Our pets have been living as we have lately their whole lives: largely confined to house arrest except for a short outing for exercise each day. Now they're joining us online, natural Zoom-bombers. Will we rethink animal relations? Realise, like Jean, our symbiosis: 'I'm their predator. I'm their prey. *They're hunting me back*' (87). Will we not just reimagine, but remake what work means? When our children go back to school, will we immerse ourselves in our homes' silence and solitude rather than seeking stimulation? What kinds of experiences will thrill us – overseas travel, fancy meals, live music in loud bars, or will just hugging another human, 'talking' to them with our full face and body, be enough? The importance we place on some things – or, rather, the lack of emphasis we previously placed on others – must, surely, shift.

Or will you let the old world start up again?

'Time's like a road, see?' Jill tries to persuade Sam in *Dyschronia*, 'And now's like a car. It goes straight along in one direction' (38). Except that for Sam it doesn't: she's continually thrown out and back through time into 'Another now. The next. This time ...' (38). *Dyschronia*'s constant refrain is that Sam's visions are a warning. All these books are that, and more: not just creative speculations of what might be, but literal as well as metaphorical stories of what already is.

In an interview with *Electric Literature* the month the World Health Organization declared COVID-19 a pandemic, science fiction author Ted Chiang wrote:

> [T]raditional 'good vs. evil' stories follow a certain pattern: the world starts out as a good place, evil intrudes, good defeats evil, and the world goes back to being a good place. These stories are all about restoring the status quo, so they are implicitly conservative. Real science fiction stories follow a different pattern: the world starts out as a familiar place, a new discovery or invention disrupts everything, and the world is forever changed. These stories show the status quo being overturned, so they are implicitly progressive ...

Chiang's advice is that we must distinguish between what is desirable, and what is familiar; between what we want because we identify it as worthwhile, and what we want unthinkingly, because it is known.

As speculative fiction writers – and readers – we might have thought ourselves progressive, but even we have sometimes longed for a 'normal' world. Even we have conservative impulses that catch us unawares. James Baldwin famously said in a *Paris Review* interview that when you're writing 'you're trying to find out something which you don't know', but what is often forgotten is that he went on to say writing is 'finding out what you don't want to know, what you don't want to find out, but something forces you to anyway'. It is this not-wanting that seems so relevant to our current speculations: we read and write not only to find out what we (as individual artists, and a human collective) don't know, but to face what we don't want to. In this case, perhaps we are uncovering that we too felt comfortable in our 'non-acute-crisis' world, where crises were happening to other people, where we felt safe. We too preferred our own safety to a world where change is possible. This is what we grapple with, as we face the page: what don't I want to know?

What will you, Dear Reader/Writer, do?

If there are no guidebooks for this future, what other purpose might dystopian fiction serve? Ursula Le Guin writes in the introduction to *The Left Hand of Darkness* that the artist 'deals with what cannot be said in words. The artist whose medium is fiction does this *in words*. The novelist says in words what cannot be said in words'. This is the challenge of novel writing that speculative fiction addresses, even if it cannot answer it: how to say what cannot be said, how to live with crisis.

'How long till you find a cure?' *The Second Cure* asks, on behalf of all of us. And answers: 'Soon, I hope.' 'When, though? Tomorrow? Next week? Next year?' 'No ... Not for a while' (165).

If reading dystopian fiction can change the way we live, as we considered at the outset, does living in a dystopia change the way we read, and write, novels? In May 2020 the US *Publishers Weekly* reported that trade publishers were looking for 'escapist' fiction – as they described the realism of historical novels and domestic drama, and as we suggested earlier in this article. But writers will write what they must, regardless of what publishers – or the market – wants. (Despite the arts industry being in such crisis, books are not doing as badly as some feared. And fiction is faring surprisingly well.) Some authors will leap into 'coronavirus novels' because they can think about nothing else, others may allude to COVID-19 allegorically, or retreat into history – whether to write about past plagues or ignore plagues altogether.

In the first few months of the pandemic, literary social media was full of writers terrified by how they would address 'these times' in their contemporary or forward-looking novels. But this problem has been with us for decades, thanks to climate change, and most fiction writers have successfully ignored it. For one of us, writing about our own opinions (including in this essay) has become fraught – who cares what she has to say in a time of global crisis? – and she has found herself tongue-tied. Her retreat has been writing historical speculative fiction that comments on our times only allegorically. For the other of us, who has had her typing hands tied with homeschooling responsibilities, her speculative fiction has begun to turn from issues of environmental consequence to those closer to home: genetic inheritance.

Ultimately, as we wrote earlier, readers will decide what a book is 'about', regardless of the writer's or publisher's intentions. And they – who are also, of course, us – will seek out the stories needed. Thanks to our own obsessions, we have read Sandra Newman's *The Heavens* (2019) as a meditation on humanity's effect on the environment, and watched *Russian Doll* (2019) as a parable of climate change, though their creators probably intended nothing of the sort. This pandemic will infuse all our subconsciouses for years to come; everything we read will feel like commentary on this time. Already Otessa Moshfegh's *My Year of Rest and Relaxation* (2018) has morphed from being read as a novel subtly about September 11 to one less subtly about quarantine. For the next few years all novels will be pandemic novels, however they were written. As Elizabeth Outka writes in the *Paris Review* about those penned during the Spanish flu: 'The continued sense of living death, of an experience that marks us with its shadow, echoes even after a pandemic passes'.

Instead of pondering such thoughts in isolation, with only future readers in mind, we chose to write about dystopian crises together. Fighting viral loneliness, timelessness, and stultifying self-doubt, one of us reached out to the other one of us to embark on a critical collaboration that could reach across the Bass Strait and turn the constraints of lockdown into an opportunity for connection. The current social distancing restrictions mean our Melbourne–Hobart relationship is now as close as any. This creative writing practice proved one way of processing what we cannot. Yet.

The sad old flesh:
How we use non-human
characters to interrogate
humanity

Anna Spargo-Ryan

What does it mean to be human? Perhaps only the animals
can know. – Boria Sax

If you were ever a primary school student, you were probably tasked
with writing from the perspective of an animal. *Imagine you're a cat*, the
exercise asked. *What happens in your day?* As children, we tried to put
ourselves into the mind of the creature. What *did* cats do in their day?
What did they think about? When we weren't home, what antics did
they perform?

In writing them, we did not make them human. They were only
imagined as their animal selves. 'I want to catch a mouse', we wrote. 'I'm
sleeping on my favourite chair.'

The role of animal narrators has evolved in contemporary literary
fiction. Rather than being an autobiography of the animal, they hold a

mirror to the human reader. They are able to offer insight outside of the boundaries faced by a human narrator, to critique social, political and economic behaviour with an implied objectivity.

All writers come at their practice from their own context. It is impossible to separate the story we want to write from what makes us human and not animal – race, gender, sexuality, class, ability. We're affected by the time in which we're writing, the way we have been raised, the country where we live, the current political climate and so on. For contemporary fiction writers, animals offer something more than an imagined day in the life of a creature walking from bowl to bed. They are an opportunity to follow lines of inquiry without the assumed or explicit framework of everything that makes a human life.

To a degree, they are not about the animal at all. Many modern animal stories anthropomorphise non-humans to critique human structures without being a participant in them.

It's not a new technique – George Orwell's *Animal Farm* and Franz Kafka's Red Peter in his short story 'A report to an academy' did this decades ago – but perhaps it is exactly what posthumanism demands. Trusting a non-human narrative voice immediately equalises it. If language is what sets us apart from the animals, putting words to their experience is a leveller. That makes it the perfect way to force us to consider our position in this hierarchy.

Authorial context is important. When we write, we respond to what is happening, in one way or another. Our authorial context affects everything from the way we express an idea to the depth and nature of our knowledge on a complex social structure. The demand for #ownstories has never been as visible as it is now – the author's story is in many ways just as crucial as the one they have written.

We also know that a character within a story has all of these same inherent biases. Although readers only see the person on the page, we can imagine (if they are well developed) their whole life outside of the story. They are not only the woman on a mission to save the world, but the product of her childhood, the city that broke her spirit, the opportunities she missed. Everything the character does in a story is coloured in some way by all that came before that moment. We know this because we are human, too.

The animal's naïvety targets the prejudices of the reader. The non-human seems to ask: 'What is the foundation of your bias? Explain yourself. Because from where I'm sitting, you and all your terrible ideas are totally baseless'. They take the reader outside of the context of the character and instead draw attention to the reader's own shortcomings.

A story that employs an animal narrator says: here is a creature. It has not been socialised into any human constructs. It has not been oppressed by other animals of its species, or been deliberately excluded, or suffered under systemic disadvantage. It does not bring any *additional* stories to the new story. It is not this story *and* the culmination of every other story that has happened to it – this is the only implied story it carries. They are independent adjudicators, of a sort. The animal narrator is able to function as both a participant in the event and a critic of it.

For the purposes of storytelling, animal narrators are the perfect blank canvas. They come without human experience, but still with the believable degree of sentience required to observe and report back.

*

Ceridwen Dovey introduces us to ten animal narrators in her 2014 book *Only the Animals*. Roundly acclaimed, the book won the 2014 Readings New Australian Writing Award and the Queensland Literary Awards' Steele Rudd Award for a short story collection, and was co-winner of the 2015 NSW Premier's Literary Awards' People's Choice Award for Fiction. It now appears on various school and university curricula.

Structurally, the book comprises ten short stories that move us through a little over a century of history. It opens with a camel observing the nineteenth-century 'poet drifter' Henry Lawson and evolves through women's suffrage, world wars and the space race to end on a woman and her parrot living in Beirut in 2006. Each piece draws stylistically on a great writer of the period, in a way that often approaches satire. They are each narrated by a different animal observing, in one way or another, humans living through noteworthy historical times.

It's clear from the first pages that our superiority complex is about to be challenged. The blurb itself promises: 'An animal's-eye view of humans at our brutal worst and our creative best'. Dovey sets us up to bear witness to our own recurrent ghastly behaviour.

These animals are employed specifically to explore constructs of humanity: war (Soul of Mussel), religion (Soul of Dog), poverty (Soul of Bear), gender (Soul of Cat) and spirituality (Soul of Elephant). Each story begins with the animal's year of death; each animal dies through the abuse, neglect or wanton irresponsibility of a human.

Every human in these pages is dreadful, as is necessary to provide the posthumanist critique, but the animals largely don't know it. For example, in 'Hundstage', we follow the story of a dutiful canine companion, the brother of a dog named Blondi. The human reader knows Blondi – she was Hitler's German Shepherd, killed to test a cyanide pill. We know that she was used to support Nazi propaganda, portraying Hitler as a gentle animal lover. Unlike the narrator, we come to the story with all of this pre-existing knowledge.

In this passage, the narrator and his sister have met their new owners and learned of their laws to ban the use of dogs in fox hunting:

The scientists at the Society were very proud of this law, and of the many others we had heard them discuss at their meetings. Yet it was not until Blondi and I met our new Masters that we began to understand the significance of these laws, and the fullness of our Masters' compassion for animals. (77)

As readers, we are forced to consider what the narrative is asking us. Is it: do you see how easily a mass murder can be humanised? Or is it: have you noticed that even the most reprehensible people have a softer side? And then the next layer of reflection: what does that say about me?

Without an animal narrator to take 'sides', the reader must find their own position.

＊

Many of Dovey's stories explore the Other; for example, in 'A letter to Sylvia Plath' – 'human women need no reminder that they're animals' (206) and 'The bones' – 'There was a painting of some Aborigines hung on the schoolroom wall, but they looked more like you, like camels, peculiar creatures that shouldn't exist ...' (6). The stories demonstrate empathy for non-humans, but Dovey's narrators aren't precisely non-human; because they are not animalistic in their nature, it translates as implied empathy for the marginalised humans the stories aim to represent. The animals are anthropomorphised to expose their human-like shortcomings, prejudices and disadvantage.

Without the human constructs the text itself critiques, the animals decay. This occurs throughout, with abandoned or chained-up or shot-into-space creatures meeting their demise without humans to care for them. Most explicitly, the epistolary 'Red Peter's little lady' tracks the correspondence of the chimpanzee as he regresses into his former self. Again, we are forced to reckon with what it is that makes him 'less' – he reflects on his transformation from chimp to human, remembering a fitting for a velvet waistcoat and discussing politics.

On humans, he says:

What sets them apart is their talent for masochism. Therein lies their power. To take pleasure in pain, to derive strength from deprivation, is to be human. (51)

Red Peter has no skin in the game, as a non-human narrator. He necessarily sees us for what we are, and we must, too.

Even Dovey's choice of animal is significant. We already have relationships with domestic animals, and so we have personified them. Who hasn't used a weird baby voice to pretend their cat is talking? In the context of humanism, we believe we understand something significant about these species – our cat is not *a cat* but *our cat* and as such has a consciousness more complex than a wild boar, for example. We have – again, in our humanness – established imaginings of certain animals. A wolf is wild, courageous, adventurous; a rabbit is twitchy, sweet, shy. We give human attributes to animals and so they, too, come to a story with an existing context.

But what do we know about mussels? Not much more than garlic and white wine, probably. In 'Somewhere along the line the pearl would be handed to me' – a strong channelling of Jack Kerouac – we meet a non-human narrator that is not only an unknown consciousness but a literal observer – a mollusc attached to the hull of a warship, watching the attack on Pearl Harbor unfold. We have no sense of what a mussel feels about being blown to bits in humanity's pursuit of total domination, and so we must take what he sees at its face:

> Something splashed into the water and streaked towards us, glittering like a school of barracuda on the hunt. We admired it, not quite knowing what it was, until it hit our battleship. A living waterspout was sucked up and over the ship's stack. The lobster was killed instantly. The piece of the hull Muss and I were attached to was blasted out into the port as our ship began to list and shudder, hit again and again and again. The humans pulled alarms – no more training drills, not now – and suddenly around us in the water were things that should never be seen in the sea: valves, legs, fittings, heads, coins, arms, helmets. (115)

In her 2014 review of *Only the Animals*, Delia Falconer writes:

> Over the last decade, scholars have been moving away from the
> assumption that animal protagonists are only furry stand-ins
> for human dramas. Instead, they are re-reading fiction to trace
> what it tells us about animals themselves, or about the complex
> entanglements of our lives with theirs.

As she contests, animal stories in modern literature are not the stories
we wrote in kindergarten. *Only the Animals* takes this a step further, to
dissolve the human–animal relationship almost entirely.

Dovey's use of non-human focalisers avoids witnessing the fall-out.
The choice to use an 'outsider's' perspective gives her certain freedoms;
she is writing without the constraints of culpability, offering comment
and criticism of human history without requiring resolution of it.
Her animals experience the vast range of human emotion but are not
responsible for its consequences. They see humanity's impact on their
environment – literally, through war and famine, and figuratively,
through technology and psychology – but do not seek to understand
how they arrived there.

In a sense, all they offer is an invitation to the human reader to
insert themselves into each scenario. They don't offer explicit critique;
without the social constructs that make us human, they also lack a
framework through which to critique it. They can merely comment,
inviting the reader to (hopefully) employ some self-awareness. The rest
is on us. We must infer our role in all of this mess-making.

In the same year as *Only the Animals* appeared, literary theorist Pramod
K Nayar published *Posthumanism*, a text that examines posthumanism
mostly through the rise of technology. In it, he writes:

Literary texts ... have now begun to show that the human is what it
is because it includes the non-human. (12)

That is, humanness is illustrated through comparison – we are human
because we are not animals. In literature, we have an opportunity to see
what we are when written in the context of the Other.

Humanism is a philosophical position centred on scientific
reasoning and the agency of human beings over spirituality and the
supernatural. While posthumanism – *beyond* humanism – has a
number of definitions, philosophical posthumanism is concerned with
humanity as *part of* ecology and technology, not separate from it.

In a text like *Only the Animals*, the distinction between human
and non-human is deliberately blurred. The narrators exist somewhere
between these two options, both embodying what is problematic
about humanity and being far enough outside of it to offer meaningful
critique.

Using non-human narrators for this function is a posthumanist
paradox, of course. We not only assume we have enough self-awareness
to write subtextually about our own experience, but that we understand
animals well enough to also convey their perspective on it. Our
superiority remains intact, and we reassert it by declaring we also speak
for them.

However, this method can also be an effective storytelling device.
The dissociation of humanness from the animal narrators means we can
look at our own biases, prejudices and oppressive structures before we
have a chance to realise what's happening.

It runs a high risk of being didactic, and certainly *Only the Animals*
is heavy-handed in parts. We understand the conceit immediately, so
in some ways the remainder of the text has an undercurrent of 'now,
remember that you're bad'. But does that matter? Aren't these stories
simply a kind of modern allegory?

Literary theorist Anna Barcz writes:

... entering the field of a literary text which necessarily affirms the nonhuman, always using tools external to man and other animals such as the constructed language, we open up to possible mediation in literature but also in a broader context – in the language of art – to other points of view. Despite the technological nature of the language and the feeling of its alienation, animal narratives may be an example of familiarising these strange elements within which we function and which – by means of another stylised voice – give the possibility to go beyond the narrowly defined world of selfish human kind. (269)

We – especially 'we' the privileged, the wealthy, the lawmakers, the self-interested – have millennia of practice at centring ourselves in stories. We do it without hesitation, even when the central characters are openly, achingly not even the same species. Dovey's animal narrators prey on our need to make everything about ourselves – and punish us for it.

Dovey's animals are not animals at all, but an 'us' with which we can be forced to reckon.

*

Narrative theorist David Herman considers the question of narratology beyond the human thus:

... Bernaerts et al. have, for their part, established an important precedent for inquiry into narration by nonhuman agents, laying foundations for a narratology beyond the human more generally. They argue that narratives told by nonhuman narrators engage readers in a dialectic of defamiliarization and empathy – defamiliarizing (at least in some instances) human-centric frames of reference while also promoting empathy with other-than-human ways of being-in-the-world. (82)

By contrast to *Only the Animals*, the non-human characters in Laura Jean McKay's 2020 novel, *The Animals in That Country (TAITC)*, are much more *like* animals. In this frighteningly timely story, a highly contagious flu is infecting humans across the country. As well as the usual symptoms, the virus allows humans to hear animals 'speak'. In fact, it gives them no choice. Suddenly, the air is flooded with new voices, from the central character of Sue, a dingo, to a pod of whales and millions of frantic insects.

What makes McKay's writing so interesting is the creation of a kind of dialect for these animals. While they all speak English, each species uses it differently from the next. The cadence of a mosquito isn't the same as a cat's. A snake makes dissimilar word choices from an eagle. And while they are given language – that distinction we draw which makes us superior – they are not 'made human'. They use language to bely the truth about the way we treat not just them but each other and the world at large, through a syntax that is recognisable to us while remaining animalistic.

Maria Takolander, reviewing for the *Saturday Paper*, wrote that McKay 'refuses both anthropocentrism and the philosophical position that non-human animals are inevitably alien to us'. We know what we do to them, but we choose to dissociate from it.

TAITC takes a different approach from *Only the Animals* to judging the human condition. The language these animals use – which is our language, that is human language, in this case English – draws links with postcolonialism. The way an invader uses words to create meaning is not the only or best way.

The animals in this story take those same words and create new meaning and interpretation; their own meaning. This is **rain**:

(Sky meat,
poison water.) (209)

A person in mourning:

The sad (old)
flesh. (221)

And **life**:

If you smell down
(deep)
the
long day ends. (235)

Rather than relying on the human reader to draw their own conclusions, the focalising character of Jean witnesses the animal's perspective and judgment of humans while it happens. Cleverly, it's not only because they tell her she's bad but because the syntax and vocabulary they have created implies it: 'poison water' carries a judgment, but the animal doesn't know it. The language these creatures choose from our own vocabulary convey a violence that's not inherent in the words themselves.

Living is *too*
big. Living is too
big. Small *piss*, there.
There. (197)

Literary scholar Lars Bernaerts and his colleagues describe a '*double dialectic* of empathy and defamiliarization' through which 'Non-human narrators prompt readers to project human experience onto creatures and objects that are not conventionally expected to have that kind of mental perspective' (69). McKay's writing encourages us to reflect on the impact of our human constructs – disease, climate damage, globalisation, industrialisation – on animals, both because we understand the words they use and their meaning, and because their way of using them is completely unfamiliar. Their near-humanness discomfits. We have been *seen*.

*

In *Only the Animals*, anthropomorphised narrators serve two functions that might be employed by other writers. Their personification is familiar to the reader, so we can easily understand and empathise – it's simple for us, with our gigantic and complex human brains, to imagine what it's like to be this animal, to feel the same basic biological sensations of hurt, abandonment, hunger or vulnerability.

On the other hand, the fact that they are *talking animals* means that we also carry a sense of strangeness that defamiliarises them. It is impossible, as a reader, to be entirely comfortable in the story. The use of an animal narrator asks the reader to consider and reconsider, reminding them that they *don't* understand the experience. As Bernaerts and his colleagues describe, 'What is often at stake in non-human narration is the ability to acknowledge similarity and otherness at the same time' (74).

Dovey's animals are us, and not us. They know what we know, but they force us to acknowledge what we do to them. Once again, they present a posthumanist paradox: the reader will only ever be the invading species. As long as the defamiliarisation exists, we are not equal.

Human–animal studies scholar Margo DeMello wrote in *Speaking for Animals*, 'Increasingly today, animals are allowed to speak for themselves, demonstrating a new awareness of animal subjectivity, and a desire on the part of many animal lovers to give that subjectivity a voice' (4).

But these are not strictly stories about kindness to animals. They may not require an animal-loving author at all. An author may create a non-human narrator not to invoke empathy or awareness of that creature, but because it is impossible for us to see ourselves without it.

Starting from place: An introduction to a different way of thinking

Felicity Castagna

Place can be a source of comfort and belonging and a site of anxiety and shame. Our complex relationships with place are fundamental to our identity. Where do you come from? It is often the first question we ask of someone, without stopping to consider how deeply personal it is. For the writer, place is where they stand, it is the experience out of which they write, it provides the base of reference, the point of view.

Whoever made up that creative writing mantra that stories are either plot- or character-driven wasn't telling the whole truth; stories can be place-driven as well. In both Alexis Wright's *Carpentaria* (2006) and Luke Carman's *An Elegant Young Man* (2013) the story is embedded in the physical setting. We experience place as a driver of plot, place that determines the voice and style, place as a spiritual guide, place as politics, place as transformation, place as the core of our identity, place that at times is even a character in itself.

Carpentaria is a novel that draws from the rhythms and stories of an oral Indigenous culture deeply rooted in the fictional rural town of Desperance near the sea in the Gulf of Carpentaria. The novel tells the interconnected stories of several Indigenous people of the Pricklebush clan and centres on the infighting between local Aboriginal communities, and the greater challenge that befalls the region when a multinational mining corporation sets up on sacred land.

An Elegant Young Man is a series of connected stories about a character who, like the author, is named Luke Carman and grew up in the working-class neighbourhood of Mount Pritchard in Sydney's western suburbs, where the community is often defined by racial conflict, anti-intellectualism and a strict adherence to traditional gender roles. *An Elegant Young Man* is essentially the story of Luke's coming of age as he makes his way to adulthood and unemployment while obsessively navigating the suburbs that both define and reject him.

What I want to do is to look at both these writers' work, though not in an exhaustive way, because both books are really too complex and dynamic to do them justice here. Instead I want to make you read as a writer, which means asking you to contemplate what they have to teach us, to look and see and think about their words and what they might have to say about how you can make your own writing spring forward from the ground on which you stand.

Map making

Look at a map. There's a lot there. Streets and streets and houses and houses and parks and important buildings. Maps do the thing that we should never do as writers, which is to put everything in, rather than to surrender our stubborn adherence to replicating the real and focus on the detail that has weight. In his book *How Fiction Works*, the literary critic James Wood argues that 'literature differs from life in that life is amorphously full of detail, and rarely directs us towards it, whereas literature teaches us to notice' (52) – to notice and make larger, so that we can focus on the significance of say, a particular river or garbage heap that comes to represent an entire history of colonialism and its resistance in *Carpentaria*, or that one street or home in *An Elegant Young Man* that defines the neighbourhood and the character's position within it. Both these texts take larger questions about who we are as a nation and explore them through the local, specific places where we can begin to really unpack these ideas. The philosopher Michel de Certeau called these kinds of personal maps 'spatial stories', which he argued are important 'because they locate individuals with regard to larger structures, providing ways of understanding how we react with others and locate our own identities within the practice of everyday life' (115).

A writer's map of a place is punctuated only by the significant things that most people wouldn't take time to look at really hard. In *An Elegant Young Man* a series of stories entitled 'In Granville' forces the reader to look closely at one street:

> For a while Clyde Street went to war with itself. Houses were firebombed, and a charcoal chicken too. It didn't make the news, or if it did, I didn't see it. I stayed at my dad's every second weekend and he took me to see the burnt out carcasses of houses and cars gutted and smoked in the daylight, a thin line of blue and white tape hanging around the ashen remains that seemed so obscene between green even lawns and tidy fibro homes set in tight rows (33–34).

The specifically chosen detail here shows us that place is not just a thing but a social, physical and mental process, in which the imaginary, memory and desire collide to form our observations of where we are standing. It's all in the well-chosen detail: the 'green even lawns and tidy fibro homes' stand in contrast to the 'burnt out carcasses of houses'. The image of the 'tidy fibro homes' and 'green even lawns' is an iconic one of a safe, idealised suburbia. Suburbs are a crucial landscape of the imagination onto which Australians situate ambitions for upward mobility and economic security, ideas about community and family.

These small markers of suburbia have tremendous weight because the image of the safe suburbia they connote is juxtaposed with 'the burnt out carcasses of houses', suggesting an extreme violation of this ideal. The carcass here goes beyond its associations with death and destruction to suggest something primitive and animalistic. Much of the conditionality of living in a difficult place is expressed in terms of the pressures and distortions on the place itself. The setting comes alive through specific verifiable detail. These details aren't there as a kind of painted backdrop for the plot, they are a place onto which the character's feelings of anxiety, fear and shame are projected: to quote another clichéd creative writing mantra, they show rather than tell.

As Lynda Ng argues in her introduction to a collection of essays on *Carpentaria*:

> ... writing is all about creating an explorer's map of the unknown. Your map is about you. It is about the way you see your place. The story of the community of Desperance in Alexis Wright's *Carpentaria* partakes of this visceral sense of belonging to a particular place. The sense of belonging and displacement felt by the inhabitants is the reverberation of a disempowerment of the Indigenous people that had begun with European settlement two centuries before. Locality is thus not only a felt presence on the literal level but, allegorically, a trope of resistance against European invasion. (10)

In other words, Wright chooses the spaces that are included on her map not just because they show her character's deep connection to place, but because all those spaces have not only a literal but a metaphorical meaning as well – they stand for a wider idea that she is exploring.

Like Carman's, Wright's map is populated with small, significant places that often become strange or otherworldly. This is a specific writing strategy that forces us to sit with familiar images and think harder about their significance as we are forced to navigate through our disorientation. Literary critics Carol Ferrier and Nicholas Jose have argued, furthermore, that there is a politics to the surreal and fantastical elements of Wright's landscapes, because by blending the carnivalesque and magical realism with Aboriginal storytelling, which also relies on 'symbol, imaginary presences and magic' (Jose in Molloy, 2) she is challenging the idea that the realism so valued in western literary cultures actually tells us anything more 'real' about life than these methods.

In the first few pages of *Carpentaria* Wright maps the places of primary significance in Desperance from the earth's creation to the present, beginning when the serpent came down and created the rivers by slithering across the land, to the present, in which mining is an ever-present threat to the land and its people. It feels epic to read, as though we have just been handed the history of the world and asked to comprehend it in a few pages. What pulls this scene together is that there is a tight focus on specific parts of the town that have a heavy metaphorical weight. Take this section for example:

> Normal Phantom was an old tribal man, who lived all of his life in the dense Pricklebush scrub on the edge of town. He lived amidst thickets of closely growing slender plants with barely anything for leaves, which never gave an ant an inch of shelter under a thousand thorny branches. This foreign infestation on the edge of Desperance grew out of an era long before anyone in the Phantom family could remember. They had lived in a human dumping ground next to the town tip since the day Normal Phantom was born. All choked up, living piled up together in trash humpies made of tin, cloth, and plastic too, salvaged from the rubbish dump. (3)

Trash, the waterways and Pricklebush are the three primary markers of place that Wright returns to over and over again, and they do in fact hold the weight of the history of the world, particularly to the Indigenous inhabitants of Desperance. In the above passage Wright isn't just trying to locate Normal within the town; she is trying to locate the story of Indigenous people represented by Normal. 'Pricklebush' is an important symbol because it is an imported European weed that infests the town, taking space and soil nutrients without giving anything in return. The emphasis on its 'thickets of closely growing slender plants' and 'a thousand thorny branches' enforce the fact that it is inescapable, much like the effects of European colonisation. The locating of Normal and his family next to the rubbish dump is indicative not just of his socio-economic position but of the lack of respect for his people. These geographical markers are heavy with history, metaphor and symbolism. It's only when you choose a few very specific markers and make them the focus of the reader's attention that you are able to invest them with such power.

Place is atmosphere and mood, but most importantly, place is emotion

There is nothing less interesting than an author trying to tell the reader how their characters feel. *She felt sad*: the problem with a line like this is that it's not only boring but undermines the way that real feelings work: the deepest emotions are often hard to articulate and sometimes we won't or even can't acknowledge those feelings are there at all. Our feelings are often bound up and expressed through our attitudes towards place in much more complex, nuanced and meaningful ways.

Take, for example, the opening passages from *Carpentaria*, which like some other parts of the text, are written in the collective voice of the Indigenous people of Carpentaria: 'Can someone who did not grow up in a place that is sometimes under water, sometimes bone-dry, know when the trade winds blowing off the southern and northern hemispheres will merge in summer? Know the moment of climatic change better than they know themselves?' (2). In these few short sentences Wright sets the mood, the atmosphere, the tone, and lays out the emotional investment that the Indigenous people, past, present and future, have in the place they stand in. Describing the place is a way of describing one's self and how one feels as much as it is a way of describing the feelings one has towards a place: the above few lines are a way of saying 'I am of this place, its changes in mood are my changes as well, they are in my body, they are who I am.'

In a similar way, internal conflict, anger and rage are often depicted as distortions of the landscape. The palpable anger and dismay of the Pricklebush people at national as well as international attempts to claim, know and control the region aren't often literally articulated in dialogue; rather they are viscerally felt through the descriptions of an enraged, volatile landscape in resistance. Toward the end of the novel a cyclone rises up to wipe out a controversial mine and the lack of respect for the traditional landowners that it represents:

> So, even though we were shaking in our old work boots, thinking we got busted eardrums, we watched the fire rage like a monster cut loose from another world. It might even have come from hell. Even the devil himself would have least expected us weak people to have opened the gates of hell. But we watched full of fascination at the fire's life, roaring like a fiery serpent, looking over to us with wild eyes, pausing, looking around, as if deciding what to do next. Then, we could hear it snarl in an ugly voice you would never want to hear again. *Alright, watch while I spread right through those hangars like they were nothing, hungry! hungry! Get out of my way.* (470)

There are so many ways that one could read this and similar scenes in the text but I read it as being purposely ironic. The Pricklebush clan have been forced to occupy the position of 'weak people' living on the outskirts of town. Maybe they are frightened people even, 'shaking in our old work boots', but the enraged earth is on their side with its snarling and 'ugly voice'. They've definitely got the most power here, and we feel their rage.

In *An Elegant Young Man*, the protagonist has multiple homes: his mother's home, which is a place of maternal comfort, and his father's home, often a volatile site of anger and shame. In Gaston Bachelard's seminal text *The Poetics of Space* he argues that home is a manifestation of the soul, a place of great intimacy and memory, and that therefore when we write about home we are trying to articulate something deep about who we are. Take, for example, this one, ordinary, intimate memory that Luke has of his brother and his mother at home together in Mount Prichard:

> She stood above us, watching him eager for breath as he drank
> from a frosted cup with Michelangelo, the Teenage Mutant Ninja
> Turtle, on the glass. Sometimes, I noticed, she would watch us in
> those ordinary moments as though for the final time, and the loud
> fluorescence of the kitchen flickered as if to do her blinking for
> her as she stared. Adam ate in a trance, lost in his inner world, the
> idyllic daydream of youth was always around him like a nakedness
> in the decline of our little mountain. (177)

This passage transcends a mere recounting of space to give us an understanding of how home is felt as an internal experience. It does this through a persistent concentration on figurative language as a way of making the reader internalise the external environment. Time itself seems to slow down as we are presented with images such as 'loud fluorescence' and 'the idyllic daydream'. This is what good writing does, it uses the fewest words possible to say the largest number of things. The simile, 'like a nakedness in the decline of our little mountain', for example, simultaneously implies both an intimacy and a vulnerability. It is their mountain, but also a space where they feel exposed. It says many things at once about who the protagonist is, how he sits in the world, and all of that is reflected in his description of place.

Speaking places: When place becomes the voice and style

There are many reasons for the wholly unique voice and style of Wright's *Carpentaria* but one of them, I would argue, is that it is a book that comes so strongly from place. Wright herself has spoken many times about trying to find a uniquely 'Aboriginal voice', in her words 'literary fiction that wanted to portray all times as being important and being intertwined culturally to place, and which I thought was a fundamentally important principle for any kind of story about place in this country' (*Meanjin*). *Carpentaria* begins with a chapter called 'From time immemorial' which collapses past, present, memory and future to address the collective experience of Indigenous peoples. The first two paragraphs are given in all caps – a visually aggressive choice which reinforces the conflict set up between the nation-state, which demands complete attention and subservience, and the 'human fallout' of a community for whom it will not even extend an 'olive branch':

THE BELLS PEAL EVERYWHERE.

CHURCH BELLS CALLING THE FAITHFUL TO THE TABERNACLE WHERE THE GATES OF HEAVEN WILL OPEN, BUT NOT FOR THE WICKED. CALLING

INNOCENT LITTLE BLACK GIRLS FROM A DISTANT
COMMUNITY WHERE THE WHITE DOVE BEARING
AN OLIVE BRANCH NEVER LANDS. LITTLE GIRLS
WHO COME BACK HOME AFTER CHURCH ON
SUNDAY, WHO LOOK AROUND THEMSELVES AT THE
HUMAN FALLOUT AND ANNOUNCE MATTER-OF-
FACTLY, *ARMAGEDDON BEGINS HERE.* (1)

This is immediately followed by a passage that seems to counter the
above narrative by taking us back to the story of the land's creation,
a story which is given far more space and poeticism: 'The ancestral
serpent, a creature larger than storm clouds, came down from the stars,
laden with its own creative enormity. It moved graciously – if you had
been watching with the eyes of a bird hovering in the sky far above the
ground' (1). The voice and the style here is driven by the back and forth
between the nation-state's patronising view of the local inhabitants
and their attempts to authentically articulate the materiality of its own
particular place. There is an acknowledgment of the wrongs colonialism
has wrought on this place but the far more distant past of the earth's
creation offers us a version of the landscape that is hopeful and carries us
forward. The style and voice is dictated by the two different conceptions
of territory that need to compete here, in a novel that embodies a
complex mesh of Indigenous realities of place.

Carman's unique style and voice also arises from his attempt to
encapsulate the complex realities of living in the western Sydney area. In
the first three pages of the opening story the author weaves quotes from
Dr Seuss, Dylan Thomas, Walt Whitman and Richard Dawkins around
seemingly random arguments about heritage listings and a crumbling
local leisure centre. It is in this space of excess that both the reader and
the narrator begin to make some sense of the text's landscape. Take, for
example:

I found someone the other day. It was Walt Whitman. Under a
broken cabinet outside the Whitlam Centre. The Whitlam Centre
is a place in Liverpool where they have swimming pools and boxing
rings. It's sort of a big deal. Anyway there was the complete works
of Walt Whitman just lying there. It was the first time I'd come
across him. He was in an Allen Ginsberg poem I read once. It was
a poem about finding Walt Whitman in a supermarket. I liked the
idea. I still like it. I took Whitman with me around Liverpool for a
bit. (3)

Just as Ginsberg finds Whitman in a supermarket, Luke finds Whitman
at the Whitlam Centre. The word play here conjoins two powerful
figures, one of Australian politics and the other of American poetry.
Both these important figures are placed into a suburb, Liverpool, which
is shown to be a neglected outpost of Sydney. The pairing of these
grandiose figures with such a landscape is farcical but important. It both
mocks the idea that grand figures can represent local spaces and asks the
reader to question why a place like Liverpool isn't considered a greater
part of the national story. Neither Luke nor Ginsberg find Whitman
by accident. Rather, they conjure his presence as a sage guide to help
them ascribe meaning to place. *Leaves of Grass* (1855), Whitman's epic
collection, created a tradition of opening up and embodying America,
using lists to build imagery representative of as much of the country and
as many of the people as possible, and incorporating the poet into this
celebration of himself and his surroundings. Luke takes Whitman on his
walk because he is looking to history to help him answer the economic
and social questions about what his modern world has become. But
the truth is that Whitman, with his visions of uniting the diverse
landscapes and peoples of America under a common national imagery,
just doesn't work in Liverpool. This is not because Whitman is speaking
of America; the idea that a diversity of peoples can be united under a
common national image is a frequent trope in Australian literature as

well. Whitman doesn't work here because western Sydney is a place that has never quite fitted into national imagery, or at least Carman refuses to allow it to be engulfed.

Walt Whitman, the man who can find poetry in everything, the poet so famous for his long verbose sermons, has nothing to say here in Liverpool. It is a silence that seems to speak symbolically to a larger silencing of such a place in Australian national imagery. This is in fact how the passage, like much of the book itself, works – by pairing what seem like opposite symbols, metaphors and statements in order to form a sly commentary that gets at the important issues Carman wishes to discuss. The seemingly paradoxical descriptions in the opening scene also immediately conjure spatial uncertainty. They signal immediately to the reader the difficulty of Carman's project and the anxiety he experiences when trying to narrate the story of a landscape that offers so many contradictions; but those contradictions inform the style and make for an arresting sense of voice.

'Nothing is random', Luke insists in the opening pages of *An Elegant Young Man*. It should be a mantra for any writer. Writers make specific choices that inform the texts they write and those choices are often bound by or come from place. Place drives story, voice, emotion. It can help us to articulate ideas that are larger than ourselves: as Wright says, 'country hears its people, it is listening all the time, and it will speak back to you' (2019). So before you sit down to write something, consider what the place and the characters' actions in that place – the details they notice and how they interact with them – will shape what you write.

Read to find yourself

Peter Polites

The Glebe Point Road Blues:
Reading to look for myself in a book

Being gay is not a monolithic experience, everyone has a different relationship to it; one of the reasons I read is to find myself in Australian writing.

As a youth I snuck into the library that my mum worked at and read Christos Tsiolkas' *Loaded*. I never borrowed it because I didn't want it to be on my record. But it was a map to me. It showed me what my future would be. Feelings of pain that were covered up with dangerous sex and illegal drugs.

The easiest place to find myself is in the writing of gay Greek men. I'm privileged in that way, that the Greeks of Greece and her diaspora have had countless same sex-attracted writers. But when I picked up Vrasidas Karalis's new book, I realised I wouldn't understand it from the departure point of myself. I'd need to go outside of my body, myself, and my experiences.

His latest is called *The Glebe Point Road Blues*, and is written in prose and verse. Part One, in prose, forms a series of fantastical portraits of characters who appear on what he calls 'The Road'. Part Two is written as a series of poems. There is no way I can claim to understand it in its totality. I'm not smart and haven't had the classical and academic training its author has had. There are numerous references to classic literature, philosophy from all eras and the Bible. As a man it's radical to admit to your shortcomings (that's for another essay) but even in my limitations there are recurring patterns that strike me. The people portrayed in the first section would probably be called quirky in a publicity release, but really they are damned souls. Thematically I identify a consistent grief, links to the occult and the alienation of settlers from the landscape. Many of the characters have untimely fates. One changes genders and becomes a murderer, a queer monster of sorts. An ageing Nazi must be redeemed by his occult nurse.

One thing that presents itself to me as a Greek is the writer's concept of the blues, conveyed here as a deep and unique form of melancholia expressed in the Greek musical form of *rebetika*. Rebetika as a form emerged in the 1920s and was a combination of Ottoman and European folk traditions played in a then-contemporary western style. The pioneers of this music were refugees from the Asia Minor catastrophe who lived as an underclass in Greece. Rebetika is a mood; the songs sing about loss of love, manifest from the loss of an imagined homeland.

All the characters in the prose section of *The Glebe Point Road Blues* are out of place, living in exile. Some have had to come to Australia because they've lost their homes to the forces of Thatcherism or neoliberalism. Others are escaping their provincial families. Many of the First Nations people in this book are lost in Australia because of policies enacted by the state. More cerebral characters find themselves lost from contemporary ideologies. All in all, the characters' experience of exile creates a melancholia I identify as uniquely Greek, pioneered by the discarded people of the Ottoman empire. As a reader, I imagine that this is the mood of the author, conveyed through the characters that inhabit

Glebe Point Road. The discarded Greek Ottomans were my literal and biological ancestors. Therefore, the tone of *The Glebe Point Road Blues* speaks to me, or rather sings to me. I recognise the mood of the book in myself.

The writer of this book is a professor of modern Greek at Sydney University – a knowledgeable and respected pillar to us peasant Greeks in the community. When I first encountered his prose and essays, I mistakenly read them as high camp cruelty under the guise of postmodernism. The concept of camp cruelty has a long tradition in the gay community. Cruelty is a method for showing affection. More unsophisticated selfie anthropologists (aka social media tumblr millennials) might call this a form of lateral violence, but gay cruelty is seen as a way of transferring critical thinking skills and resilience to younger generations of queers. In one of the prose pieces the floating voice laments a missing person they remember and speaks a familiar form of camp cruelty. The piece is called 'Did he really exist?' A character called Alkis sings a song, 'Put the blame on Mame', from the movie *Gilda*, made famous by Rita Hayworth. He is 'defiant and condemned, but irreverent, standing tall and singing' (23). Alkis prefers the consolation of a glossy women's magazine to that of the Bible. In a scene describing his assault and his pain, Alkis confesses stoically the most painful memories of assault and never breaks, disturbing those around him as they go to church. The character talks about 'the flowers he loves, the trees, the cars, the sunsets' and then seamlessly discusses 'the rape by his father and brother'. A hallmark of high camp is creating an uncomfortable atmosphere for those around.

Beyond the high camp comes a different understanding of his work. As I discuss this work with other people, I gain a more complex understanding of it as Baroque. There are riffs and references that seem like decorative gilding but are really part of its architecture. They become part of a spiritual framework for the building, for example: the heavy themes, as discussed above, next to language of beauty; describing a death from AIDS-related illness and including descriptions of the 'Sweet breeze, gentle silence, soft sunlight' (25); this play with metaphor, extended in the writing.

One of the limitations that stops me from reading this Baroque aspect in the work is my knowledge of the writer himself. Vrasidas means something significant to me. It's his significant stature to me as a Greek gay man, someone I look up to and respect, that makes it hard to read the work. Being awestruck makes it hard to separate the text from the author. He experienced the great upheavals in history that many of us same-sex-attracted cis gay men fetishise. For example, his experiences of growing up at a time when homosexuality was criminalised, and men were beaten, of the Greek community excommunicating queers and the insufferable and provincial homophobia of the Greek community generally, living and loving through the AIDS crisis and 'just being friends' with the only descendant of Byzantine royalty on Australian soil, Manoly Lascaris. It's because of his standing in the community and his experiences, being at the centre of so many things that I hold as crucial to my identity, that I read his work for wisdom and as a chance to refine my thoughts on art and practice.

One of the stories in the prose section is called 'Ode to the new millennium'. It delivers wisdom about art and life and should be a fable for all young artists. The story is about a poet called Charbel from suburban Sydney. He writes terrible poetry that celebrates his erotic experiences and triumphs with women (all this kind of poetry is terrible). He is a character who is obsessed with his own experience. He writes poems 'about his beautiful body, his triumphant penis' (61). Quite narcissistic. After the failures of his poetry, he doesn't do any self-reflection and never wonders what it means to be creative. He finds a different method to centre his own experiences in the public domain, through long political screeds and manifestos. He lacks the abilities of self-reflection, playfulness, and sympathy – all qualities one needs to be an artist. So, he dies as an artist and moves towards a self-destructive path that is manifest in his personal life. He is a young man whose pig-headed emphasis on himself leads to a shallow identity politics and self-destruction. I know this person; I have met this person and I have been this person.

Voss: Read the letters to your love

Patrick White's most famous book. Part of the Australian canon. The story is about an explorer who tries to conquer the landscape and fails. Quintessentially Australian, in that it's about failure. But for me the best part of this esoteric epic is its intimacy: the relationship that develops between Voss and Laura Trevelyan. Laura is the love interest in the story, but she and Voss only meet once. And as Voss travels deeper into Australia they appear in each other's dreams and connect through letters. In the letters he expresses a humble love for her but there is an element of rationality in them. It's clear that her love for him doesn't mean the world, he has other things going on his life and looks forward to meeting up with her eventually (even though they never do). I read the letters to my boyfriend when we were courting. They are romantic. And express themselves in a formal way, where the feelings are muted by convention. Repression is kinda hot. Despite this, I hope my relationship is more successful than that of the couple in this book.

Ransom: Read it to know what it is to be a man

People don't know this but Greeks alive today don't make a distinction between Ancient Greeks and themselves. We see the ancients as ancestors. The first time I said this in a public forum, elderly members of the audience gasped in horror. Later I got too many follow-up questions. I explained that Greeks still name their children from these ancient times. Today you can find Athena, Socrates or Hercules running corner shops or driving trucks. So many of the pagan traditions are still incorporated into the yearly calendar of Greeks. About four months a year around the ceremonial holidays Greeks eat no animal products, oils or sugars, in order to purify the body for ritual. And even though I am no eugenicist, studies show that Greeks from the bronze age still have the same genetic structure as contemporary Greeks. I take a very shallow comfort in this DNA information.

What brings me more comfort and connection to my Greek heritage are stories about Hercules, the goddess Athena, or the philosophy of Socrates. These were the stories that were told to me as I lay in bed under my doona. And *The Iliad* is one such story connecting me to my heritage. All Greeks, whether diasporic or on Hellenic soil, feel these stories are in our custodianship.

In 2009 when David Malouf attempted to write one of the minor narratives in *The Iliad*, I decided I really wanted to read it to see if he had done justice. Malouf dedicated a whole novel of prose to the moment when the King of Troy tries to get his son's dead body back from Achilles. His novel *Ransom* is basically a posh form of fan fiction about *The Iliad*. After reading it, the novel became instantly pressed into my heart as one of my big favourites. It's been more than ten years since this book has come out and every time I go back for a reread I discover something I forgot, something surprising. *Ransom* isn't usually the first book you talk about when you reference Malouf. But to me it's his best.

It excites me when an established poet writes prose. Toni Morrison teased her poet friends that they wrote beautiful poems and she wrote beautiful prose. But David Malouf has had the resources to have a practice in poetry. He has written nine books of poetry and four librettos, the words to an opera. And when someone has the time, regardless of how they acquired it, they will create interesting work.

Firstly, the language describing the landscape is striking: such an important job for a writer. It's particularly important for those writing in the southern hemisphere and many have theorised that it's a defining aspect of our work. Not only do the landscape descriptions set the tone for the novel but they also help form an image for the reader in their mind's eye. In the opening sequences of the book, the sea is described as a 'lustrous silver-blue membrane' (3). Using the colour blue and the metallic silver puts an image in the reader's brain of something impermanent but shiny. But describing it as a 'membrane' makes the sea a single organism with a barrier. I reflect on the Jungian idea that the sea represents the unconscious. It's these kinds of details I look for: images that represent other images, that lead me into the deeper thoughts of the writing.

The link between mother, sea and unconscious create an ecological and queer matriarchy that guides Achilles in this book. The sea membrane image introduces him: a Greek soldier fighting this battle of Troy. This scene also shows that one of the strongest influences on his life is his mother, Thetis the sea nymph. Here, when Achilles' thoughts go towards his mother, his manly and hard qualities are suspended, his will melts and the 'solid particles of which they are composed' begin to 'tumble and swarm' (172) and he is of his mother's element. In that state, Achilles is from the sea and made up of the sea, at the same time. He is a formless shape under the silver-blue membrane in which ideas, memories and influence emerge from its depths.

In this man's world, references to the gods or supernatural modes of existence are located by using queerness. The kind of queerness that I am talking about is in potential. Theorist Jose Muñoz identifies queer not as a state of being but a 'warm illumination of a horizon' (1). Queer shouldn't be a noun, it's not an identity. Queer, as I see it, is an approach and an intention. In *Ransom*, there is the sea-like quality Achilles associates with his mother, particle-less and formless. In another scene the most powerful god Zeus sends Hermes to escort Priam, King of Troy, across the battlefield. The way Malouf describes him is as kind of a femme but sexy street tough. Hermes has a rosy mouth, narrow waist, and ringlets. The god is play-acting with anger and his gestures are described as an elegant flourish. It creates a disconcerting space for the king's emotions and registers this queerness as supernatural. His limitless godlike potential, ultimately queer.

Apart from the metaphysical queerness and the use of formless spaces accessed through gender – in the real time of the narrative, this book is about homosocial bonds. It's a story between fathers, sons, soulmates and enemies. There are queer childhood narratives in this book but ultimately it's about men and maleness, exploding during a time of war.

For me it is the final scene that teaches readers what the ultimate form of masculinity is. It is in the gesture of Priam, King of Troy, who goes to the Greek camp to retrieve his son's dead body. He decides to appeal to Achilles not as a king but as a man. To do this he completely dethrones himself. He does not wear any royal signifiers of capes and jewellery. He goes there with only a donkey called Beauty and its peasant handler, Somax. He is a vulnerable old man asking for his son's body back. This action makes the case that real masculinity must be dethroned of all its ornate decorations. Emotionally bare, gentle and vulnerable, this moment is the ultimate performance of male gender and the duties of a man.

The Adversary: How to be a gay now

When I first read Ronnie Scott's *The Adversary*, I saw it as being in the tradition of novels that are written about ornate social relations: novels that centred a person's character and their experience amid the confinement of constructed and arbitrary human barriers. These books were written primarily by women in Britain during the nineteenth century and in my rudimentary experience, *The Adversary* falls into this tradition. I am in the extremely privileged position of being able to speak to many authors who have new books coming out. So, I talked to Ronnie and said that his book reminded me of aspects of Jane Austen novels. He said that I was wrong: that his work shared more of an interest with the Brontë sisters.

When coming-out and AIDS narratives are passé, being a white gay cis man is normalised. And with this normalisation, we get a different understanding of the concerns of gay men. There is a whole genre of coming-out fiction, and its concerns become another hegemony, something that new artists rebel against. It is common in queer literary circles to roll one's eyes at the shallow sentimentality evoked when the hetero hegemony discusses texts like Timothy Conigrave's *Holding the Man*. The AIDS book is a canon of its own now. I use this term loosely and cruelly because these kinds of stories centred the emergence of the virus and its effect on communities and gay life. It seems that many cis gay male authors must create a major gay AIDS novel. AIDS, like all pandemics, affected the social order as much as it did people's bodies. Just before AIDS crashed into the community, it seemed like the community was shifting into a mode to fight for rights. We had just had the 78ers protesting in the streets to decriminalise homosexuality. They all got arrested. When AIDS hit, people who would have been involved in the fights for civil rights had to start organising for healthcare.

AIDS and homophobia created what I call the monster homosexual. Hear me out. The source of discrimination that gay men experienced was based on social views that homosexuality was wrong. In a legal framework this manifested as a law against sodomy. This law stigmatised men's bodies and their acts. When AIDS came along it was literally an infection of the body. Infected blood and illegal acts were the reason why gay men so readily identified as these 'body monsters'. Littered through gay art and culture are images of half-men, half-animals, and hyper-muscled cartoons designed to terrify and arouse. For a long time, the biohazard symbol became a common tattoo and gas masks were popular objects of play in the community. And it gave rise to a series of transgressive gay texts. Examples include Alan Hollinghurst's *The Line of Beauty* and Tony Kushner's play *Angels in America*.

Recently we have seen a correction in literature that doesn't take this gay monster equation into account. The stigma of HIV is disappearing. It is no longer a tombstone, it's just a manageable illness now. In the West, all the rights and privileges that heterosexuals have are officially afforded to homosexuals. White gay men are taking their place as out politicians, business leaders and athletes. For me white gay male normalisation was cemented when the book *Less* won the Pulitzer. This novel by Andrew Sean Greer is a book about being a gay man, but there are no references to the defining issues of the gay experience. There are no references to homophobia, stigma or HIV. Instead the concerns of the book are a life well lived and travel experiences. It centres work, creativity, joy, and the quest for companionship. This book has received the highest accolades any book can, meaning this kind of gay literature is now established.

In Ronnie Scott's *The Adversary* the characters have a historical understanding of gay male identity and its struggles. They acknowledge this history and when they encounter someone who doesn't, that person is rudely dismissed. There are numerous references to their shared history with the gay community, paralleling the author's understanding of this book's role in the history of gay literature. It asks the question: 'What would be the main concerns in Queer literature if gay men weren't monsters?' And the answer to this question goes to matters of race and class. And this is what the book is demonstrating to us. The characters in this book are predominantly white or their cultural background isn't specifically mentioned. So, they read as white and what does define them is a geography: a small pocket in Melbourne's inner north. This bourgeois bohemia is enacted at parties, holiday homes, terrace houses and pubs. Setting becomes paramount, more so than characters' background or history. And this emphasis on setting parallels the emphasis on landscape in Australian literature. This foregrounding of place can be read as the characters' inability to deal with their settler backgrounds. To expand on this idea, the characters don't want to delve into their families' pasts, how they came to Australia. They don't want to delve into their whiteness, or how it is complicit in structural racism.

In this posh setting, it is easy to barrack for our main character. Although character likeability is considered a book club question outside of the role of serious literary interrogation, the question still comes up again and again. I try not to bother about whether I like a character or not, but sometimes the author renders the character into the real world, and I can't help but think about this. I find the protagonist in this book both insufferable and adorable. The reason for this is that he is bound by a limited geography and this parallels the limited social conventions that bind him.

At the start of part three, there is a Brontë quote: 'You held out your hand for an egg, and fate put into it a scorpion' (Charlotte Brontë, *Shirley*). This stylish reference to convention encapsulates the whole book. The first-person voice is enchanting and self-effacing. Ronnie is a masterful ventriloquist of the foppish, early nineteen-twenties ingénue: 'I watched the possibilities fly like currency out of my hands' (73). It really is a triumph of playful writing. The author conveys the thoughts of our protagonist very well, with lots of humour and a light touch. Our main character hates bodies, fluids, secretions and mouths. He makes a terrible gay man and he is always trying to interpret and re-interpret gestures.

The action of the book never veers into the overdramatic but its emphasis on style mirrors the central action, which hinges on a deception. Although its protagonist has an acute understanding of gay politics and history there is effortless light-heartedness to the subject matter. What is so refreshing and exciting for me in this gay book is that at its core it's not about boys and sex. This is a book about platonic relationships and their mysterious desires; it's about the kindness and curiosity it takes to search and maintain meaningful human contact. And isn't this a better way to define a man, rather than who they sleep with or what their body once was?

Postcards to Charlotte Wood: Revisiting *The Natural Way of Things*

Ashley Hay

Dear Charlotte,

It's five years now since I first met your book. Five years since I woke with your characters on their first morning of incarceration, isolation – before they (or I) knew where they were, what was coming. Five years since I first met your ten women, snatched from the world, and abandoned.

I can't remember where I was the first time I began to read its words, although I do remember that first scene, the night time, the isolated confusion, Yolanda finding the brightness of two enormous stars: the power of an opening image, an opening mood, a viscerally sharp scene.

And I remember where and how I reached its end, the pitch of emotion that your story's passage had brought me to. I remember how those pages, those last sentences felt – not their actual words, but how I felt inside them, pressed as close as I could be, as small as I could be, against the final seven women as they emerged on a bus from the other end of the story, being carried back to what they mistook as freedom. Your narrative had pressed so hard against me it had lodged inside my self.

So many diagrams have been devised to map a story's shape – jags, curves, peaks, troughs. I think about the shape you chose, or discovered, in this story as a line that climbs and climbs and climbs, foreshortening the scale of its witnesses – the word 'readers' doesn't feel strong enough – in the face of the magnificent self-preservation, the epiphany, of the two characters who make it out and away and free from participating in any remaking, any retelling of this brutal narrative. Verla and Yolanda, free from any idea of return – free, as Anne Summers put it, to 'flee the prison of their femininity, of their sex' (*Griffith Review*).

I can still feel the tightness of every part of my body, curled as small as it could be in the middle of the floor among your manuscript pages as I finished reading them for the first time, willing myself on, willing myself to believe in that potential of freedom, of salvation against the fate of those women still on that bus.

To write a story that inhabits its readers: that is some thing. The broadness of the landscape you conjure for this book against the limits of the world that it's set inside: it's an elegant balance of scales.

I'm writing these words curled in another small space, the bubble of a newly viral world. I'm thinking about the magical thinking needed to let those women on that bus – Lydia, Leantha, Joy, Barbs, Maitlynd, Izzy, Rhiannon – suppose they could return anywhere, reclaim anything. That let them believe their world could ever be the same again – or that they should want it to be. What would 'the same' mean? We live differently pressed against the reality of that idea now – and yet what (or how) the world thinks of women and of men can be also shockingly unchanged.

And what 'same' would they want to claim? The boots, the perfumes, the pretty things you give them in those showbags as they leave? Or the blame, the shame, the judgmental dismissal? The way you balance the scale: of tiny indulgence against the magnitude of a society's judgment.

The way you led us into and out of this story. Five years on, over and over, your book still tightens its coil on my imagination.

*

Dear Charlotte,

The first time I read this book, a group of us had been sent an early copy. It felt like being snuck into somewhere unknown and undiscovered, given a preview of some newly classified animal. It felt almost like spying, prying. Malcolm Knox defied 'anyone to read it and not come out a changed person'. Christos Tsiolkas called it 'a howl of despair and fury ... you can't shake off this novel; it gets under your skin, fills your lungs, breaks your heart'. Clementine Ford called it 'terrifying, remarkable, and utterly unforgettable'. Tegan Bennett Daylight said we wouldn't 'read another book like it this year. Or ever'.

I said it took my breath away.

There are no taxonomies of literature, although we pretend there are; we pretend the rules of compare and contrast can apply to let us understand one person's book through another's. Each is its own thing – and each is made finally, and made whole, by readers, all of us in our separate space. There's a strange alchemy to this external completion; an ongoing potential.

The second time I read the book, I focused on its structure and its beauty. Beauty is an important word; it didn't diffuse your story's power. Instead it was an adjunct to everything at work on every page in terms of craft and plot and pace. The lesson in that sat in the work you required of, and put into, every line, every sentence, every thought – the patience, the attention and the labour of all that. That's part of what gives this story its power.

The third time I read it, I was differently alone in 2020's differently viral world – after #MeToo, after the resurgence and resurrection and reprise of Margaret Atwood's *The Handmaid's Tale*. Your women in their bonnets, in their long, stiff, green, canvas smocks, counting, remembering, anything to hold onto the edge of their real selves, old selves, gone selves as they're marched two hours through hot landscape to be shown the fatal pulse of a high, sharp fence. The tactility of the details you gave us as we witnessed them, walked with them, sank into the story's intent. These shards of awful detail brought your images to life.

*

Dear Charlotte,

Years ago, when David Hicks was locked inside Guantanamo Bay, I saw a piece of physical theatre that imagined part of his story there. Nigel Jamieson's *Honour Bound*. The Australian Dance Theatre. The glare of orange jumpsuits against an illuminated set of chainwire and media report projections. All tucked inside the moulded smoothness of an Opera House theatre, the beauty of the harbour bright outside.

When it was over – the show, not Hicks' imprisonment – it seemed important, urgent, to hold this man in mind. It seemed necessary to hold the incarcerated reality of his situation above all other awareness, without pause.

I doubt I held that concentration for an hour. The failure of that privileged thought experiment.

This story works against that kind of distraction; it requires us to hold it in our mind and in our selves – even while its characters have been removed and imprisoned. It requires us to witness something otherwise deliberately put away, rendered unseen:

> Would it be said they 'disappeared', 'were lost'? Would it be
> said they were abandoned or taken, the way people said a girl
> was attacked, a woman was raped, this femaleness always at the
> centre, as if womanhood itself were the cause of these things?
> As if the girls, somehow, through the natural way of things, did
> it to themselves. They lured abduction and abandonment to
> themselves, they marshalled themselves into this prison where

they had made their beds, and now, once more, were lying in them. (176)

Verla who fed her father chips. Yolanda who lost the necklace her brother gave her. Who in their own world held these girls at the forefront of their minds when they were snatched and disappeared? Who kept them alive in the outside world in any way? Who let them go on living, in that sense?

You don't show us whether anybody did this, from their old lives. But we do, all of us who read and carry with us then the story of their taking, and why, of what was done in that strangely branded (Hardings') space with its dangerously irrelevant logo: 'Dignity and Respect in a Safe and Secure Environment'.

We can't speak for them back in the world of their own book; do they make us do better at speaking out for people in our own world?

Today I hear news of a 30 per cent increase in domestic violence reports in this time of lockdown. I hear about research that uncovers the impacts of COVID-19 along gendered lines. I hear reports, only this morning, of another woman who died on a roadside – an 'abhorrent' attack; her 'horrible injuries'. The woman; her injuries; her femaleness at the centre of the story (*Guardian*, 22 August 2020).

These stories just keep coming, their emphasis, their focus, still set this way. To reread your book is to think on what, if anything, has changed in the world of women, of men, between its publication and now.

*

Dear Charlotte,

A group of us went away with you once to write for a week, to push away all other distractions or occupations from this work. You brought us ideas of preparing space to be curious, engaged, actively productive.

To wonder, *I wonder what I'll learn today*. To strip away all other busynesses and doings.

We went away to write for a week on a strip of land between the ocean and the smooth disc of a wide and silver bay. A long way from the dry grass, the hillside, the vast and dislocated – unlocated – isolation of Hardings' base. *The Natural Way of Things* was printed – I'd read it – but it wasn't yet out in the world. The strange state of limbo when a thing has finished being made but has not been somehow realised.

Through that week, I thought of Yolanda, her cloak of furs, her rabbit-skin bootees. I thought of the way she had remade herself. I looked at the way you had crafted and honed your writing being, the way you honoured its power, its potential, the prism of perspective you seemed able to apply to the tsunami of response that might come. That must come.

Before the week began you said to me: think about the way you can switch the story you're writing from micro to macro, from up close to far away. The generous trick of this, of its potential: that it was always possible to change the angle, and that there was a drive, a power, in bringing a reader in so close, and then throwing them further away. It opened up a new possibility of momentum: zoom in, zoom out, keep the words moving across the page.

I've never written so much in a week in my life.

*

Dear Charlotte,

I love the idea of books finding their writers, of being buried as potential in some deep part of their differently journeying lives. Of the trick, the trigger, different for each one, that enables their making, their release into the world.

I wish I could remember you, in that late eighties, early nineties creative writing class in Bathurst. It's always winter in my memory of

Bathurst, cold air inside those fibro rooms. But I'm not sure if I can really see you there with me, in the buff-coloured space of the low buildings at Charles Sturt University, with Joan Phillip and Jan Woolley, Kate Llewellyn and Dorothy Porter.

I want to be able to see a rabbit's paw, a wide blue sky, a heavy china plate – a glimpse of bits and pieces heading towards a future page.

But I can't remember where you sat, what you wore, how you held your pen or read your words aloud. I can barely remember myself.

I can only marvel at the idea of having been there at the beginning of your writing life, and being here now to see the scale and generosity of all that you've achieved.

Dear Charlotte,

When I think about the idea of beauty in your story, I think of the image of a field full of spiders' webs in a morning, like crazy gossamer bunting. The delicacy of that, and the power; the weight of such a thing in the midst of this story. This detail invited the reader into a kind of opportunity: the privilege of seeing it; the privilege of affording it value.

> It could not be said, even if Yolanda still used her voice, but
> increasingly she found things beautiful out here in the paddock.
> This pink sky, these starry cobwebs. (237)

The first thing I want to say here is about the importance of beauty itself in this imagery; the light touch of observation. But the second is to acknowledge the great work done by the slight accent in the order of the words, in your choice of those words and their placement. You say, *increasingly she found things beautiful out here* – as opposed to *she found beautiful things*. The emphasis is on Yolanda, a change in the way she sees things, not in the beautiful externalities of bits and pieces of the world that are suddenly at hand. This tiny phrase feels like an elegant gesture to a greater change.

Beauty does particular work around the story of these women, the stories of how they are betrayed, reviled, abhorred. You pin these transitory fragments so carefully against the bigger shape the story is making, the broader themes of the narrative: the spiders' webs, caught in one moment, the right-place-right-time of seeing them as much as the capacity to acknowledge them as wonderful, and the impossibility of 'right-place-right-time' in the wrong-place-wrong-time world these women are stuck in: where they are, and what has been done to them to deliver them to this place.

*

Dear Charlotte,
There are phrases of yours beyond *The Natural Way of Things* that I carry with me always, that help me make sense of my own writing life. It's what we want, helpmates and maps along the way, before we reach the next place where the dragons are. Active curiosity. Imagining a writing place – a nook, a tent, a burrow. I learn these lessons over and over again.

This one is from your 2018 essay 'Reading isn't shopping'. It's your howl against relatability; your stake against the primacy of epiphany, empathy porn, the dangerous inadequacy of requiring common ground.

I remember it as an encouragement to work harder. Try harder. Put yourself in the space where you're uncomfortable, where you have nothing in common with whoever else is there, and find a means of being there.

That's worth something different again.

You quote Sarah Sentilles talking about her own book, *Draw Your Weapons*, in an essay for *LitHub*. You write:

Sentilles says that the embrace of 'unknowable otherness', rather than empathy, is our society's most urgent task now. Drawing on the work of other theorists and philosophers including Judith Butler and Emmanuel Levinas, Sentilles writes that 'Empathy depends on perceived likeness, a sense of sameness; I treat you justly because I recognize you as fundamentally like me'. (2018)

But, Sentilles goes on:

if it's only discovered likeness that creates the possibility for ethical behaviour, what happens when likeness can't be found? ... In this climate of fear and oppression, something more radical than empathy is needed. The faith that deep down 'they' are like 'us' won't get us where we need to go. Because what if they're not like us at all? What then?

The challenge Sentilles throws down about ethics is 'to learn to live with, and protect, what we can't understand' (quoted in Wood, 2018).

Your insistence on something other, something more, some other attention that can be paid. I go back to this essay of yours again and again; I fold it into the edges of so many things I try to do. The focus of a single point of flame that can spark a conflagration – that's how this essay feels.

The quote from the poet Jane Kenyon that other writers pin above their desks:

Tell the whole truth. Don't be lazy, don't be afraid. Close the critic out when you are drafting something new. Take chances in the interest of clarity of emotion ... Be a good steward of your gifts. Protect your time. Feed your inner life. Avoid too much noise. Read good books, have good sentences in your ears. Be by yourself as often as you can. Walk. Take the phone off the hook. Work regular hours. (quoted in *Brainpickings*, 2015)

The ways you have performed this and the work that it has made.

*

Dear Charlotte,
The line that does the most work in *The Natural Way of Things* sits on page 201 of the version I'm re-reading:

> It was Leandra who found a way to remove the bolts from their cell doors and fix them to the other side. They locked themselves in at night now.

The pivot, as we'd say in these COVID-19 times. The hinge.
    The point at which everything changes.
    In my mind, this is the equivalent of that great mechanism of steel, the hinge that holds the pure weight of the Sydney Harbour Bridge; the work that that one thing is required to do.
    Locks on the outside; locks on the inside.
    This single line, and its great shift. This change.

*

Dear Charlotte,
The scene I come back to, again and again. Yolanda is out in the day's first light, making the rounds of her traps. Her plan for sustenance, for survival; her plan to feed them all. The rabbits, the morning, the work of this thing. Three cockatoos screech overhead. A cloud moves across the sun. Yolanda shivers.

The visceral impact of reading these sentences. The beauty of the sunrise, of a new day coming on.

And then, the impossible assault of sight, of sound. A hot-air balloon heaves up over the landscape, an unthinkably flippant witness; an impotent bystander. The majestic displacement of it, and the privilege of its height, its separation, its safe passage across the surface of Yolanda's story. 'It was like a planet from another universe, almost touching hers and moving fast, and soon it would be gone' (238).

Hello! The people call down from their basket – do I imagine this, or are they sipping champagne? *Beautiful morning,* they call, looking but not seeing and presuming that a woman waving would be nothing more than some happy morning thing, a thing that is a part of their segmented world.

The safe space, the protected space that allows them not to notice who she is, how she is, where she is; that allows them to scoop her into the narrative of their pleasure, their entertainment, and to dismiss her as some slightly curious and unexpected detail in its shape. Surprising. Piquant.

Perhaps later that day they'd say to each other: *Did we really see someone out there this morning? And I wonder who that was?*

John Stuart Mill, in 1867: 'Bad men need nothing more to compass their ends, than that good men should look on and do nothing'.

And away it sails, that beautiful balloon, privileged to be able to be somewhere else, and not to have noticed anything amiss as it went by.

The power of this scene, of its disruption to the world you've made; the power of the unexpected appearing – and disappearing again. The impotence of witness without action.

The power of Yolanda unseen, unrecognised, unnoticed as this impossible possibility of assistance slips away.

*

Dear Charlotte,

I think I have this memory from when you were working on *The Natural Way of Things*: a post on Facebook where you asked how much current would have to go through an electric fence to kill somebody who tried to climb it.

My unreliable memory: I can't remember when, or what anybody told you in reply. Maybe I'm imagining all of this.

But I think that I hold one phrase from your inquiry. That you said that you were 'asking for a friend'.

That makes me smile.

*

Dear Charlotte,

I turn this book back to its first page; I step into the story again. The unwashed hair, the bonnets, the scratch of something like canvas, the sachets of dried soup powder. The lady and the unicorn. The hiss of a spear gun in the narrative's shape, like Chekhov's pistol – if it's there in the first act, it has to be fired.

The bright stars framed in Yolanda's window.

The week I went away to write with you, the star through the window of that house in which we stayed was so impossibly bright I had to look it up, to make sure it was real. Alphard, the brightest star in the constellation of Hydra, 177 light years away. Cooler than the sun, but larger and more luminous. This name, in Arabic, means the solitary one.

The seduction of the lag between the instant of the light's pulse and its arrival here. So much can change in 177 years; other things, not so much. Power. Equity. Potential. Respect.

And 177 years from now, when the light of this now reaches from Alphard as far as the Earth: what will have changed here by then?

The two streetlights she had seen in her dream turned out to be
two enormous stars in a deep blue sky. (3)

Yolanda wakes up for the first time: we come into being with her.

In each of your books, I feel you take another stride. I feel you reach
for some further, clearer thing. Impossible to always pin down where
they set out from, stories, or how long it might take them to be realised.

These are the quantum physics of narrative, of time and inspiration.

But I know – as a reader, and a writer – how grateful I am for their
power and their worth.

You shine a light onto the page that you're writing and across
whatever timespan it finds us, reading, later, all the way out here.

Its brilliance and its beauty and its truth.

Thank you for your words.

Fearless:
On Christos Tsiolkas

Nigel Featherstone

There is a mystique to the writer, particularly the novelist, and much of it is cliché, if not worse. The commonly imagined scenario: he (for, it seems, in this scenario, the novelist is male) is sitting at an oversized antique desk; there is an expensive, preferably French, bottle of red wine off to the side, and a clunky old typewriter waiting for the next masterpiece to appear, one that will put the author on a plane and flown around the world before being paraded in front of an adoring festival audience. Of course, the reality is much less glamorous. Most writers spend years juggling 'real work' and domestic responsibilities while trying to wrestle a manuscript to the ground, with only a flickering hope that the book will see the light of day and find a readership. Most industry surveys suggest we are reading less, especially literary fiction, so most contemporary writers will inevitability ask themselves, again and again, a particular question: why am I doing this?

George Orwell penned 'Why I write' in 1946, as the world was beginning the slow process of rebuilding after the devastation of the Second World War. In it, he gave four reasons for why he wrote:

'sheer egotism' (a need to seem clever), 'aesthetic enthusiasm' (perceptions of beauty), 'historical impulse' (a desire to document facts), and 'political purpose'. Of the latter, Orwell claims:

> When I sit down to write a book, I don't say to myself, 'I am going to produce a work of art'. I write because there is some lie I want to expose, and my initial concern is to get a hearing. (2)

One of Australia's most politically attuned writers of recent generations is Christos Tsiolkas. Born in Melbourne in 1965, Tsiolkas is the son of Greek migrants; he is also gay and identifies as a socialist as well as an atheist. Despite, or because of, the conservatism that has been a part of Australia's political landscape since John Howard rose to power in 1996, Tsiolkas has had one of the rarest experiences in Australian letters: a literary career that is commercially successful while – in the main – being critically lauded. That he has achieved such success while encouraging, if not forcing, his readers to reflect on unpalatable aspects of society is truly remarkable. He is the author of short stories, novels, plays, screenplays, and essays of criticism covering art forms such as film and music. Even though he is widely regarded as a fearless artist, Tsiolkas is well known as a warm and affectionate man who has supported generations of emerging writers.

Looking deeper, how might we describe Christos Tsiolkas the writer?

Words such as audacious, dangerous and ambitious come to mind. From the evidence of his considerable output to date, it is likely that Tsiolkas would agree with Orwell's political motivation to 'expose lies' and 'get a hearing'.

Justifiably, and perhaps reassuringly, Tsiolkas has been getting a hearing since the publication of his first novel, a relatively slim book called *Loaded*, which was first published by Vintage, an imprint of mainstream publisher Random House, in 1995. In *Loaded* – the novel was adapted for the silver screen and called *Head On*, starring Alex Dimitriades and directed by Ana Kokkinos (1998) – Ari is a nineteen-year-old son of Greek migrants. He is actively gay though expresses considerable hatred of himself and the world around him. We see him as he works his way through a day and night in Melbourne, taking an almost death-defying quantity of drugs, having sex, and interacting with family and friends with both animosity and affection.

What is most striking about *Loaded* is its audacity.

Here is the opening paragraph:

> The morning is ending and I've just opened my eyes. I stare across the cluttered room I'm in. I scratch at my groin. I yawn. I feel my cock and start a slow masturbation. When I'm finished, and it doesn't take long, I get up with a leap, wrap a towel around my naked body and make a slow journey downstairs. (2)

There is much to learn from the above about the craft – or the 'trade', as Tsiolkas himself has called it – of writing: the life in the language, the boldness of the prose, and the fact that the DNA of the entire novel appears to be contained in those few opening words. We immediately know the story will be told in an uncensored way, and we know there will be shocks; we also know, by the very fact that Ari makes a 'slow journey downstairs', that the narrative will be one of descent, potentially into some kind of hell. It is the audacity that is the most striking feature here: this is writing that believes in its own worth, even though Ari himself openly believes in nothing but short bursts of sexual connection and chemical-induced pleasure.

Three pages later:

> Riding on a bus always makes me horny, something to do with the sensation of moving while looking down into the world below. I sink behind a seat in the back and shift my tight cock. The music

enters my head and I rock back and forth a little to a pulsating electric beat. (7)

In lesser hands, this writing could come across as unnecessarily crass. However, the reader has the sense – conscious or otherwise – that Tsiolkas knows what he is doing. This is confident writing, and readers need confidence. In the case of *Loaded*, why stay with this in-your-face narrative if we felt otherwise?

That is an important question. Especially when the narrative does not let up one bit:

> I detest the east. The whole fucking mass of it: the highways, the suburbs, the hills, the rich cunts, the smacked-out bored cunts. The whitest part of my city, where you'll see the authentic white Australia, is in the eastern suburbs. A backdrop of Seven Elevens, shopping malls, gigantic parking lots. I was picked up by a guy once, he lived in this shit-hole suburb somewhere, Burwood or Balwyn or Bentleigh or Boronia, and I woke up in this strange man's bed, got up and made myself a coffee, went into the front yard, looked down the street and thought oh-my-fucking-god-is-this-America. I didn't feel sane again until I reached the corrosive stenches of the city. Lead and carbon dioxide in my lungs to make me forget the Disneyland I had woken up to. (41)

There we see some of Tsiolkas's main concerns: class in Australia, and the power and privilege of whiteness. One of the writer's many strengths is his ability to explore political concerns through the depiction of the everyday. An example is in the irony of Ari not feeling comfortable again until he has lead and carbon monoxide, those by-products of capitalism, in his lungs; he has made room for the reader to put herself in the story, to do some of the work.

Christos Tsiolkas is a writer who is truly unafraid:

The Polytechnic is history. Vietnam is history. Auschwitz is history. Hippies are history. Punks are history. God is history. Hollywood is history. The Soviet Union is history. My parents are history. My friends are history. I will be history. This fucking shit-hole planet will become history. Take more drugs. (87)

For some readers, it might be tempting to conclude that this is just another example of nihilistic fiction: there is no meaning to human life, so find pleasure wherever you can, say whatever you want, and offend as many people as possible. But again Tsiolkas knows exactly what he is doing: as is made clear in the novel's epigraph – 'The immigrant child … cannot have a life identical with that of his mother or father' (which is from *An American Writer* by Richard Rodriguez) – he is revealing to us the notion that migrants and their children are living in different worlds even while sharing the same city. There is deep melancholy in that, and tragedy too.

Before we move on from the above passage, it is worth noting the way Tsiolkas pushes his prose towards poetry, in that the language is doing more than one thing at once. As well as being provocative, he is revelling in the double meaning of 'history': the past is worth knowing, essential even, but it is also dead and therefore meaningless.

Is it possible for a writer to be audacious without purpose, including political purpose? Sure, but that is likely to lead to writing that falls flat on the page; it would become a directionless sludge. It would certainly not resonate with readers in any kind of deep way, nor would it have any kind of long-term significance in Australia's literary life.

How is an emerging writer to write with audacity?

Perhaps, as is always the way, the answer is multi-faceted. There is a need to care deeply about the work of writing: to invest all of ourselves, including our bodies (every part of our body), in the words as they go down on the page; writing is not just a brain activity – it is also a chest and gut and crotch activity. Further, there is also a need to care deeply about the characters even – especially – when they are flawed: selfish, messy, incommunicative, inconsistent, cowardly, callous, vain. And then there is a need to *not* care: about what others may or may not think of what we are writing; about whether or not readers will decide that we are a degenerate, or inarticulate, or insane. It is a difficult juggling act, but in *Loaded* Christos Tsiolkas gives us a commanding example of how it can be done.

*

Tsiolkas is also a writer who gives himself permission to be dangerous. In his short story 'Tourists' (from *Merciless Gods*), two middle-class Australian travellers, Bill and Trina, are in New York and hoping to see an exhibition of contemporary art at a prominent museum – friends have told them that it is a 'must-see'. Despite Bill and Trina displaying the petty tensions of couples travelling, they are clearly in love and on the cusp of settling down to start a family.

However, when a young man behind the museum's counter acts in a condescending way towards Bill, the narrative goes awry:

> They walked towards the lift, then as they waited there behind
> an elderly couple, Bill exploded. 'What a stuck-up black cunt,'
> he hissed at Trina. (53)

In that two-sentence paragraph, Tsiolkas again writes without fear or favour. He is willing to do what some novelists would not even consider: allow racism, ugly as it is, damaging and never justified, to be expressed. Quite rightly, the consequences for Bill are potentially life-changing. Trina decides that she does not want to spend time with him; she storms off. Towards the end of the story, there is reconciliation, albeit a harsh one:

Her lips curled, her face fell and he thought for a moment she
was about to cry. 'You bastard,' she said up close to him, 'when
we do have kids, you dare say one racist thing to them, just one,
and I swear I'll leave you and take them away from you.' She was
thumping her chest, hard. (65)

While in *Loaded*, Ari may not experience any repercussions for his wild
and at times lawless behaviour (though we sense that in time he will),
in 'Tourists' Tsiolkas ensures that Bill's outburst comes back to unsettle
him. In this relatively simple tale, the author reveals the racism that
exists at the core of Australia's masculinity, and the violence that courses
through the nation's vernacular.

The fact that Tsiolkas courts danger, seeks it out perhaps, plays with
it, tempts it, gives his narratives purpose and his prose – even when
delivered in a matter-of-fact way – a power that is both shocking and
memorable. It is writing that has the capacity to change the way readers
think and act.

Note Tina's gesture at the end of the extract above: the hard
thumping of her chest. Not only do we experience her state of mind, we
see the physical manifestation of her anger and frustration, as though we
are thumping our own chest, as though we are all thumping Bill hard. It
is an observation like this that reveals how much Tsiolkas knows about
his characters, including their dreams, desires and motivations, which,
time and time again, he connects directly to his political purposes.
Christos Tsiolkas is a social critic as much as he is a writer of literary
fiction.

Tsiolkas has always been an ambitious writer, and he appears to be
getting more and more so. In his best-selling novel *The Slap*, Tsiolkas
uses a single event at a family barbecue – the slapping of a child – to

again dissect Australian contemporary life, exposing the fault-lines of class, race, and barely submerged violence. Each section of the novel is from a different character's perspective, as the slap echoes through their lives, changing them forever. It is an epic and forceful novel, which Irish writer Colm Tóibín believed 'confirms Christos Tsiolkas's reputation as one of the most significant contemporary storytellers at work today' (jacket endorsement).

Perhaps the reason *The Slap* has had such an impact on Australian readers (and television audiences) is because it is an unflinching exposé of that most beloved, even sacred, of activities: the backyard barbecue. For most people, a barbecue is an opportunity to relax with a drink and some good, easy food. But in this novel, Tsiolkas is not going to let us get away with that; once again he proves that beneath our polite, easygoing surfaces, we are seething with complexities, contradictions, prejudices, and violence. Should an emerging writer be looking for a topic or theme to explore, she may wish to choose something that is 'every day', and then, without caring a jot about what her readers (and critics) may one day think, dive deep and reveal to her readers what is really happening – the true, potentially ugly, motivations, but also the love and tenderness.

Undoubtedly cementing Tsiolkas's reputation as an eminent Australian writer is his latest novel, *Damascus*, which sees him bring to life the early decades of Christianity, focusing on the troubled but revered man who would become Saint Paul. The ambition is obvious: here is a gay Australian man, an atheist, taking on one of the most powerful stories – and institutions – of the modern world.

The novel opens in the way Tsiolkas almost always does, hinting at the whole:

The world is in darkness. The hood the guards have placed over her head scratches at her cheeks and neck. She takes fleeting comfort from the smell of the greasy fibre, the odours of the sheep and goat. From her first memory their bleating was part of her life. They were her companions during the day and over countless nights, when she'd join them in their rough stable to escape the drunken violence of her father and her brothers, and then that of her husband. The warm bodies of the goats had been her solace and her bed; they had been her work and her friends. (5)

She also recognises another smell, far more noxious. Fear. How many others has this hood covered?

Tsiolkas's writing in this passage is both considered and precise. There are a number of meanings in the 'darkness' of that first sentence: the literal, the political, the spiritual, and the metaphorical. The reader then becomes the woman who has been imprisoned by the hood; with just a few lines, we are shown how she was a shepherd, and a tender and affectionate one at that. And then we are placed directly in one of the themes of the novel: fear. The fear of the stranger. The fear of the marginalised. The fear of the feminine. The fear of the misunderstood. The fear of the new.

All that and we are yet to turn to the second page.

One of the many elements of the writing craft that new writers can learn from Tsiolkas is the importance of contrasting the heavy with the light, the big with the intimate, violence with peace, hatred with love. Tsiolkas is a master of drawing out acts of tenderness and affection from his characters and the situations he puts them in. While some may be tempted to describe *Damascus* as relentlessly grim, he illuminates his worlds with meaningful interactions between characters that reveal their humanity and their need for true – and deep – connection.

Here are three examples, all from the final third of the novel.

In the first quote, Saul (Paul) is experiencing absolute reverie; he is singing for his people and for the kingdom to come, which has been a constant promise. Wanting to share the moment:

> Saul grips his beloved's hand, raises it to his lips and kisses it.
> 'Thank you, Timos,' he says, breaking free for a moment from
> his song, 'for making me promise to bring you along'. (251)

And:

> Brother Impetuous is my favourite. We are not meant to favour one
> over another – we are all equal in the eyes of our Lord. But I have
> been able to master such a virtuous equilibrium. Impetuous is still a
> youth. Even in the faint light from the moon, the wispy beard that
> he is attempting to grow is comical. I resist the urge to tickle him
> under the chin. (289)

And:

> The two old men, eyes unyielding, face each other. Saul sees it, the
> fall of Thomas's shoulders, a peace that scatters a passion. Thomas
> reaches for Saul's cheek again, he strokes it gently. (401)

So easily can we experience those beautiful moments of affection, and, as mentioned, they offer a contrast to what can sometimes be an onslaught of questions and suggestions. We can also see – and hear – the way Tsiolkas uses a different style of prose to explore his themes from book to book. In *Damascus*, his writing style is almost biblical, which, of course, is appropriate. Almost every sentence carries a profound spiritual yearning. He also draws on the complex dynamics and literary fireworks of Australia's first Nobel Prize-winning novelist Patrick White; evidence of this is in the way Tsiolkas both bends time and pushes language. Tsiolkas wrote about White in *On Patrick White: Writers on writers,* which reveals another side of the author's practice: being aware of literary elders, respecting them, learning from them.

Any writer can express ambition, but Tsiolkas's ambition is informed by an intelligence that is both artistic and political. He also knows what tools to use and when and why. This leads us back to his reference to writing being a trade: all writers should have a box of tools to use, and take the time – years, decades – to know how to use those tools and for what purpose.

*

In a brief interview published in the *Guardian*, Tsiolkas responded to accusations of misogyny in *The Slap*:

> What surprised me and angered me about that was that there was a confusion between the writer and the characters, which was really annoying. I wonder if there's a tameness to the modern novel when it comes to writing about certain people or experiences. When I remember the novels that made me want to be a writer, they were the ones that had characters that were difficult, complex and ambiguous.

That answer suggests something important about Christos Tsiolkas: he fully understands the novel's purposes, which can be summarised as being the expression and revelation of complexity, in a way that is both new and exciting; but he also appears to be constantly looping back to the books that turned him on as a young reader. It is a worthwhile reminder that everything we do as writers is for the reader. We can be political. We can be audacious. We can be dangerous. And we can be both ambitious and achingly tender. But we are nothing without our other half: the reader. If we are lucky, our work – our blood, sweat and tears, our fears, our body's various needs and energies, our desire to tell a different story, even to want to change the world – lives on in the reader.

Yes, if we are lucky.

And fearless.

Caught in the rip:
The first seven pages of
Tim Winton's *Breath*

Cate Kennedy

A student remarked recently, after we'd been talking about dramatic structure and how it operates in films: 'Now that I know what it is I can't *un*see it'.

It's true that once we try to explore just *why* a work of art we admire is working on us, the pleasure becomes a little more diagnostic, the awareness of the craft a little more alert. The first draft of a story may be full of 'happy accidents', but by a final draft, nothing is accidental. Everything has been taken out, weighed, polished and reset carefully in place, everything redundant has been removed. Everything that is left is there to serve the story, so everything feels intentional, causal and consequential.

Once you are aware that the effect and impact of the story is made up of a series of the author's deliberate choices, it's more difficult to feel obliviously immersed as you read. You are aware, instead, of the tiny, invisible stitches which hold the whole thing together. You're alert to the skilful building of effect, the precision of an image – its placement, a pay-off withheld, a glimmering of metaphorical subtext suggested early and kept implicit.

I'm not saying that the enjoyment I derive from reading fiction is diminished by an understanding of craft – far from it. My attention is just more appreciative. My admiration for what is unspooling in front of my eyes is greater, if anything, through an awareness of its elements and how the author has ... what? Woven them? Amalgamated them? Synthesised them?

Conjured, is a closer word for me. A story is like close-up magic, and even if you try to practise magic yourself, it doesn't ruin the thrill of it for you when you sit in the audience and admire somebody else doing it with passion, skill and bravado.

Tim Winton is one of the authors, for me, who makes something ineffable and transformative happen with his fiction. I remember hearing him talk about the writing process on the ABC interview program *Enough Rope* with Andrew Denton, just before he released his collection of interlinked short stories *The Turning*. He spoke about the strange process of inspiration in a striking way. 'I just rock up to the desk in the morning and hope something shows up', he said with typical candour:

I figure if I don't show up then nothing else could show up, or it could show up and I'm not there, in which case there's a day gone ... The process is not very intellectual. It's not very rational. I don't plan things. I'm just trying not to be bored ... There are some days when you just can't believe your luck and other days where you know it's just not going to rain for five years [...] The only other analogy I can give you is it's a strange way to live a life where you have to live by your wits – like pulling a rabbit out of a hat, and some days you're not sure if there's a rabbit in the hat and other days you're not sure if you've got the hat. But you've just got to go there and hope that something shows up. And there's a kind of discipline in going to the empty desk, the empty page, and waiting. It's not for something to fall out of the sky on you. It's something to ... for you to be in the right space, to remember where you're at. And once I achieve a certain kind of momentum, then I'm okay. But it's sort of getting up to warp speed that takes me a lot of energy. (quoted in Denton, 2004)

The rewriting is done with an eye to craft, of course, but the early intuitive leap, the desire to create something out of what shows up, is made with a sort of dream-like instinct. Learning confidence in that process is as important as any 'nuts and bolts' elements of writing, such as dialogue and characterisation.

The desire to be disciplined about turning up in case today you get into the right frame of mind and momentum to 'get up to warp speed', as Winton puts it, is a practice every artist understands. You dream it up, and work yourself into the right psychological space to try to render it.

For myself, the more I write, the more the process begins to feel like a kind of lucid dreaming. (When it's going well, that is. When it's not working it's more like having root canal.) I've learned to do it through nothing more complex than working out what I love to experience when I read, and trying, in turn, to create that experience for somebody else.

The author and critic John Gardner, in his guide *On Becoming a Novelist*, describes the pleasure of reading as slipping into a vivid and continuous dream the author has created for us, so that instead of seeing words printed on the page, we are imaginatively immersed in that story, experiencing it rather than 'thinking' about it. This transference of imagistic meaning is what I want to discuss here. There's a lot to admire about Winton's much-lauded body of work, but for the sake of brevity, and since I want to find a more manageable snapshot that demonstrates just what he masterfully creates with language, I am going to settle for one book: his 2008 novel, *Breath*.

And not even the whole book, just the first section, only 1579 words in length, which feels more like a preface than a chapter – or the door he opens a crack to conjure up the world of the story which is thrown open, from there, in all its detail and dimension.

I want to walk through those first few pages with you, pointing out what he's directing our attention towards, and how subtly he is building the implicit tensions to be explored. I'll address these elements in sections which represent, to me, what many inexperienced writers struggle with the most: immediacy, pace, dialogue and control over metaphorical subtext.

*

The opening section launches us, *in media res*, straight into a disturbing experience which pushes the narrator, an ambulance officer on call-out, back into the traumatic territory of an adolescence he spends most of his time trying not to think about, although the damage shows through in his life like an unhealed wound.

After this beginning, the book seems to almost start again in a more controlled, conventional narrative form ('I grew up in a weatherboard house in a mill town and like everyone else there I learnt to swim in the river ...' (9)) but this first section is the story's clear catalyst which precipitates the narrator's deep dive, or slip, back into the treacherous waters of time and memory.

In fact, a deep dive is a good metaphor, since the whole book employs an 'image system' of a metaphorical set of incoming waves the narrator must ride, pouring in to engulf him then draining back to leave him beached in the fractured, rueful present. This creates its structure: a long, extended recollection and return.

If there's one thing Winton is famous for, it's writing about the ocean. He's a master at capturing the transcendent feeling of swimming in that ocean, of surrendering to it, surfing it, experiencing it as spiritually transformative. Across his body of work, his language is so lyrical and his grip on this imagery so relaxed and naturally expansive that it often doesn't feel like the reader is doing anything more than taking a breath and ducking under that wave with him, yet in *Breath* the extended metaphor of fighting the current, gasping for breath, being immersed and in play with the loss of control, becomes the propulsive shape and swell of the narrative itself. While this is emblematic of how troubled and unresolved memory works, the undertow of many other dark levels and currents is also evident.

Another set of motifs – the chemical addictions of adrenaline, endorphins and testosterone, the glamour of heroin, and the crucible of adolescent masculinity hellbent on testing its limits – are also provoked uncomfortably to the surface by this opening scene of a distressing call-out involving a teenage boy's death.

While the writing starts out crackling with pace and tension, replicating the urgency of the ambulance trip, once the implications of this death are revealed, Winton slows everything down as we are invited to carefully observe and comprehend everything which is not being explained to us but which is clearly there under the surface. Within this short section, he finds time to embody a dreamlike, disassociated recollection which mirrors a birth, to show a character in inadvertently revealing action and to suggest an ocean of suppressed, haunting pain. He does this through a first-person voice which is both terse and laconic, giving away very little but hinting at this looming hidden past trauma only because, we intuit, the narrator has absolutely nowhere else to go.

The whole section is a remarkable feat of compression. It operates as a microcosmic version of the whole book, pivoted around a single event which draws down like a hook into the deep and brings up something long-hidden there.

How does he do it? And how does he orient us so we are compelled, after a few short pages, to take this disquieting dive with this particular narrator?

Immediacy

First, we are plunged in:

> We come sweeping up the tree-lined boulevard with siren and
> lights and when the GPS urges us to make the next left we take it so
> fast that all the gear slams and sways inside the vehicle. I don't say a
> thing. Down the dark suburban street I can see the house lit like a
> cruise ship. (1)

Immediate, real-time narration means the reader begins visualising
and listening to everything unfolding in the scene, which makes it
intrinsically dramatic. Every detail matters, like the 'establishing shot'
in a film – the boulevard is tree-lined (suggesting wealth and prestige),
the vehicle has sirens and lights, and 'gear' inside that sways when they
take the corner, so we know we're not in an ordinary passenger vehicle.
'I don't say a thing', establishes not only a first-person, present-tense
narrator, but the suggestion that he or she is not the one driving but
the one keeping silent and withholding judgment. And finally, their
destination, a house 'lit like a cruise ship'. Again, a cruise ship suggests
wealth and prestige, but when it's chosen as a simile like this, when we
already have a suspicion that sirens are wailing and this vehicle is either
law enforcement or an ambulance, it's the incongruity of the imagery
which is arresting, because it creates a feeling of dread. This is no cruise.
Something terrible has happened. And what is the narrator, Bruce,
keeping silent about? Does he have an inkling that there's no point
rushing, or that the people in the house will be distressed by the lights
and sirens?

All this is packed into these opening sentences.

The narrator doesn't stop the action to explain that they're two
ambulance officers, racing to a call-out, or that he has his own private
misgivings about the speeding, lights and sirens. We don't know the

names of the people in the ambulance, or what they look like, or what's brought them to this point. We have to keep up, and assume we'll pick up on those things later, as we do in real life when we're thrown into a dramatic or unexpected situation.

What's more, Winton assumes we will keep up. He's not going to patronise us by explaining, creating the kind of authorial intrusion that not only puts the handbrake on dramatic action but suggests the reader is too slow on the uptake to work things out for themselves.

Immediacy works to compress all salient details into a compelling blow-by-blow experience that we are immediately engaged in, and to promise we'll soon be completely oriented as to what matters – so hold tight. It achieves this through specific detail – the 'boulevard' rather than 'street', the 'gear' rather than 'equipment in the back of the ambulance'.

After a brief exchange of terse dialogue, we do get a morsel of backstory: 'It's been a long, slow shift and there's never been any love lost between Jodie and me. At handover I walked up on a conversation I wasn't supposed to hear. But that was hours ago. Now I'm alert and tingly with dread. Bring it on' (1).

Names, context, a brief hint of an overheard conversation suggesting potential conflict. Then Bruce's particular mindset: he's tingly with dread, but he wants it. He's anticipating it. Despite these details being referred to so glancingly, in the heat of the action, they are actually setting up plot and foreshadowing the story's larger 'undercurrents', in terms of both this narrative character and his interactions with others. Again, Winton doesn't stop to explain why they're important. He does not sacrifice momentum for exposition; because we are in the vivid, continuous moment, we're feeling it, not analysing it:

When she hits the handbrake and calls in our arrival at the job I
jump out and rip the side door back to grab the resus kit. Beneath
the porch steps on the dewy grass is a middle-aged bloke hugging

himself in silence and I can see in a moment that although he's probably done his collarbone he's not our man. So I leave him to Jodie and go on up to announce myself in the open doorway.

In the livingroom two teenage girls hunch at opposite ends of a leather couch.

Upstairs? I ask.

One of them points without even lifting her head, and already I know that this job's become a pack and carry. (2)

We're in Bruce's mind now; the author has stepped back into the shadows, getting out of the way so that the narrator is speaking directly to us, in a voice which feels real. Bruce is our guide into this conjured world, so we're both 'hearing' his voice (rather than reading words on a page) and 'seeing' just what he's seeing, through the particular focus of his sensibility. What's a 'resus kit'? I don't know, but I can make a pretty good guess, and I'm completely oriented now that we're in the head of an ambulance officer. What does this narrator notice about the man on the lawn, and how does he know just by looking that he's broken his collarbone, but he's not 'our man'? And what's the awful confirming dread of the 'pack and carry', slang that suggests exactly what's waiting for us upstairs at the big 'cruise ship' house?

It's writing that signals to us to stay awake, to pay attention to every small thing we're being shown, because we are, by our own volition, in the dream now, both in Bruce's head and alongside him, about to face something devastating.

The girls, 'hunched' numb and disconnected on opposite ends of the couch, pointing upstairs, confirm this.

Up we go. We don't want to, but we do. Further searing small details await us: 'a little mat of vomit in the hall. Splinters of wood' (2). With Bruce, we step into the bedroom where a mother sits with the body of her son. The amassing of more crucial detail brings everything into focus: 'The room smells of pot and urine and disinfectant, and it's clear that she's cut him down and dressed him and tidied everything up' (2).

The discipline of keeping within the narrative character's viewpoint, 'seeing' only what he sees, noticing exactly what he observes, 'hearing' what he says in the following exchange with this grieving mother, creates a constraint which is one of fiction's superpowers.

It is not a broad, sweeping, generic examination of 'themes' and theories, swamping the reader with authorial intervention. Instead, through the narrative character's eyes, it zooms in on a close-up – the small and specific – and Winton understands perfectly how these are the things which lodge in the reader's mind and stay there.

As the author Richard Price, well-known for his scrupulous research and excellent screen dialogue, once said: 'You don't write about the horrors of war. No. You write about the kid's burnt socks lying in the road.'

Writing which is sensory is viscerally 'felt' and experienced by a reader, rather than just intellectually comprehended. It elicits a physiological reaction, and that's how you know it's working. The sensation when the knot in our stomach tightens, or our pulse goes up and our mouth goes dry, when we feel provoked to tears, laughter or the blinding flash of realisation, makes that scene memorable to the point of being unforgettable.

There's a lot to learn about immediacy, which works to make prose as dramatic as live action unfolding in front of a reader's eyes. Once we're settled into 'hearing' the narrative voice: Bruce's inner thoughts and the way they're progressing, the author can use syntax and punctuation to mimic this flow of the way a character 'thinks', in everything they are saying and not saying. The use of 'jump cuts' – segueing from one panicked thought to another seemingly unrelated one, for instance – can convey psychological blank spaces, elisions, avoidance, or something we intuit that the character can't bear to attend to. We attend to it, though. When immediacy is combined with first-person narration in this way, we're reading, constantly, for what is between the lines, what is unspoken, pushed away, or too incendiary to acknowledge.

Pace and control

It may be vivid, but it also has to be continuous, and here is where an author needs to sort out what to show and where, what to withhold and why, how to ratchet up the pace to convey urgency and slow it down again when things get quiet. While the pace of this opening section is almost literally breathtaking – it skims and crashes along, covering time, gliding over depths, skirting submerged reefs – once Bruce is alone with the mother in her son's bedroom, navigating the rawness of her grief, everything slows right down. Simultaneously, narrator and reader take in the implications of what we're seeing together. There's a visual echo of *Pietà*, the Michelangelo sculpture where a grieving Mary sits with her son Jesus's body when he was taken down from the cross, but Winton is much too skilled a writer to explicitly refer to this or the extended meanings it implies. Instead there is a murmured exchange in which he tells her the boy has passed away and she says she knows, and he asks if he can open the wardrobe. She demurs.

Now we are deep in raw, unspeakable territory as their exchange skirts around something terrible at its centre that this woman and her family now must live with. The dialogue holds all the tension, especially as Jodie steps into the room just as Bruce asks about looking inside the wardrobe. This triangulation – of introducing a third party to a scene who is 'tone-deaf' to what's going on between the two characters already present – is a masterful device in accelerating tension (Shakespeare does it all the time) and here, within the confined space of the bedroom and the unspoken knowledge between Bruce and the mother, it reaches boiling point. The interjections of the emotionally oblivious Jodie, the suppressed grief already palpable, combined with the urgency of time

– the police will soon be arriving, and some straight answers will be required, no secrets will be possible – all create exquisite tension even as the physical pace slows.

Winton builds this accumulation of detail – a hand caressing a head, the scent of soap, incongruous earrings, teenage posters and sports trophies decorating the room, the sound of car doors in the street below – like a fire, stoking implication upon implication. Again, he gives us the credit for reading what's not said as well as what's said, and since what's inside that wardrobe is the catalytic push-point into freefall for the narrator himself, the juxtaposition here between stillness and rapidly escalating stakes is masterful. For decisions about pacing alone, this short but powerful encapsulation of buried psychic pain in unexpected confrontation with its 'trigger' incident is worth close re-reading.

Dialogue fuelling plot

After the elliptical exchange between Bruce and the grieving mother, he and Jodie leave the family to their pain and the police, and when they are almost back at the depot, they also have a revealing exchange of dialogue.

Good dialogue in a story is used to convey conflict, but it is adversarial rather than a screaming match, clearly 'about' something more than its stated subject. Clumsy or 'wooden' dialogue tends to state true inner motivations and prematurely reveal the stakes the characters are trying to keep hidden, while good dialogue makes these stakes clear to the reader but keeps them unvoiced, until increasing pressure makes it impossible for the character to hide them any longer. Once that peak point of pressure is reached, the dramatic tension culminates and there can be no more 'build'. So a character 'blurting' the truth needs to have arrived, plausibly, at a climactic point of no return, to convey the extreme pressure they are under. That hidden interior conflict drives the story forward, and once it's exposed, it's very difficult to stuff the genie back into the bottle – the character must act on what has been revealed.

It seems a very common problem, for inexperienced writers, to eagerly play all their good cards early and reveal the character's true psychic turmoil the first chance they get. This gives the reader no time to infer and anticipate building pressure about what the character is fighting to keep hidden. Because this hidden interior conflict dictates the story's forward momentum, once the character reveals it, the vehicle of the story rolls to a stop, suddenly out of fuel.

There's a discipline in withholding your good cards. Plot doesn't exist without a character to live through it, and the reader needs to understand the interior state of the character, particularly – and most effectively – when it is very different from their external behaviour. This gives dimension, and reader engagement hinges on it.

First-person narrative – or close third person which allows passages of 'interiority' – allows a reader to see and hear what a character reveals to other characters, while still being privy to what they are masking, or keeping quiet about. When this is done well, the reader will be absolutely attuned to the inner conflict driving the character, whether the character recognises that conflict or not. When it's done particularly well, the character both knowingly and inadvertently reveals themselves to us.

We tend to read these kinds of elliptically voiced exchanges avidly, because they are evidence of both an interior and exterior power struggle, as characters fight to get what they want, often through barbed volleys.

In Bruce and Jodie's exchange, both interior and exterior conflict converge as Winton makes the dialogue do 'double duty' through the bickering:

So when were you planning to let me know what all that was about?

All what?

With that poor woman. For a moment there I thought you were flirting with her.

Well, you can add that to your list of complaints.

Look, I'm sorry.

Arrogant, aloof, sexist, bad communicator, gung-ho. Obviously I missed a few things, coming in late. But for the record, Jodie, I'm not a Vietnam vet. Believe it or not I'm not old enough. (5)

Bruce mentioning that he 'came in late' harks back to the earlier mention that Winton included, seemingly in passing, of the 'something I shouldn't have heard' at handover. Only now, when the heat of the moment is past – and a great deal of this story is about being in the adrenalised state of purpose and heightened awareness of the moment – he returns to it. By listing all the characteristics that Bruce has overheard Jodie complain of to a colleague prior to the callout, Winton neatly encapsulates how other people 'see' Bruce, and how he knows they 'see' him. He then denies that he's a Vietnam veteran. What a richly suggestive seam this mines: the notion of repressed trauma, introduced via a casual and unexamined rumour used to explain away his demeanour and behaviour at work. His workmate may speculate on whether or not this behaviour might be a result of PTSD rather than just general prickliness and remoteness, but the reader senses a deeper truth.

And while the spoken dialogue throughout this section is stiff with anguish, bitterness and guarded acknowledgment of pain, the reader is also aware of Bruce's unvoiced thoughts, conveyed as unfiltered and revealing asides.

Winton understands just how to utilise interiority. The character is in silent dialogue with us, his intimate confidantes. His is a weary, resigned voice, laconically male and terse, more discomforted than it cares to admit by this catalytic fatal event, which he has assessed instantly and correctly for what it is.

Just as something terrible has befallen this family which must now be processed and endured, we sense something terrible has also happened at some stage to this character, and by the end of the section we are oriented towards revelation: that as the story dives deeper we are going to have that reluctantly addressed. We turn the page, then, into the more conventionally structured chapter (past tense, a long view) with that promise pulling us forward.

Metaphor

Dialogue may do all the heavy lifting when it comes to conveying what a character is fighting (and failing) to keep under wraps, but metaphor creates a navigational device through the story's thematic material.

Even in this brief section, Winton expends just over 120 of his 1579 words treating us to an extended metaphor, wrenching us out of the chronology of the events described into a stand-alone hallucinatory description of almost drowning but being rescued, by someone he recognises as himself. The imagery: 'my caul of bubbles'; 'someone to pull me up, drag me clear, blow air into me hot as blood', conveys a sense of birth or rebirth, juxtaposed with the death he has just witnessed. Suddenly he 'wakes with a grunt on the sofa', still in uniform after his shift (7). He surveys the disordered mess of his life then goes out onto his balcony and blows on his didjeridoo. 'The wind goes through me in cycles', he says, 'hot and droning and defiant' (7).

This is only a snapshot of the expanded metaphorical material yet to come, which will operate to give such rich subtext to its themes of breath, blood and surviving the threshhold moments of growing up, in which death contains its own mysterious glamour. But unambiguous elements are set in place here, in the aftermath of Bruce's destabilising experience of recognising the boy's death for what it was. The damage, it suggests, is beginning to rise unbidden already, as nightmares and uneasy subconscious thoughts of suffocation. The didgeridoo, with its requirement for 'circular breathing', seems to offer some kind of symbolic power and agency, as he 'blows until it burns' (7). The sound of it as he blows its music at the world outside suggests a heralding, a battle trumpet which allows him to feel 'defiant'.

Winton sets the book surely on its course, ready to descend from the shallow ledge of the here and now into the turbulent submerged undertows of the past, to 'do battle' with its spectres. No wonder the prose of the book itself can be so lyrical, and full of such elegy and loss, when the scaffolding has been so quietly and skilfully set in place.

Ending, unfurling: *The Life to Come* by Michelle de Kretser

Roanna Gonsalves

I

The act of reading a story is often propelled by an anticipation of its ending. Sometimes we read the last page first, possibly as a way of bracing ourselves for the journey to come. At other times, we are so absorbed in the world of the story that we resist its closure, wanting to prolong the experience, to hear that textual music, for just a while longer. The act of writing must also, therefore, be marked by an engagement with endings. As creators of stories, one of our tasks is to find a way to take the reader to the concluding page, to bring the story to a close. Yet creating an ending that is enchanting, moving and powerful can be a challenge. A close reading of one magnificent Australian novel can help us think through the question of how to write an ending.

The award-winning Australian writer Michelle de Kretser's novel *The Life to Come* (*TLTC*) has elicited praise from a wide circle of critics and reviewers. The most cursory of searches finds international homage being paid to de Kretser the stylist, de Kretser the satirist, de Kretser the creator of sparkling sentences. Lindsay Duguid, writing in the *Times Literary Supplement*, for example, says of *TLTC*, 'There is an enjoyably acute observation on almost every page ... Above all, there is the pleasure of her writing'. It is especially the final section of this book that has drawn wide acclaim. The literary scholar and critic Mridula Nath Chakraborty notes that, 'The last chapter in the novel, "Olly Faithful" is arguably de Kretser at her best. The tale of Bunty and Christabel, sharing their lives in the detritus of empire, in a young country where old age has no place, is both implacable and affecting in its instantiation of the here and now' (*Phoenix*). James Ley describes the novel's closing pages as 'elegiac' (*Sydney Review of Books*), and Marcel Theroux calls the last section 'the book's brilliant final act' (*Guardian*).

This essay is a reader's attempt to understand why the ending of *TLTC* works so well. It is an endeavour to think through what Chakraborty, Ley, Theroux and many other readers and critics are responding to in this last act. Pippa, the only character appearing in each of the five sections of the book, provides one kind of connective tissue. Yet I was curious about how the last section of the novel was held together, how it could feel so powerful and surprising and alive – despite the introduction of completely new protagonists, despite the story careening in astonishing ways. An answer may be found by considering a question that lies at the heart of this novel. At the end of the first section, the narrator asks, 'Who was the cat and who was the mat?' (de Kretser, 20). It is a question that makes us interrogate our notions of power and privilege and provides a guiding frame through which to read the book. I suggest that the force and dynamism of *The Life to Come* lies in its formal responses to this question. The re-arrangement of narrative time, the use of the technique of omission, and the scattering of a trail of figurative breadcrumbs throughout the novel build anticipation, create a sense of deferred understanding in the aftermath of events and lead to a subversion of power hierarchies.

In doing so the novel stages an ending that resists closure, gesturing instead towards a sense of unfurling. It is this that makes us want to keep reading and gives the final section its power and its magnificence.

II

Right from the skein-like syntax of its opening sentence, *The Life to Come* labyrinths us towards its end through a web-like re-arrangement of narrative time. Complicated relationships, such as the one between George Meshaw and the man whose house he lives in, are rendered from the first page onwards and followed through until we come to the relationship between Bunty and Christabel in the final section. Here, the intimacy and the yearning for companionship between the women draws attention to deep connections across geographies and race. Chronology is re-arranged and duration is manipulated as time is sometimes stretched out and sometimes compressed. This radical re-ordering of time is a literary strategy that has been employed by writers to varying effect, most skilfully in novels such as *A Visit from the Goon Squad* by Jennifer Egan and *Man Out of Time* by Stephanie Bishop. In *TLTC* it may be seen as a formal response to our age of social media saturation. In performing a mimetic response to the fractured nature of our consumption of literature, it offers a rejoinder to our web-like experience of the world. It uses this networked sensibility to weave a story that sways sideways rather than lurches forward in a predictable fashion.

The book is structured around five chapters, each narrated in the third person. The chapters are mainly focalised through characters whose lives, to a greater or lesser extent, imprint the other chapters too. Time is orchestrated at two distinct yet interconnected levels throughout *The Life to Come*. At one level, the story grows in a loosely linear fashion over an unspecified period of a few years as narrative time is measured in writerly time, the time it takes for a writer to work on a book, to get published, to achieve success. This timeline serves to incrementally set up and solidify the quest towards literary success before vapourising it in the final section. The novel, in one sense, is thus held together through its ironic depiction of the spectacle of authorship and the subterfuges it demands, through what Chakraborty calls its 'trenchant incisiveness of tenor and piercing clarity of perception' (*Phoenix*), through the use of its characters as portals into other times.

In the first chapter, 'The fictive self', we are told the protagonist George Meshaw is a PhD student at a university in Sydney, working as a tutor to augment his scholarship, and sustaining writerly ambitions. As the chapter progresses, we are told that 'George's own novel sang inside him' (12) and that while he wrote his thesis on his laptop, 'his novel had woken an instinct that mingled superstition and veneration, and he was writing the first draft by hand' (12). This chapter is layered with the relationship between George and Pippa, setting up both characters in such a way that their cruelty in the final chapter is heightened but also understood. Pippa is George's former student and current housemate, 'whose knowledge of history was cloudy' (12). Through the flashes of their relationship, through rain and a rising river, we see a creative commitment to a novel-in-progress unfolding as 'George went on with his novel at night' (13). It is towards the end of the chapter, after the news of his father's death, that we are told: 'George had just finished the first draft of his novel. It was called *Necessary Suffering*' (19). The time it takes to finish a first draft is stretched out.

As the novel progresses, George's fragmentary presence hovers over each chapter until he becomes whole again in the final section as a renowned author. In the second section, we hear about George's career from Pippa. The third section provides a discussion between Pippa and Céleste of George's novel. There is a brief interaction between Pippa and George over text message, and Pippa's reflections on George's narcissism, her professional envy of him. By now George Meshaw has had some success. We are told that 'his novels were published without acknowledgements, which Pippa considered a typically male move' (184). Pippa then reflects on a crucial moment in her writing journey. 'Long ago, George Meshaw had encouraged her to look inwards for material. He was smart, George. Pippa never forgot that he had set her on a path.' (204) In the fourth section, a character, Rashida, mentions that 'she loved George Meshaw's latest book' (221). A discussion between her and Pippa ensues, with Pippa's envy of George manifesting itself more distinctly. Further along in this section, Pippa googles George Meshaw to find that his latest novel has won a prize. Finally, in the fifth section, de Kretser draws George Meshaw back into the narrative, first as the subject of gossip at a party hosted by Pippa and her husband Matt and then in the closing pages where the architecture of social and cultural power, finely constructed as the novel progresses, is irrevocably subverted. As this writerly timeline progresses, we see that Pippa proceeds to mine her own life as well as the lives of those around her for material for her next book, with devastating consequences. This may also be seen as a delicious narratorial satirising of the genre of autofiction. Fittingly, in a novel about reading and writing literature, this final act takes place at a writers' festival and explores its aftermath.

III

The second level of the orchestration of time includes the novel's deep narrative time. Late in the final section, we are told that 'Time made a loop, hauling back the years' (344). This curling rearrangement of chronology is at its most radical when de Kretser weaves in and out of memory and dreams, including those dreams narrated within imaginary letters, and visions of the future calibrated to current desire. This re-arrangement of narrative time is compelling because it is used in conjunction with the techniques of omission and delayed disclosure.

The fluid omission of explanatory transitions between an interrupted narrative linearity builds anticipation of the progression of Christabel's story. Delayed disclosure then creates a sense of deferred understanding in the aftermath of events. The text itself reinforces these effects as we read that Christabel writes an imaginary letter to Pippa, saying 'One of the things Bunty and I shared was a mistrust of disclosure' (346). In the absence of explicit explanations, it is up to the reader to make connections between the gaps created by this radical re-organising of time.

Time is experienced as a web-like entanglement rather than chronologically laid out. This disruption of linearity is not random, but networked, evoking a system. On re-reading *TLTC*, the critic and teacher Dr Michael Moller insightfully suggests that 'Time is a tapestry in this novel where there is no single thread, no discernible point of origin that is more essential than any other. Pull anywhere on any thread, and the whole tapestry is compromised' (personal interview). The novel's networked re-arrangement of time, then, is reinforced through its structure, as the shape of the novel is held together by a complex associative logic, a connective logic, the logic of memory and of contemporary social media, rather than any easy, linear adherence to the logic of causality.

This associative, connective logic, as time is radically re-arranged, as stories are told within stories, serves also to muddy the boundaries between real life and fiction. For instance, in the final section a Russian story is retold as if it were a real-life incident (288). We have a sense of novels being 'at once removed from and more vivid than life' (294). This blurring of boundaries is employed to strongest effect when, towards the end of the book, Christabel thinks back to the beginning of a sense of dread, unseen at the time, when Pippa follows her back home, her opportunism and instrumentalised curiosity masked as concern. In the final extended scene at the Sydney Writers' Festival, Christabel asks George Meshaw, 'How could someone reading this book know what is and isn't true? It's Pippa who's mixing up fiction and life' (355). When sequenced with Pippa's mining of her own life and the lives of others for novelistic material, this blurring of boundaries between real life and fiction reinforces the interrogation of the genre of autofiction.

As we read the novel we understand that there is a lot that we are not told, right from lexical omission, such as the use of the appellations Fa and Moth, where the second half of each word has been dropped, to the omission of exposition, backstory and transitions between time periods. The less de Kretser tells us, the more we want to know, particularly in relation to filling in the gaps between events and the observations of these events by various characters. By disrupting the chronological progression of time, de Kretser withholds information about intervening moments, days, years, providing explanations well after key facts have been made known. The final section is thus narrated in the aftermath of events, leading to a deferred understanding, a sense of the truth being just slightly out of reach. One of the characters in the third section, Céleste, a translator who has been at the receiving end of Pippa's hurtful smugness, wishes to tell her something: 'You should have deleted the first sentence in each paragraph of your novel and looked closely at the last' (126). We receive this as a mirroring of the formal strategy of omission enacted by the novel.

In a novel without a traditional single protagonist, if there are characters around whom the story swirls, they are Bunty and Christabel. Pippa may be the only character who appears in every section. But it is Bunty whose detestation of disclosure reflexively models the formal strategy of omission and delayed disclosure that infuses the novel. And it is Christabel who best exemplifies the novel's myriad responses to the question at its heart, 'Who was the cat and who was the mat?' (20). We are not introduced to Bunty and Christabel until the final section, 'Olly Faithful'. Yet our encounter with Bunty, and even more with Christabel, does not seem sudden, because there has been a trail of figurative breadcrumbs leading us to them right from the start. These include specific motifs and images sprinkled through the narrative in a way that builds up certain expectations if only to destabilise them at the end. Bunty and Christabel's echoes precede them so that when we do meet them they are old friends to us, as they are to each other, people we seem to know well and want to know even more.

In keeping with the use of omission and delayed disclosure leading to a deferred understanding, many questions are left unanswered throughout the book. When Bunty points to a building that reminds her of Kuala Lumpur, Christabel notes, 'Somehow it was impossible to ask what she had been doing there, and when' (287). We are not told how Christabel finds work, only about details of her working life, such as her superficial interactions with 'Jone from Payroll' and then, more intimate interactions with her husband. We are unsure whether the toast to the buffalo occurs before or after the onset of Bunty's dementia (298). We don't know why Bunty refuses to stay in their accommodation in Jakarta (303), nor what happened on their holiday in Turkey (305), nor the details of Kiki Mack's death (306). All of this information remains undisclosed, enhancing the sense of resistance to closure that marks the ending of the book. It is Bunty, focalised through Christabel's memory of her, who unlocks the key to the inner workings of the novel, '"There are no secrets left now," said Bunty. "Only mysteries"' (318).

The networked re-arrangement of narrative time creates large gaps, omissions, at yet another level of the narrative. In their analysis of de Kretser's earlier novel *Questions of Travel*, literary scholars Anne Brewster and Sue Kossew write, 'The issue of horror lies deeply coiled in the centre of the novel. De Kretser gestures both to the "unspeakability" or incomprehensibility of horrific violence and to the efficacy and importance of narrative and storytelling in commemorating war in diasporic, transnational contexts' (193). This use of omission is used to great effect in *The Life to Come* too, particularly in the fifth section, to heighten the sense of the unspeakability of horrific violence, perpetrated by the state and by individuals.

IV

The fifth section, 'Olly Faithful', is structured around one long scene. However, in this scene, narrative time is radically altered as the scene bulges with memory, imaginary conversations and wishful foretelling. The scene begins one morning, approximately a year and a half after Bunty has died, when Christabel is anxious about what to wear to the Sydney Writers' Festival. The reason for this anxiety, indeed for her desire to attend the festival, is revealed over the next one hundred pages, as a meditation on the aftermath of exertions of social and cultural power.

Our empathy for Christabel has been finely calibrated and shaped by the withholding of backstory and the provision of only flashes of detail, so that Pippa's betrayal of her is felt all the more keenly by us. This is done through a build-up of compassion for Christabel, another trail of figurative breadcrumbs, as she experiences debilitating loneliness: 'Days passed, and weeks, and no one said her name' (334). Our compassion is strengthened as we see her experiencing betrayals of differing intensities. The first betrayal we are made aware of is when Len, the man Christabel might marry, leaves for Canada. The second betrayal is colder and foreshadows the bigger betrayal to come, when one of Christabel's lovers tells her, 'I don't think much of your face' (308). Christabel also experiences another unexpectedly cruel betrayal when she smiles and waves to a child. Instead of reciprocating her kindness, 'The child's voice reached her, bold as a bell: "Bitch!"' (310). It is only nearly halfway through this final section that we meet Pippa again, the character who spouts clichés of the writing life and whose actions will bring forth the denouement of the narrative. Christabel feels a sense of dread several times in relation to Pippa but ignores this or masks it with other more charitable emotions.

At the start of the fifth section, we are quickly transported to a time in Ceylon, present-day Sri Lanka, where Bunty and Christabel are students at the same school. We go further back in time and memory as we are shown Christabel as a young child:

> She had risen while it was still dark and wandered out of the house.
> The crows were already calling. The lawn lay in deep shadow,
> but the upper part of the air was full of light. It announced the
> approach of something loose and strong and expansive. Christabel
> sat on a step and waited for her life. (275–6)

The narrative threads back to the juxtaposition of Christabel with a trail of breadcrumbs of light, of brightness and hopefulness. Sometimes this moment is rendered just before a moment of shame and pleasure: in the crush of a Colombo train station we see Christabel, whose 'small sharp bones were full of light' (283). Sometimes it is rendered via a moment of saving grace: 'Christabel picked up the kitten by his scruff. "You are sentenced to life", she said and stowed him in her broken bag' (284). At other times it is rendered as a stabilising, if unreachable, 'assurance of a different life ... enormous and astonishing. Sometimes it lay in the future, like an infinitely suspended wave. Sometimes the wave had already broken and receded, leaving only darkly gleaming sand' (302). Christabel has also felt this hopefulness early on in her interactions with Pippa, bathing in Pippa's attention: 'Christabel's soul expanded, pulled upwards by the light' (312).

The nature of this sprawling 'something loose and strong and expansive' is never divulged explicitly. Instead, this moment, possibly the first moment in terms of the chronology of the events in the story, yet revealed only towards the end of the narrative, performs two gestures. It provides a clue about the heart of the book and its title, as little Christabel waits for the life to come. It also prepares us for the capaciousness of the book's ending, a vision of the closing scene.

Immediately after this childhood memory, we are taken through an unexplained gap of time, to another key scene that explains the name of this section. Bunty and Christabel sing 'O come, Olly Faithful' as the school choir rehearses for the carol service in Colombo. From this point onwards, we hear this choral refrain often, in different circumstances, but always with the heightened omission of the space between 'all' and 'ye'. This particularly, if not exclusively, South Asian linguistic proclivity leads to the popular Christmas carol 'O Come All Ye Faithful' sounding like 'O Come Olly Faithful'. The consequences of this contraction, its tendrils extending from Christmas carol to dog, are an invitation to reconsider the finitude of the past. The memory of an image from the first section rises up, the image of George Meshaw's mother, a woman whose roots are showing. For the reader, there is a deferred understanding. This image may be seen as a potent symbol for the concerns of this book: the persistence of the past, the squalid heritage of George Meshaw's and our present.

This section proceeds to loop backwards in time, sometimes providing fragments of narrative unconnected to what has come before, sometimes providing longer scenes convex with memory, within the larger scene set on the day of the Sydney Writers' Festival. For instance, we are taken to another key moment when Bunty and Christabel are schoolgirls but not friends, when they suddenly encounter each other on a street:

> The girls drew close and halted – uncertainly, as if they might yet
> pass each other without a sign. The face Christabel saw was as
> white as a bandage and as blank. For comfort, she thumbed a hard
> object in the pocket of her skirt. The sweet, held out, was round
> and orange in a cellophane twist. For a frightening moment, she
> thought Bunty would strike it out of her hand. (278)

While Bunty accepts the sweet, the context around Bunty's sudden appearance is not disclosed to us. We are unsure if she has come out of a violent experience or if the situation is more benign. So too, the far-reaching if lopsided consequence of Christabel's gesture of kindness is not revealed until much later in the narrative, after we have whorled back and forth in time. At a later point in the narrative, in a coiled memory of this sudden meeting, we get a sense of a deferred understanding in the aftermath of vital events. '"I don't understand," said Christabel. Then she did' (318). The purpose of this fractured looping is to withhold information, to delay disclosure, until a later point in the narrative. Its consequence is one of deferred understanding and deferred epiphany, a literary technique employed to astonishing effect throughout this book: a tantalising sense of the narrative unfolding as aftermath, until we come to the final unfurling into the future in its last lines.

V

Earlier in the book, the narrator offers a lucid observation about the process of reading, focalised through the character Céleste. We are told, 'Translation had taught Céleste that every book had an internal rhythm: energetic or languid, jittery or calm. That was its *hum*' (149). The hum of *The Life To Come* is its quietly subversive turbulence.

This hum is felt keenly in the final section, where the novel opens up to the future, while being chained and buoyed by the past and the present. From the house by the river in the opening line we are now returned, a little chastened, a little jubilant, to another house, other scenes by the river, involving Bunty and Christabel. From valorising the writer George Meshaw on the first page we are brought to a subversion of the power between writer and reader. The cultural authority bestowed upon the literary field is set up and satirised in the first section, with many in-jokes about professional envy and literary clichés. This build-up of authority reaches its climax at the writers' festival during Christabel's encounter with George Meshaw. It is then cleverly subverted, as the position of reader assumes dominance over that of writer, as Christabel dumps both George's and Pippa's novels into a bin by the door of a public toilet.

In the novel's final lines, Christabel's character is conveyed as if in a state of grace, as a dog seeming to connect Christabel to Bunty approaches her. These lines suggest a resistance to closure, an unfurling rather than a termination, throughout this concluding section:

> It was Bunty's dog – Christabel was sure of it. He had come to lead her to Bunty. 'Olly Faithful!' she called. He lowered his head and started moving towards her. Her arms rose, joyful and triumphant. And still he came. (373)

Christabel's arms raised towards the dog, with their suggestion of soaring hope, the juxtaposition of her character with the figurative breadcrumbs of light throughout this section, as noted earlier, provide the rhetorical force of this ending. This force is compounded by the culmination of another set of figurative breadcrumbs, the motif of human interaction with dogs. This is achieved through Bunty's refrain 'O come Olly Faithful' and Christabel's love of and longing for Pippa's dog Hank. This love is foreshadowed throughout the novel even before we get to know Bunty and Christabel. In the first section we hear of a dog called Bruce whose barking is alarming. In the second section, Ash mentions 'a tale about a white dog that brought misfortune to whoever saw it' (81). In the third section, 'The dog entered this idyll and passed through it, lending it fullness and truth' (164). In the fourth section, we are told 'an aversion to dogs is a cultural thing' (232). Finally in section five this is turned on its head in those beautiful closing lines.

The question posed explicitly and implicitly throughout the novel in a variety of ways: 'Who was the cat and who was the mat?' (20) holds the work together in anticipation of a response. This question may be intuited as 'Who needs saving?' In response, the narrative retorts with a resounding 'Not the reader':

> Christabel dropped George's novel into the bin and followed it with
> Pippa's. A lit fuse sparkled the length of her spine. She was a woman
> on a screen, renouncing love or claiming death with one stark,
> superb gesture. How wonderfully light her bag felt now! (363)

This is a moment when Christabel exerts agency, personal power, and demonstrates, once and for all, that she does not need external redemption. Her actions clearly indicate that while she may not be the cat, she is certainly not the mat. Christabel, the object of Pippa's pity, does not need saving. The novel's other cultural outsiders, Ash and Rashida, similarly refuse to be rescued. As Dr Michael Moller notes, 'The characters, all of them, grapple with the problem of how to express and solidify personal agency. Riven with the ordinary doubts and insecurities of existence, they seek ways to assert some sort of control over their circumstances and to reassure themselves they are leading meaningful, fulfilling lives. Except, perhaps, for Christabel, who does not appear to need such reassurance. Her agency seems stable, for she is more certain of who she is' (personal interview). In this final section, it is Christabel's 'joyful and triumphant' moment that closes the book. Christabel's redemption comes from within herself.

Stories curve around other stories. Christabel dumps George Meshaw's and Pippa's novels into a park bin. But the novel doesn't end there. De Kretser re-arranges narrative time yet again to give us one more assemblage of stories, set in Romania, where Bunty and Christabel took a holiday. At this point, one more belated disclosure is made: '"I didn't know you played chess," said Christabel' (368). In the Romanian countryside, bulging with its own ancient stories, we are returned, further back in time, to that first moment of light in Colombo: 'For no reason, Christabel was five years old, alone in the morning. Everything was about to begin' (370). The effect of this return to the chronological beginning of the story, now told achronologically, is to imbue the last scene with all that has gone before it, with the magnitude of a past filled with darkness but also with light. So when we finally circle back to the river where this book began, we return to this old place with a new understanding, ripe with the lives of the characters whose desires, failings and vulnerabilities we have come to understand. This lucid ending, capacious and exhilarating, does not force a rigid closure. Instead it feels like another beginning for Christabel, another moment of unfurling possibility, the weight of loss and betrayal behind her, as she opens her arms to the coming of life.

An uneasy anticipation:
Tension in MJ Hyland's novels

Angela Meyer

MJ Hyland's three novels are intimate character-driven works. *How the Light Gets In* is about an exchange student, Lou Connor, caught up in fantasies of empty houses and other lives. *Carry Me Down* is about an eleven-year-old, John Egan, who believes he has a unique sensitivity to lies and liars. And in *This Is How*, Patrick Oxtoby starts a new life by the seaside but one terrible action alters his future irrevocably. Each novel is an absorbing page-turner. Hyland is skilled at creating narrative tension and a compelling sense of unease. The devices she uses to infuse her novels with this tension, and how she draws the reader into the story through her protagonists' experiences, are particularly instructive for fellow writers.

Tension in a novel arises from conflict. Conflict is often referred to as being 'what happens' in a novel. It is, essentially, the meeting of two opposing forces. Tension arises from the overarching and minor (often connected) conflicts in the work. Tension anticipates conflict, by sitting in that space between opposing forces. Tension, for the reader, is a sensation of pleasant discomfort where we are compelled to read on to know what is going to happen and how it will play out.

Tension is a key driver of narrative. It can be related to plot, preceding action, but tension can also be present in works that are not plot-driven. Strong works without an easily definable plot structure still have conflicts. The tension arising from these conflicts is enacted through characters and their actions (or inactions), rather than marked 'plot events' such as an inciting incident, crisis and resolution. Tension can also be present in place, mood, and other elements of the novel, though the focus here will be on character. In other words, it is possible to have a page-turning novel where not much 'happens' if the writer is sophisticated at imbuing the work with conflict and its associated tensions.

The overarching conflicts, from which the tension derives, may be between any number of opposing forces and a novel often has layers of different conflicts at play. Some examples of conflict are: between people, between a person and an obstacle, between a person and a closed environment (trap), between a person and an external force (society, nature, technology, god), between a person's perceptions and reality, between a person and their own self. There can also be an overt versus an underlying conflict, such as between what one person knows and another doesn't, or conflict through dramatic irony, where the reader understands more than the character does.

This Is How is a deceptively straightforward book that contains a multitude of conflicts, and the layering of each of these within the novel creates its tension. The protagonist Patrick Oxtoby has conflict with other people, which leads to the plot point upon which the novel pivots; he has conflict with obstacles, which are in the way of him achieving professional or romantic goals; he has conflict with a closed environment, particularly in the second half of the novel when he is in gaol; he has conflict with reality (a certain disjointedness between the way he perceives a conversation or moment and how it appears to others), and certainly he is in conflict with himself, as he consistently fails to be in touch with his own emotions and motivations.

Similarly, in *How the Light Gets In* and *Carry Me Down* Lou Connor and John Egan experience conflicts between their expectations and reality. Much of the tension in *Carry Me Down* derives from the central conflict of John's desire for truth and his unique ability to detect lies versus his perception that others live in untruth and deception. And in *How the Light Gets In*, a central conflict for Lou is her desire for a shinier life versus the much more complex reality of the ordinary and, creating additional tension, the way she self-sabotages her own 'dream'. There are multiple devices present in Hyland's novels that act to infuse them with the tension related to these overarching conflicts, and it is worth going into detail about each of them.

Tense and point of view

A writer has to make choices about *how* to tell the story. Through the eyes of the character, with immediacy, or at a remove? Differing effects can be created with each, and sometimes a particular choice will feel more 'natural' to the writer. A writer must consider how choices in tense and point of view will shape how the narrative unfolds. All three of Hyland's novels are written in the same point of view and tense: first person, present tense. These choices limit the information the reader receives to the protagonist's moment-to-moment thoughts and interpretations. We see through their eyes. This creates tension partly through dramatic irony – the reader must interpret how other characters perceive events while only receiving limited information via the vantage point of the protagonist-narrator. There is also dissonance between the protagonist's thoughts, which we witness, and their actions. We know that what they tell themselves doesn't always line up with the words they speak, the actions they take, or their thought process in a different situation. We then read on partly to know if we have interpreted this correctly. There is a sense we 'know more' than the protagonist, though

Hyland manages this in such a way that we are often not sure *what* it is we know. Nevertheless this dissonance creates tension and makes us uneasy.

In *This Is How*, Patrick arrives at the boarding house in a new town where he is to start a new job. He has arrived late and the first-person point of view immediately alerts us to his being on guard in the second line: 'I don't bang hard [on the door] like a copper, but it's not as though I'm ashamed to be knocking either' (1). Hyland gives us no clues as to the tone of the landlady's voice, to begin with, as she and Patrick converse, so we are partly to guess whether she is bothered by his lateness or not. The exchange is awkward – she offers to take his coat, he leaves it on, then acquiesces because he wants to be shown to his room and 'get it over with'. He wonders if she is nervous, the way he is. His internalising invites us to wonder, too, but also alerts us to the fact his own nerves could be clouding his interpretation of her.

We are also immediately present within him 'bodily', and this is another way that Hyland's first-person narration creates tension: 'My mouth's gone dry', 'my hands hang heavy' (1). Experiencing the protagonist's physical sensations enhances our ability to empathise with them. We also have access to their desires and cravings, bodily and otherwise, through this point of view: 'I wouldn't mind a ham sandwich and a cup of coffee. After that, we could lie down together and I could put my head in her lap' (3). This intimate access reveals vulnerabilities that can both stimulate our sympathy and simultaneously intensify our unease.

In the opening of *How the Light Gets In*, Lou Connor is on a plane. We don't know where she is going yet or why (which adds tension in itself) but there is a sense of frustration as Lou notes her seatmate eating while watching a show about death row. Lou needs to stop herself 'from screaming' (4). As with Patrick, we are also bodily acquainted with her, a few pages later: 'This sudden intimacy makes me acutely aware of my teeth and the way they don't sit properly in my jaw' (7). By the end of the chapter a little anticipation creeps in: 'the smell of Henry

[host father] tells me that, from now on, I will sleep on cleaner sheets'
(11). An element of Lou's inner conflict (fear vs hope) is introduced
in these pages, as she lands in the US and meets her host family, and
the first-person, present-tense narration means we feel the tension that
sits between these opposing forces alongside her as the moments of this
new experience unfold.

Withholding

One way to create tension in a novel is to *withhold*. To write 'just enough'
that the reader can follow, but to avoid over-explaining: to hold back,
to tantalise. This can be in terms of plot information, but it can also be
in terms of character. In some novels this is done cheaply, and we're a
little too aware of the writer's manipulations. Not so with MJ Hyland.
Hyland withholds subtly, creating a series of open-ended questions in
our minds, enhancing the tension and inviting us to read on. In the early
pages of *This Is How*, Patrick gives clues as to why he has changed his
life – why he's come to the boarding house. We don't receive the full
story. We get a partial flashback scene, which reveals how he'd felt in
the moment: his fiancée Sarah had told him the relationship was over.
'I wanted to push her down the stairs, make the kind of impression
I didn't know how to make with words' (4). He reveals the loop of
thought that had been playing in his head, in the moment, and a fantasy
of violence he'd had, and then how he had left. Five short paragraphs,
and then the narrative returns to the present. Elaboration on this
relationship is then withheld until page forty. Often, and especially in
a first draft, writers feel the need to put everything 'up front' lest the
reader become confused about the what, why and who. It takes practice,
but giving 'just enough' detail helps to create tension – here, an insight
into Patrick's motivations, a hint of his difficulty processing emotions
and of women being a trigger for him.

Not giving a character what they want

The writer will understand, or discover, while writing a novel, what the character wants. There could be overt desires and hidden ones. There could be desires hidden even from the character themselves. In building tension it's important not to give the character what they want. A very basic example of this is a zombie story. What do the characters want? They want to be safe. The story is resolved when they are safe. The desires of a character like Patrick, in *This Is How*, are much more complex and multilayered, but we can figure out that, essentially, he wants to be accepted, praised, even loved. He wonders why his new boss, Hayes, doesn't compliment his work more. When Hayes says he's a 'pretty good' mechanic, Patrick thinks: 'Pretty good? I'm better than he is, better than most. Why doesn't he say so?' (88). He also, without realising it, has a desire to *possess*, hence his difficult and violent feelings towards those who seem to 'own' women so easily, like Welkin. Both of these complex motivations are still present after the turn in the narrative, when Patrick is in gaol. He desires to be accepted by other inmates, and the psychologist. And he is discomfited by the paedophile (who has 'possessed'). By refusing to fulfil these desires, Hyland holds the tension relating to them.

A further desire is set up in this second half of the novel: to undo what has been done, and for others to understand that he did not mean it. So Hyland holds off on giving Patrick what he wants, giving him only brief moments of satisfaction (that also act to reignite his desires), and adds new desires on top. Additionally, she gives him constant physical discomfort – pains, sickness, and the inability to sleep. She also adds a layer of tension by weaving in other characters' *opposing* desires, and holding off any satisfaction or resolution of those, such as Patrick's father's desire for him to take responsibility for his actions. In a commercial fiction narrative, reader satisfaction would often come from characters' desires being met at the end, as part of the resolution of the plot. In a more character-driven, literary novel such as this, satisfaction comes from the shift, at the end, towards awareness, for Patrick. So his unconscious desires and motivations become more conscious for him. But there is also a complex resolution in the irony of confinement becoming somewhat comfortable for Patrick, in him finding a life that unexpectedly might suit him. So that, in a way, *is* an unconscious desire being met, one that was beautifully withheld from both us and him.

Early on in *Carry Me Down*, young John Egan states: 'One day I will be in the *Guinness Book of Records*, along with all the other people who do not want to be forgotten or ignored' (5). Writers do not always overtly display their characters' desires, and of course there are unconscious desires (for approval, admiration, love) that underpin the specificity of this one, but the reader knowing this goal of John's helps to aid the tension all the way through *Carry Me Down*. The conflict between achieving admiration and being thwarted brings tension to various scenes with other characters, and is behind many of John's actions and reactions. When he connects with a new teacher, Mr Roche, it is because Mr Roche has paid him positive attention and humiliated one of John's bullies, a seeming alignment to John's side of the conflict. John pins hope on the teacher so quickly, as a person in whom he can confide, that the tension for the reader around being thwarted or disappointed by this obviously sadistic man is immense. In general, Hyland holds this tension not only by denying John his desires but by giving him such an elaborate and fanciful desire in the first place. Therefore, an added layer of the tension for the reader is: will he ever realise just how fanciful his desires are? And worse: how will it affect him when he does?

Put more things in the way

To create tension, a writer may not only prevent characters from getting what they want, but may place even more obstacles in their way. An obvious example of this technique would be a crime novel where, besides the central plot thread (solving a murder), there are accumulating and complicating plot events such as a second body, lack of evidence, and so on, but *also* secondary tensions inhibiting the protagonist/s' ability to solve the crime, such as fraught relationships, complicating work factors, personal trauma or whatever trope the author chooses. In a character-driven novel, like *This Is How*, Hyland 'makes things worse' for Patrick by having him stumble through a series of interactions with other characters while never quite developing the ability to manifest the craved connection or recognition. In either example, a plot-driven or character-driven novel, a sophisticated writer will also ensure that the character is *active* in progressing the narrative. In other words, it will be their own choices and actions (or lack thereof) much of the time that 'make things worse' and that lead to the action that pushes the story forward. For example, Patrick chooses to call Georgia, the waitress, when he is arrested, and he suffers the consequences when it comes back into the narrative at the trial. Most novels will contain a combination of both external and character-induced 'events' that create forward motion in the story. The external events help to build a picture of the character, showing how they *react* to what happens *to* them. But their activeness, being the creator and cause of events themselves, is always important to how the plot progresses and is resolved; it generates tension related to what they will do next.

Lou makes things worse for herself, too, in *How the Light Gets In*. Her host parents lay down the house rules. On top of these are the exchange student organisation's rules, including that she must not leave the house without telling Margaret or Henry where she is going. Immediately after these rules are established, Lou leaves the house. 'I like to walk around the streets at night and fantasise about being in other people's houses' (37). Despite the fact that she has flown across the world to do exactly that (live in someone else's house), she has not rid herself of the intensity of this desire. What gets in the way of what she wants is seemingly herself most of all, which creates a dual tension. On the surface, we wonder, will she find the perfect living situation? Underneath, we question if she will ever figure out what she really needs to be fulfilled.

There is something else worth considering here: how does a writer keep us engaged with a character who keeps getting in their own way? As mentioned before, Hyland creates intimacy with her characters through their point of view, their internalisation and also their physicality. By the point Lou goes out to 'fantasise about being in other people's houses', we have experienced her anticipation, her difficulty with physical affection, her anxiety at not knowing how to act, her desire to sleep; how effortful it all is for her. Though we may not entirely understand her motivations yet, this intimacy with her moment-to-moment experience means we are invested in her. We want to know more about *why* she is who she is and feels what she feels and this tension intertwines with that of *what will happen*?

Dialogue

Certain techniques with dialogue can be employed to aid tension in a novel. Hyland goes easy on dialogue tags, such as 'says' or 'asks'. Dialogue flows from character to character without much explanation of tone and without excessive use of 'ly' adverbs ('says thoughtfully', 'asks quietly' and so on). Therefore, the dialogue aids the *withholding*. Between the lines of dialogue are 'beats' in which we often have a thought from Patrick, a gesture or action, but they are rarely explanatory or expositional. When Patrick's father visits him in gaol, the conversation builds towards talking about the reason he is there:

'A normal man,' he says, 'wouldn't have gone to another man's room like that with a wrench and attacked a man in his sleep.'

'I know that,' I say.

'Do you?'

''Course I know that.'

'And what about remorse? Are you sorry?'

''Course I am.'

'You didn't say much about that in your letter.'

I thought I had.

The siren sounds.

My father gets up.

The officer shouts 'Time!'

I want the doors to open for me, to go out the gate in my father's place. (233)

Hyland creates just enough mystery within each conversation, just enough space, to infuse the scene with tension related to the various overarching conflicts of the novel. And Patrick's active role in contributing to the tension is always present. In the example above, this is related to not only what he has done but what he failed to write in his letter.

Miscommunication

A related technique to 'withholding' is miscommunication or disconnect between characters. Some authors are incredible at creating tension chiefly through this technique, like the American novelist Richard Yates. Not only does perpetual miscommunication between characters create tension but if an author is skilled at rendering it, it can make for particularly resonant fiction. Hyland's protagonists all have difficulty in being 'heard', and tension is built around their meetings and interactions with others and their inability to communicate in a way that builds a meaningful or lasting connection. In *This Is How*, tension is also created through the discord between the conversations Patrick is having and the (often desperate) thoughts and feelings that follow. After a conversation with Welkin, Patrick is pummelled by emotion:

> I don't say more, don't say goodbye, won't use his name the way he's gone and used mine. The thing is, I can't speak, not now. I've got to swallow the lump out of my throat and my mouth's clogged up and all because he's decided to make this advance to friendship, or whatever the hell it is, and he's patronised me and it riles me and it also makes me feel good and it's hard to say, but I suppose I want his friendship more than I don't, and what he's said has got me in the neck. (65–6)

The second sentence is long, full of commas and conjunctions, enhancing the effect of tumbling desperation, confusion and high emotion. These juxtapositions of Patrick's thoughts to the exchanges in dialogue (contrasting exterior to interior) build, adding to the tension as the reader wonders how he will be able to sustain a polite exterior or contain the impulses just beneath the surface.

Sentence length and rhythm

Sentence length and the rhythm of sentences and paragraphs play a part in building tension. When the conflict is coming to the fore, the tension ratcheting up, a writer will often use more paragraph breaks, shorter sentences, minimal description and more action. As with the above example, they may also use more conjunctions and create a staccato rhythm to convey emotion. Sometimes a writer slows down instead of speeding up – pauses, adds filler to the sentence or paragraph, holds the reader back – increasing anticipation. Depending on the novel's style, an effect is created by changing the sentence structure and paragraphing so that pivotal moments are built towards in a deliberate way. In *This Is How*, in the moments leading up to the violent act, Hyland gives us each piece of action, each observation, on a new line:

> I go out to the hall and knock once on Welkin's door and say his name.
> He doesn't answer.
> I try the handle and go in.
> The curtains are closed and the stuffy air stinks of his drunken skin.
> It's too dark for me to see what I need to see.
> I go out to the hall, switch on the light and go back in with the door left open behind me.
> I look at his big body asleep on its back and listen to the wet gurgling in his fat throat. His right arm hangs down over the side of the mattress and his fingers are near to touching the mouth of the empty whisky bottle.
> I stand close by his bed. (138)

The paragraphing leads to the eye slipping down the page, creating a sense of building tension. The repetition of 'I' is rhythmic, with alternation in between, leading us through Patrick's actions. The short descriptive details are selective – giving us just enough of a picture of the scene, but crucially also insight into Patrick's mood and mindset, drawing tight the tension from conflicts that have been introduced in the opening chapters. All of these clues inform us that something is about to happen.

Foreshadowing

To foreshadow is to introduce an idea, character, object or piece of information that will become significant to the story later on.

In *This Is How*, Patrick's attachment to his tool kit foreshadows both how angry he gets when a tool is not returned and his use of one of the tools to do violence. His first inappropriately intimate, but private, thoughts about Bridget, the landlady, also foreshadow how Patrick will feel about Welkin's overt, sexualised actions towards her. And the hint of violence in his thoughts about his ex in the opening pages foreshadows his capacity for it. This capacity is built upon through further flashbacks, such as his reaction, as a boy, to the death of his grandmother, with whom he had a rare connection: 'When I got the news I rode my bike to the new estate being built around behind the chocolate factory and dug a hole in the ground and screamed into it. I screamed about how fucking stupid the world is' (33). The trick with foreshadowing is to not overexplain, to instead drop open-ended clues and hints: a scattering. Also, to repeat or build upon foreshadowed elements to create a 'hook' in the reader's mind. We will realise that there is something significant about this element, consciously or unconsciously, and we might realise it is relevant to an overarching conflict, but we will not know why, or how it will play out, and that creates tension.

Repetition

Repetition creates build, expectation and anticipation. This is one reason an essentially plotless work like Samuel Beckett's play *Waiting for Godot* is compelling: its internal repetition combined with the philosophical tension it holds (the larger, unresolvable questioning that opens out and out). Besides the tool kit in *This Is How*, which foreshadows the incident upon which the story pivots, it is worth examining how Hyland holds tension in the second half of the novel, when Patrick is in gaol. There's a circuitous, repetitive nature to Patrick's thoughts. He repeats to himself and others that he did not mean to do what he did, and so he should not be locked up. With each new encounter, we wonder if this will be the person or moment to cut through this repetition (which would resolve conflict), and as each one does not, or does only partly before he springs back to these circuitous thoughts, the tension is held.

In *How the Light Gets In*, Lou's desire for newness, difference, a fresh start is repeated throughout the narrative:

'It would be best of all to go back in time, to my first or second night, or forward in time, to winter, so we could be wearing woolly jumpers. That would be best, with the open fire burning. We could start again.' (60)

'This is another fresh start and I'm going to get it all perfect.' (106)

'I know that I will start all over again; rewind this, and go back to the beginning.' (138)

'This time it will be different.' (245)

The repetition helps to maintain tension, reminding us of Lou's motivation, reminding us of what Lou (superficially) wants, and that there is more (in a non-superficial sense) to what she wants that she hasn't yet realised. At the point in the narrative beyond the last quote, when she feels concern for Lishny (another exchange student gone astray) it is a revelation for her to be worried about another person, and this new and enduring feeling is the beginning of the resolution of her character arc. The tension, however, is still held, because she does not immediately change or accept the internal shift. She tests 'the memory of him', tests herself for 'real feeling'. Finds that she does still care about him. Closer to the end, he plays out a fantasy with her about the future which acts to acknowledge her inner world, her turmoil. Thereafter, she better understands the fantasy as fantasy. And the tension is dissolved, the conflict resolved.

Contrasts

Contrasts can also be used to build tension. A writer may show joy when there is terror lurking, show beauty when there is ugliness, or write in a character who embodies the opposite feelings to the protagonist. Contrasts can represent the story's overarching conflicts on the page, in micro. In *This Is How*, Hyland employs the previous technique, repetition, to enhance or highlight contrast. In the opening, Patrick's observations of Bridget as 'pretty' (twice) and 'lovely', and his intimate desires, are contrasted with both his discomfort and his thoughts of violence. The encounter with his mother, who comes to visit him, is full of contrasts. He finds her overbearing and wants her to leave. He ends up walking away from her. But then he goes back, can't find her. He hopes 'she'll be all right'. His conflicting thoughts about her provide mystery, gaps to fill in, for the reader. We might suspect one thought or another is more genuine, but we need to read on to understand further.

Minor characters

James Baldwin said, in his *Paris Review* interview, that it is minor characters who 'carry the tension in a much more explicit way than the majors'. He said that 'minor characters are the subtext, illustrations of whatever it is you're trying to convey'. In terms of the conflicts in a novel, a minor character might exhibit the opposing force to the protagonist (in simple terms: good versus bad, weak versus strong, animal versus mechanical, etc.). In *This Is How*, each of the minor characters provides these kinds of contrasts to Patrick, but also act to highlight his internal conflicts. Welkin is confident, comfortable in his flesh, and sexually dominant: the antithesis of Patrick. Bridget is a replacement for both Patrick's mother and his ex – he projects onto her comfort and kindness, and he wants to be accepted by her. His interactions with her and thoughts of and around her highlight his internal conflicts. Welkin's possessiveness towards Bridget is what sets off Patrick's violence, combined with his loss of control over the items in his tool kit (a symbol of the only skills for which he has been valued and the only direction he has had). The waitress, Georgia, gives us insight into what Patrick really wants (acceptance) just before everything is taken away from him. An early cell mate, Stevenson, who tells Patrick he is 'not in touch with his own body' and who openly farts and wanks, adds to the tension by confronting and making us question the level of Patrick's repression. The more permanent cell mate, Gardam, holds tension as he may be Patrick's unexpected chance of salvation or redemption, allowing Patrick to finally acknowledge and quieten needs within himself. And Patrick's parents carry tension throughout by pushing Patrick to be different to who he feels he is. So each minor character throws into relief some aspect of conflict, by being an opposing force to Patrick and/or highlighting or exposing his inner conflicts, and therefore each interaction, each moment of action with these minor characters, while the conflicts are sustained, holds tension.

It is worth noting that several of these devices also emphasise Hyland's skill in creating character-driven fiction and, rather than existing purely for the sake of narrative tension, act to stimulate sympathy for her characters and express greater poignancy around the human condition. Don't we all miscommunicate, fail to see what's coming and, often, how our own actions lead us towards it? In literary fiction, narrative conflict and tension are often intertwined with characterisation, character motivation and the character arc, along with the greater themes of the text. A skilled literary writer is able to create this cohesion, through which we are turning the pages wanting to know what is going to happen while experiencing the novel in a layered sense: emotive, intellectual, philosophical. A literary novel does not entirely resolve its tensions at the end – in terms of narrative and character, somewhat, but its philosophical tension is often carried over, resonant and lingering, and though more ambiguous than commercial fiction's narrative conclusions, it makes for satisfying and even transformative reading.

Structure in Nam Le's 'Love and honour and pity and pride and compassion and sacrifice'

Fiona McFarlane

When I first began reading Nam Le's 'Love and honour and pity and pride and compassion and sacrifice', I was sceptical: a story about a writer writing a story? A writer at the Iowa Writers' Workshop, no less? Isn't this a little self-indulgent? Hasn't this been done before? But Le had already anticipated all of my objections, and the story insisted on countering them with a mixture of intelligence, generosity and audacity. Any anxiety or weariness I felt about the story's metafictional thickets was already written into it. We've tied ourselves in knots about who has the right to tell which stories: *look!* says the story, *I'll write the knots!* Isn't it immodest to write so blatantly, and at the same time so coyly, about your own writerly self? *What self!* says the story, and also: *no one is harder on this not-self than I am!* And, hasn't this been done before? *What hasn't been done before!* says the story, and opens with someone waking up from a dream. By the end of that first reading, I was dazzled – along with everybody else – by its self-reflective brilliance.

It wasn't until much later, when I'd read the story multiple times and was preparing to teach it, that I really came to appreciate its technical excellence. This story about a story works so well because it's so well constructed. When I teach it now, I always approach it through structure. Inevitably, the discussion of structure becomes the foundation for a complex conversation about authorship, ethics, trauma and inheritance; but anchoring that discussion in the story's craft allows writerly readers to pay attention to *how* Le has prompted these conversations. 'Love and honour' is full of stories, and the way Le chooses to tell them – in what tense, in what order, in what form of speech – is the way he generates the story's meanings.

I'll summarise the story briefly, with the caveat that I don't believe stories can be summarised; as Flannery O'Connor says, 'When anybody asks what a story is about, the only proper thing is to tell him to read the story' (96). Its narrator, an Australian student at the Iowa Writers' Workshop – whose name happens to be Nam – receives a visit from his father. This visit poses problems: Nam has a story due for class and hasn't been able to write it; he has a complicated relationship with his authoritarian and emotionally distant father; on top of this, Nam's girlfriend, Linda, is hurt by Nam's refusal to reveal her existence to his father. Nam, we learn, has resisted writing an 'ethnic story' that will capitalise on his father's experience of wartime Vietnam and the family's escape to Australia. Now, with his father in Iowa City, his deadline looming, and Linda insisting that he at least finish this piece of writing, Nam *does* write his 'ethnic story' (he titles it 'ETHNIC STORY'), drawing on the account of the infamous My Lai massacre that Nam once heard his father tell at a party. Linda reads some of his story and is disappointed. Nam's father reads it and tells him there are 'mistakes' in it. With only one day left until the deadline, Nam and his father discuss the mistakes; Nam's father reveals more about his experiences in Vietnam. Nam stays up all night and rewrites the story. He's proud of it, and believes his father will be proud. The next day, only half an hour before the deadline, Nam discovers that his father has destroyed the only copy.

Distilled like this, the plot already sounds complicated enough; maybe I should mention that, at twenty-five pages, this is a *long* short story. But in addition to this complex plot, 'Love and honour' works with three significant time periods: I'll call them 'the time of story', 'the time of the past' and 'the time of telling'. The 'time of story' is the period of the father's visit. This timeline is relentlessly linear. It begins, just as the story does, with the father's arrival, and it ends as Nam sees that his father's hands are empty: the story has been destroyed.

Throughout the linear account of the time of story, we see glimpses of 'the time of the past' via flashback and exposition. The time of the past includes everything that Nam experiences and represents *before* his father arrives. It's important that we see every moment of the time of the past as filtered through Nam's sensibility: for example, it never includes the actual My Lai massacre; it only includes Nam's memory of the father's narration of the massacre at the long-ago party. The time of the past includes Nam's childhood and adolescence; his unhappy legal career in Melbourne; his move to Iowa; the party he went to last week, on the way home from which a friend complimented him for not capitalising on his ethnicity in his work; and it includes the night before the father's arrival, when Nam and Linda are in bed, and he tells her – for the first time – about his father's visit. The time of the past is disorderly, in the sense that different flashbacks and expository passages take us all over the past timeline, so we don't encounter it sequentially. But it's orderly in the sense that it's subjugated to the order of the time of story: the time of the past is revealed in a sequence that supports the time of story.

The third significant time period is the one that makes all of this possible: the 'time of telling' is the time from which the narrator tells the story. This time is unspecified – we just know that it's after the story's events. The narrative voice speaks from this time; it already knows the end of the story, makes decisions about how to tell it, reflects on its outcomes and hints at later developments. Nam, the narrating writer, is being writerly about his story about a story, and he's doing this by drawing attention to the formal and stylistic decisions he makes in order to tell it. You'll notice the moments in which he does this: a typical example comes after his dramatisation of his father's My Lai tale, which Nam presents in full realist mode, as if we're present at the party to hear the father's every word. Afterwards, Nam admits that, 'Maybe he didn't tell it exactly that way. Maybe I'm filling in the gaps' (17).

Le manages all three of these narrative times so well that we're never confused by this mass of material or our movement through it. His transitions are flawless; the tools he uses to make them include large spaces between sections, philosophical musings that trigger memories, perfect control over tense and a plethora of time indicators. By these, I mean references to time: what time it is, how much time has passed, when something occurs in relation to something else. Phrases like 'two weeks later' or 'the night before' or 'the clock read 11:44'. Clear indications of time may feel too simple and dull to think about, but they're essential; once you start keeping track of timekeeping in great short stories, you'll see how much of it there is. The thing I'd most like my students to learn from me is how to keep track of time in a short story.

And of course, the time of story in 'Love and honour' is under pressure: both Nam's story and his father's visit share a deadline of three and a half days. Having introduced these mutual (but conflicting) 'ticking clocks', Le makes sure to account for every moment of those three and a half days. He both delays and builds toward this time-of-story deadline by introducing digressions from the time of the past and the time of telling.

Each narrative time – of story, of the past and of telling – plays out along its own dramatic arc; the story actually manages to produce a climax in each of them. The time of the past builds to the climactic scene in which teenage Nam, in freshly laundered school uniform, asks his father to allow his mother to return home. One of the most useful pieces of writing advice I've ever received came from the wonderful American writer Elizabeth McCracken, who told me, 'The past is a burning house. Only go back to take what you really need'. Le is very good at knowing when to dramatise the past and when to simply narrate it; he always rescues the right things from the flames. Notice the painful tenderness with which past-Nam is undone by his father's speaking to him as a friend rather than a father; notice that past-Nam still refuses his father, still won't come home. This interaction prepares the way for the climax in the time of story; among other things, it opens up the possibility of a confrontation between father and son in which the outcome is positive.

Both Le, the author of the story, and Nam, the writer-narrator who tells it, manipulate our experience of the father by revealing different aspects of him in a certain order, and at certain times, during the time of story. These are all structural decisions. Imagine how different the story would feel if it opened with the My Lai account, and the news of the father's severity with Nam came later. As the story stands, by the time we reach the My Lai account, we're forced to hold this trauma in the same space as the father's paternal brutality. Quite rightly, we can't resolve the complexity of this. Neither can Nam. Imagine how different the My Lai account would feel if it hadn't been preceded by the scene in which Nam's friend complains about 'ethnic literature', so that we're forced to pay attention to the act of telling it. Every moment in this story has been prepared for us so carefully; the story is relentless in this sense, and importantly so: it never wants to be experienced complacently or simplistically. At no point in this story should you feel comfortable, even when it invites you to. *Especially* when it trots out the tropes of the 'ethnic story': the trauma, the 'exotic' foods, the second-generation narrator who helps the reader navigate otherness.

Notice, too, how early in the story we're given the account of My Lai. Another story might have saved the high drama of the father's ordeal for a more climactic moment; My Lai would make a very effective climactic 'set-piece'. But that would be a different story – one, perhaps, about a son coming to terms with the way his father has been marked by his experiences, and the way this has in turn marked the son. 'Love and honour' isn't interested in coming to terms with anything. It's a story about telling stories, and good stories rarely come to terms: they complicate terms, they unsettle accounts, and they suggest new possibilities. The time of story in 'Love and honour' contains multiple stories: Nam writes two, neither of which we get to read. The father tells two stories, which we don't really hear – we only hear Nam's reconstructions of them. The first My Lai account is visceral and vivid; it inspires pity and horror. But the story's earlier comments about 'ethnic stories' should make us uneasy about this response. 'Love and honour' doesn't want us to settle in the complacency or piety of pity and horror; it doesn't want us to 'read and clap ... and forget' (25). When Nam's father does tell him, first-hand, about Vietnam – expanding on My Lai, adding more information about what happened before and afterwards – we're given very little direct dialogue. Unlike the My Lai account, the reader *isn't* there, listening in; we're not even given the opportunity to *pretend* that all of this information isn't mediated through Nam. This is crucial to the story's proposal that there *is* no unmediated version of the father's 'ethnic story': not the realist, first-person version and not the narrated, third-person version; not the first draft, which disappoints Linda, and not the second draft, which the father destroys.

The reader is propelled through all of this – the many timelines, the layers of metanarrative – by the steadily ticking clock of the story deadline and the expert way in which the stakes of 'Love and honour' are pinned on it. Nam's relationship with his father and his relationship with Linda are both caught up in it; notice, too, that there's probably no scenario in which Nam can write the story in time for the deadline and please both his father and his girlfriend. These are classic story mechanics: complication, conflicting goals and a time limit. 'Love and honour' functions beautifully as a traditional short story, all while questioning the traditional short story's capacity to represent complexity.

The time of telling doesn't really assert itself until the end of the story, but it's present throughout: in the use of the past tense, in any reference to memory, any discussion of new wisdom gained through the passing of time, in the self-consciousness about the truth of the My Lai scene and in the suggestion that Nam is writing something 'close enough' to a 'eulogy'. When Nam wakes up on the morning of his deadline – his father's last morning in Iowa City – and finds his story missing, we're firmly in the time of story: so firmly in it, that we participate in Nam's wishful projection of a future time in which his father has read the story: 'He would recognise me. He would see how powerful was his experience, how valuable his suffering – how I had made it speak for more than itself. He would be pleased with me' (29). We're being prepared for a climax in this timeline, the time of story. It's reasonable to expect that the climax will involve some kind of confrontation over the story, and that this confrontation will give us further insight into the characters of both Nam and his father and into the complexity of the ethical and aesthetic questions raised by 'Love and honour'. Although the reader suspects that this confrontation is unlikely to end in the simplicity of fatherly recognition and pride, we can still hope father and son may come to a new understanding or an uneasy peace; there may be gestures of forgiveness or compassion; old wounds may begin to heal. Surely, we'll learn that Nam's efforts to re-listen to his father and re-tell his father's story will have been worth it, even if only in a subtle way. Nam goes looking for his father only thirty minutes before the story is due and finds him on the riverbank. He's talking to a homeless man they've met earlier in the story; this man presides over a fire, in which Nam knows the only copy of his story has been burned.

This is as climactic as the time of story will ever get: it remains poised in the moment in which Nam waits for his father to climb the riverbank toward him. In the last paragraph, the time of telling steps in, and this is the point from which we see (or don't see) the meeting of the men. We don't see the confrontation of father and son in scene; we only know what Nam says through indirect speech, and we don't know how the father responds. The voice from the time of telling is able to tell us that 'If I had known then what I knew later, I wouldn't have said the things I did' (30). We don't know what Nam knows in the time of telling that he didn't know in the time of story. We can speculate: it may have something to do with his father's health (remember, this is 'close enough' to a eulogy). I suspect it's less concrete than that – that it has more to do with the general passing of time. The Nam who tells this story has lived longer than the Nam who acts in it. He's experienced, written, thought and read more. He knows, now, that 'time can hold itself against you, how a voice hollows, how words you once loved can wither on the page' (25). Once again, the story resists resolution and draws attention to storytelling.

By the way, I think the story plays one final trick – on the reader? On itself? I think Le *has* written an 'ethnic story', and the ethnicity of his story is North American. It might take an Australian – or, at least, a non-American – reader to notice the specificity of the story's local colour: elms, sidewalks, girls on tree swings, Washington Street, falling leaves, snow and men on porches with guns. The story veers subtly and gorgeously into various American genres: it summons a flaming gasoline drum out of American urban grit (even the story comments on the unlikelihood of this); it strays (hilariously) into hard-boiled crime fiction (Nam, in terse sentences, imagines killing the boy with the air rifle and never speaking of it to anyone); it toys with American realism (the apparently random and ambiguously significant concrete detail, like the racialised and objectified 'black woman' who leans forward to kiss the handle of her shopping cart), and it draws on American naturalism (that final, symbolic image of the freezing river). There is no moment at which this story hasn't run out ahead of its reader; it simply can't be caught unawares. But it's never merely clever. It's also deeply moving, and this combination – ingenuity and emotion – is the source of its brilliance.

If you see the Buddha
in suburbia kill him –
Anguli Ma: A gothic tale
by Chi Vu

Hoa Pham

The works of Vietnamese-Australian writers commonly grapple with issues of trauma and postmemory, the inherited memories of the generation before from the Vietnam/American War. Chi Vu's work, and my own, explore the complexities of this experience among Vietnamese communities. Vietnamese diasporas are characterised by silence in regards to the war-torn past and it's the 1.5 generation (those born in Vietnam and brought up in Australia or the US), and the second generation, who often seek to question what is accepted and remembered (for example, in the work of Viet Thanh Nguyen and Isabelle Thuy Pelaud). Vu's creative works and reflections on them demonstrate that she is ethical in her representations of Vietnamese people, seeking nuanced depictions of complex experiences, and her writing has much to teach from a craft point of view. In her texts, trauma is not easily resolved by coming to a new country or by the written word; the Vietnamese communities she depicts are still haunted by war. As well, Vu incorporates Buddhism and mindfulness practice in her novella *Anguli Ma: A gothic tale* in a way that I greatly admire as a compatriot Buddhist writer.

Vu is an example of the transnational cosmopolitan writer, able to draw on more than one literary tradition and culture. In *Anguli Ma* Vu uses literary forms such as the gothic tale and Buddhist parables to create a horrific story centred upon a group of Vietnamese refugees. She creates two worlds, one that is timeless and mythical, the other set in the mid-1980s in the western suburbs of Melbourne. Retelling the Buddhist parable of Anguli Ma, she interweaves vignettes titled 'The monk' and 'The brown man' respectively, managing to incorporate Buddhist concepts and teachings in the novella – one of only a few works of Australian fiction to do so.

I too seek to explore and portray common Buddhist principles and practice, to share them with a non-Vietnamese audience. My novel *The Lady of the Realm* is about my protagonist Lien's search for peace, which she eventually finds through mindfulness in Buddhist practice. She learns through compassion that all things are connected through interbeing – that we *inter-are* – and that all humans have the potential to be good or evil. My novella *The Other Shore* is about a Vietnamese government psychic who reunites the war dead with their descendants, and the conflict between her Buddhist principles and the Communist government directions she receives.

Chi Vu retells the original Buddhist fable of Anguli Ma, which is about the Buddha being stalked by a serial killer who wears his victims' fingers around his neck. The Buddha is able to transform Anguli Ma into an enlightened being by teaching him mindfulness, and by showing compassion to the killer instead of fear. Vu places this fable in a modern setting to show how even a traumatised killer might be transformed by Buddhist teaching. She uses Buddhist theology to show a way out for her Vietnamese refugee characters, who are haunted by the past, while at the same time alluding to the Australian gothic tradition. She pulls this off in a masterly fashion, and the execution of the novella in its structure and narration speaks of sophisticated planning and design, using the Buddhist concept of 'interbeing' not only as content but embedding it in the narrative structure of the work itself.

There are at least two narrative structures at work in *Anguli Ma*. The first unfolds in the sections titled 'The brown man' and 'The monk', which appear to be out of chronological time and have the qualities of myth. The 'brown man' is a representation of Anguli Ma, who discovers the monk meditating by the river. The second narrative structure plays out in the main body of the work, which is narrated from a number of points of view in the novella's present – some time in the mid-eighties. This structure works on multiple levels, and the narratives can be read in counterpoint. There is a range of voices and characters: from Dao, the shrewd landlady, to Bac, the wise elderly tenant; Sinh, the younger, more innocent woman and Tuyet, Dao's seven-year-old granddaughter.

One example of this method is when Tuyet's point of view alternates with her grandmother Dao's to reveal that Anguli Ma has stolen Dao's money from the house. Tuyet goes with Anguli Ma to buy lollies and it is through the little girl that Dao learns that the money she has been holding for her community has been stolen. The narration switches points of view to provide different perspectives on what happens. Tuyet comments: 'She didn't know that people could be wolves as well. There was so much to learn about adults' (67).

Another illustration is when Dao begins to go mad after the theft: the reader sees her son Trung's point of view when Tuyet tells him that Grandma is burning her clothes, and then Bac's point of view, when the old female tenant tells him about what has been going on in the house. Vu is able to provide commentary about Dao's state of mind through the perspective of Bac, a wiser woman. Bac reflects 'that Dao would wallow in the circle of pain for years before she would become aware of her animal situation' (94). This is an allusion to the Buddhist understanding of suffering: that Dao is unconscious, and not mindful of her pain.

In *Anguli Ma*, all the narratives are connected, reflecting the nature of inter-being: everything is interconnected, all things inter-are (2008). The quote at the beginning of the book is from *The Way of Non-Attachment* by Buddhist monk VR Dhiravamsa: 'The truly present moment has no connection with the past or the future – it is independent of what has gone before or what will follow – it is a different dimension to the flowing of time'. The inclusion of this quote foreshadows the Buddhist content of the novella and Vu's incorporation of these concepts flows naturally and is unforced. This quote reveals the nature of the present moment, explaining the relation between the brown man and Anguli Ma. Anguli Ma, in his manifestation as the brown man, touches the present moment in a different interpretation of time and finds peace, while Anguli Ma in the eighties is still damaged by the past and is driven to bloody acts. The present moment can be touched through mindfulness and observing the flow of emotions away from chronological time. According to Thich Nhat Hanh, the Vietnamese Zen Master, time has a historical dimension and an ultimate dimension. This can be understood through a metaphor of the ocean. One experiences history and the ultimate dimension, with the wave being historical and the water being the ultimate dimension. Through mindfulness practice you can experience and perceive both dimensions.

Vu successfully incorporates mindfulness concepts in the interactions between the brown man and the monk. The chapters titled 'The monk' and 'The brown man' provide a counter-narrative to Dao and the other realist characters and their concerns. These chapters are more surreal, providing a moment for the brown man and the monk to pause and reflect on Buddhist teachings. The writing here is beautiful: evocative and poetic, a contrast to the sparse utilitarian prose of the main narrative. An example is the monk's reading of emptiness in nature and man, just before meeting Anguli Ma:

The monk lowers his eyelids, returns to his breath. The large trees in this park have within them light from the sun and the nutrients from the soil. These non-tree elements have transformed into tree elements: trunk, bark, foliage, roots like strands of hair digging into the sandy earth. This is the nature of Emptiness, contemplates the monk, and he lifts his eyes a third time. The brown man is right before him, drenched, his gnarled fingers curled around a pair of meat shears. (14)

Man is connected to nature and vice versa. One could also argue that Anguli Ma is made up of non-Anguli Ma elements such as the monk, and the violence he may have perpetrated or witnessed in Vietnam. Everything is interconnected and the monk becomes part of Anguli Ma too.

Vu manages to depict the practice of mindfulness in an accessible way, showing the internal thought process of the brown man and his experience of meditation. The transformation of the brown man into an enlightened being takes place as a result of the practice of mindfulness taught by the monk. This includes raising insight and strengthening the observer so that the practitioner can watch the emotions, rather than engage in them. Anguli Ma catches a glimpse of this in his first encounter with the monk and discovers a taste of calm and peace despite his darkest emotions. He is told to sit down, and he experiences the present moment for the first time, under all his anger:

Then he has an experience that is completely unknown to him. Without willing it or choosing it, his mind drops between the churning waves of anguish into something underneath, as though submerged momentarily into another world. Resting beneath his wandering, agitated mind is the clear and still truth. He has his first taste of not grasping at the future or the past.

Then, just as suddenly, it is gone and the brown man is back on
the choppy surface, scarcely understanding what has happened. As
quickly as the truly present moment has come, it has vanished, and
inside his mind again swirl a thousand thoughts of violence and hate.

The monk tells him, 'The human race needs to practise to know
itself as an animal.' (25–6)

Vu describes meditation practice and mindfulness as a possible path to
enlightenment for Anguli Ma. According to Buddhist understanding,
the nature of 'interbeing' and emptiness means that all things are
interconnected. Vu explains the nature of emptiness in simple terms:
'Everything is inside everything else. The river red gums have within
them sunlight and soil and rain clouds and wind. Within each thing
is its other. That is the nature of Emptiness' (105). Nothing exists
independently of other things; all things are empty. Everything depends
on something else for its nature. Vu takes this concept of interbeing
and not only embeds it in the structure of the text but also uses it as a
theme and content in the work, executing this idea with deceptive ease.
She signposts her theme by having the monk reading about emptiness
and reflecting on 'interbeing' with the trees, that the trees are made
up of non-tree elements such as soil and sunlight. Thus, the violence in
Anguli Ma is connected to the latent violence in Dao, the violence
in the land and the peace that the monk has found. The violence visited
on Sinh, the youngest tenant, is connected to the violence inflicted on
the Indigenous people on the same land. She is murdered where fish
traps were once set by these local people.

Vu acknowledges the previous inhabitants of the land by their
absence:

Their car drove through the western suburbs, with neat gardens
and milky overfed children. A land so sparse and peaceful that the

newcomers believed that it was empty space, unmarked and un-
storied, a barely populated land uninhabited by wandering demons
and limbless men from wars that dragged on for millennia. (49)

In *samsara*, in the cycle of suffering, everything is connected and,
according to Buddhist thought, the only way out of the cycle is to
follow the Noble Eightfold Path. The noble path is illustrated in the
novella through the meditation practices that the monk tells the brown
man to follow. The brown man achieves enlightenment through his
interactions with the monk, meditating by the side of the river. At
the end it is unclear whether Anguli Ma dies at the hands of Dao his
landlady, or is redeemed as the brown man by practising mindfulness
with the monk. Both endings are possible, reiterating the Buddhist
potential of human beings for good or evil.

The violence that the refugees have escaped from has followed them
to Melbourne, and that violence is still present, as is portrayed by Dao's
transformation into a potential killer. She is driven to contemplating
murder after finding the sawn-off fingers of Sinh, her young female
tenant who goes missing:

It was a necklace made of fingers with knuckle joints and nails
intact.

Dao let out a gasp as she recognised whose they were. She was
tossed in the murky waves, churning, churning, churning in
violence.

An idea awakened in her mind and Dao was horrified by it. Yet,
she obeyed it. Lifting the gory lei high above her she put her head
through ...

Equipped for vengeance the woman crouched down. She was ready
… She will not even hear the words of an enlightened being. She
will make a wreath of his fingers that will hang outside her garage
door. (104–5)

In the realist sections, the Buddhist references are extended to include
the female refugees; a comparison is made between them and hungry
ghosts – the souls of the dead that need to be fed continuously to be
sated. The narration is polyvocal, with each section being given to a
different character, from the female tenants to Anguli Ma. This device
creates a multi-layered universe in Vu's fiction.

The family is suffering from the past, with Dao hoarding fabric
offcuts just in case she needs to hide things in a hurry, and Anguli Ma
himself drowning his memories in drink after eating a dog that he hit
with his car. The post-traumatic stress that the characters endure is merely
hinted at, through the violence that is latent within both the male and
female characters. All have survived the wars in one way or another. But
Vu does not give details of the characters' pasts, merely alluding to their
bad memories and the terror that came before that. Vu deals in silence
and absence, not going into detail of the war or flashbacks of characters'
memories, describing only Anguli Ma's drunken tears in the present.
The terror is only implied not spelled out.

The function of writing and the creative act can be to re-narrate
and empower the writer to heal from traumas like these. However, some
stories do not provide this positive release and serve merely to bear
witness and to articulate the pain of survival. For instance, the grief and
trauma of Anguli Ma and his workmate from the fall of Saigon in 1975,
when they lost the war, is reduced to the depiction of drunk men crying
their separate tears:

In that stillness they avoided each other's eyes, for losing a
homeland was like losing someone who knew you intimately,

and whom you knew intimately. In this abyss, Anguli Ma and the workmate realised that their old life, and youth were gone forever. (52)

Their Southerner grief is not one acknowledged often in Western stories about the war.

Writing can be a form of testimony; as Isabelle Thuy Pelaud writes: 'for some the act of writing itself is intimately linked with the wish to reify history, to serve as witness to the past' (51). In my novella *Lady of the Realm*, my protagonist Lien searches for peace from the mid-1950s to the present day, witnessing and surviving Vietnam's history. Through Buddhism Lien comes to terms with violence and finds peace; even though it is short-lived, she realises its possibilities. She struggles to find compassion for all, including her enemies.

I too, have seen peace, and witnessed the possibilities of healing through retreats run by Thich Nhat Hanh for Vietnamese people in Vietnam. I attended a retreat attended by a few thousand people at Prajna Monastery in aid of relieving the suffering of those affected by the Vietnam/American War. Through meditation and mindfulness practice and dharma discussion I came to a greater sense of peace and saw the effects of Thay (teacher)'s teachings on survivors of the wars. It inspired me to write my novels *The Other Shore* and *Lady of the Realm*. Kim in *The Other Shore* struggles with her Buddhist ethics, which are at odds with the government directions she is given to use her psychic powers. Buddhism does not take sides in wars. This dilemma is at the core of my novel, inspired by Thich Nhat Hanh's teachings.

In *Anguli Ma*, the characters are trapped by the past. Even though Anguli Ma attains enlightenment he cannot escape what he has done, and neither can Dao. He is described as having the 'dead countenance of a man severed from history. It is a form of liberation, he thought, from your own conscience, from all your expectations of life' (37). Vu's characters serve as witnesses to a bloody past, with Buddhism the only way out of the vicious cycle of violence. The tale comes around full circle with Anguli Ma meditating in the sun like the monk in the beginning – just like in Buddhist theology, there is no end or beginning.

> He arranges his hands into beautiful mudras ... The river red gums
> have within them sunlight and soil and rain clouds and wind.
> Within each thing is its other. That is the nature of emptiness. (105)

Vu is a conscientious writer, who acknowledges that 1.5 generation writers can either be 'translators' of or 'traitors' to their culture of origin, like myself. In writing and being published in Australia one has to be aware of writing for a non-Vietnamese audience when depicting Vietnamese content. One may choose to represent Vietnamese communities with this sensitivity in mind, translating culture of origin material for non-Vietnamese consumption, or being a traitor by not being ethical about one's representational choices. I see Vu's work as that of a translator, portraying different Vietnamese refugee trauma stories for Vietnamese and non-Vietnamese audiences. I too see my work as that of a translator of Vietnamese diasporic experience. I consciously explain elements of this experience in my fiction for Australian audiences, such as the obligations born of filial piety, which Vietnamese people take for granted.

Vu suggests that 1.5 generation writers use either realism or 'impressionism' in order to avoid stereotyping and invisibility (2011). By consciously choosing a mode of representation one is aware of what one is representing and how it is represented. Vu uses both modes in this novella. The descriptions of the monk and the brown man are impressionistic in nature, interspersed with a mostly realist narrative. The reader's expectations of a 'gothic tale' foreshadow the fear and horror of Anguli Ma. Vu also uses Western references to hell: for example, she refers to 'this other layer of Hades' (52) when the men continue drinking after eating the dog.

In retelling this parable in the Australian setting, Vu allows the work to be read in a number of ways, due to her sophisticated rendering of an open narrative. According to Bac, the older tenant, who talks of the 'hungry ghosts' of their loved ones who died untimely deaths: 'We think we have a new beginning because we escaped the terror, and came to a new land. But we haven't left them behind, they came with us' (54). Thich Nhat Hanh suggests that if you are a hungry ghost you may find other like-minded people, thus creating a community of hungry ghosts. In Vu's novel Dao invites Anguli Ma into her home and community. Dao is a hungry ghost, hoarding fabric offcuts, obsessed with money in her running of the *hui* circle (credit scheme). The potential for her to become a murderer is realised after the disappearance of Sinh. According to Hanh we all have this potential, if the seeds of violence are watered inside us (2002).

Vu's realist depictions of the lives of the refugee women are detailed and specific, and do not allow the reader to pass them off as 'typical' refugees. Vu herself has stated that heterogeneity in representation of individuals can mitigate against stereotypes (2011) and *Anguli Ma* is an example of Vu as a writer of conscience. In this novella, the refugees have complex experiences and motivations. Bac is an old woman with wisdom on her side. She is shown as having insight into the *ma hon* hungry ghosts that they brought with them to Australia. Sinh is the innocent young refugee who is murdered, while Dao is a shrewd but clearly troubled woman who collects fabric samples and hides money among them. The novella is superbly narrated from multiple points of view, including the monk and the brown man. This polyphonic approach prevents the reader from drawing on Orientalist stereotypes and from having a simplistic idea of what refugees are like. The depiction of the characters, their stories and how they cope with trauma serves as a counter-narrative to media and political portrayals of refugees.

Depending on your reading of Vu's tale, one can see people as either being trapped by the cycle of violence, or as gaining hope through Buddhist practice. The potential for violence in all individuals is accounted for in Buddhist psychology. Dao's seeds and potential for violence are watered: she could become a murderer. Vu leaves the ending of the novella open to interpretation, honouring the sophistication of the narrative threads. Dao lies in wait for Anguli Ma to return to the garage, wearing the necklace of Sinh's fingers around her neck. The reader does not know whether she actually kills Anguli Ma or not.

Vu has rendered a complex representation of the potential for violence in Vietnamese communities and of transgenerational trauma. However, titling her novella 'a gothic tale' shows the deliberateness of her intentions in translating this experience for a broader audience. Vu has successfully avoided writing stereotypes, with the violence of Anguli Ma counterbalanced by his time as the brown man, and the possibility of him becoming an enlightened being. Dao and Anguli Ma are haunted by the past, and neither is able to leave it behind. A simplistic application of trauma theory cannot account wholly for all Anguli Ma's suffering though. There are no easy conclusions in the book and, it appears, no healing outcomes.

Vu's diverse depiction of her characters is something I aspire to do in my fiction. Her use of myth and allegory as a device is to be admired and in particular her adaptation of Buddhist concepts of interbeing in a way that is accessible to the reader. Her prose ranges from understated to lyrical and poetic, creating a beautiful polyphonic work.

The complexity of the ending includes her depiction of Anguli Ma's experiences of mindfulness, in which she conveys a profound experience:

'The human race needs to practise to know itself as an animal, this is not the same as to *be* an animal,' the monk says quietly to his disciple, and his own heart.

On his next attempts the man experiences increasingly longer moments without the prattle of plans or hopes or conversations recreated inside his head. His body is aware of itself as breathing, pulsing, pulled down and sagging in gravity, heating the air around it, slowly burning in time. This thing we call time. The storms of anger and violence accumulate and break across his being until they empty him out completely. Then he is ready to experience loss. (96)

This moment comes close to the end of the novella; the brown man seems to be on the path to enlightenment. But the inconclusive nature of the ending provides possibilities of another murder that may or not be carried out. All the characters have the potential to be seen as hungry ghosts. Anguli Ma is given an opportunity for salvation through mindfulness, but Sinh is murdered and Dao may become a murderer. The reader is left with a vision of horror in the string of fingers necklace.

This conclusion is open to multiple readings, including hope for those who follow the Noble Eightfold Path or despair for those caught in the cycle of suffering – samsara. Another interpretation is that Vietnamese war trauma cannot be easily resolved, even with Buddhist assistance.

The novelist Viet Thanh Nguyen suggests that a just memory requires an acceptance not only of our potential humanity but also our potential inhumanity. Ethical storytelling includes how our own side makes ghosts as well as how the 'enemy' does (chapter 9). The story arc of Dao in *Anguli Ma* demonstrates this premise – we all are capable of being hungry ghosts and killers in the right conditions.

In my novella *Lady of the Realm*, the protagonist tries to find compassion for all after surviving the war and its aftermath. She too learns mindfulness and encounters the possibility of peace. I explore the different kinds of love, from intimate love to love of people more generally. I also explore the challenge of fully embracing all of the Buddhist teachings, given our humanity and the tragedies people have to survive. I do this by detailing the journey of Lien witnessing historical events in Vietnam such as the immolation of monastics during President Diem's regime, and the wars themselves. Her physical journey is accompanied by her spiritual journey as she tries to find peace through mindfulness and meditation. The novella ends with the destruction of Prajna Monastery in Vietnam in 2007. Religious oppression in Vietnam continues in reality. In *The Other Shore* Kim is Buddhist and wishes to help the war dead of all sides. However her Communist bosses wish to disregard the Southern Vietnamese war dead, causing her an ethical dilemma that drives the narration of the story.

For those of us with such intentions Chi Vu has written an exemplary work. She explores the theme of interbeing not just as content but as a structural element of the work – which is polyphonic and inter-connected. Her rendition of Buddhist principles is accessible and poetically executed, and her prose is understated and beautiful. In *Anguli Ma*, Vu has achieved much to admire, and to inspire.

*

Parts of this chapter were derived from the author's doctoral exegesis, supervised by Gail Jones and Ivor Indyk at Western Sydney University.

Sabotage and repair:
Intertextuality in Carrie Tiffany's
Exploded View

Maria Takolander

'Each new thing is just a version of something else.'
– Carrie Tiffany, *Exploded View*

Intertextuality – the generative relationship of text to text – is the secret force that powers our writing. I say 'secret' because, unless we write fan fiction, we are often unconscious of how we write from a grounding in tradition. Given the messages we receive about the innateness of talent and the evils of plagiarism, we may even feel nervous about admitting that our original creative interventions are inspired and informed by the work of other writers. In an essay called 'The ecstasy of influence' – the title itself an intertextual nod to Harold Bloom's *The Anxiety of Influence* (1973) – the novelist Jonathan Lethem shows no such qualms, provocatively describing cultural artefacts as the product of 'appropriation, mimicry, quotation, allusion, and sublimated collaboration' (61). His argument is twofold. First up, artists are 'converted to art by art itself' (61). When it comes to writers, we absorb plots, character types, rules of genre, voice, technical tricks or mood-scapes from other authors' works, which we then reproduce (instinctively or intentionally) in our own work. Lethem's second point underlies his first, though its implications are more far-reaching. We are, he writes, 'born backward into an incoherent realm of texts, products, and images, the commercial and cultural environment with which we've both supplemented and blotted out our natural world' (63), so that we are inevitably late to an absurdly crowded creative scene, so that we see the world through the prisms of others' stories, so that our imaginative *vision* can only ever be a *re-vision*. While such a picture of an already-storied world seems to leave us creatively handicapped, that richly teeming environment of words – rather than the blank page – is what makes our writing possible. In fact, if we become *conscious* of the intertextual context for our writing practice, we can find ourselves empowered in all kinds of important ways.

Lethem's argument is consistent with a 'postmodern' celebration of an aesthetics of remaking and recycling, apparent in texts as diverse as singer Ariana Grande's mash-up of 'My favourite things' to poet Kenneth Goldsmith's re-presentation of a year's weather forecasts as poetry (as part of his 'uncreative writing' project). However, intertextuality is hardly a postmodern discovery. While the term was invented by the literary theorist Julia Kristeva in 1966, the Ancient Greeks drew upon its generative power thousands of years ago. Reprocessing stories – in poetry recitations and theatrical performances – from a repository of myths, Ancient Greek audiences were a community (or, more precisely, an elite class of men) experiencing a sense of *communitas* through repeated engagement with a communal repository of stories. The repetition of certain stories in our culture today – of the kind we see with the Marvel Universe – might be viewed as serving a similar purpose, bringing together its audiences through a powerful imaginary (and one that also thematises power).

However, postmodern writers often re-mine texts in order to under-mine the authority of their story-worlds. Women writers have led the charge in this regard, challenging the marginalisation of female voices in the classics and, in the process, producing their own classics of postmodern revisionism. Jean Rhys's *Wide Sargasso Sea* (1966) reimagines Bertha, the Creole madwoman in Charlotte Brontë's *Jane Eyre* (1847), as a woman rather than a monster. Angela Carter's *The Bloody Chamber* (1979) re-envisions fairy tales from a feminist perspective. With *The Penelopiad* (2005), Margaret Atwood rewrites *The Odyssey* (c. 800 BCE), one of the canonical stories inherited from the Ancient Greeks, from a woman's point of view. The US poet Adrienne Rich's essay 'When we dead awaken: Writing as re-vision' (1972) – another title with an intertextual reference, this time to Henrik Ibsen's *When We Dead Awaken* (1899) – was a notable call to arms, calling on women writers to 'wake up' (Rich, 18) to the power of cultural tradition in order 'to break its hold' (19) over how women imagine themselves.

Carrie Tiffany's *Exploded View*, the Australian novel I want to discuss here, is an innovative extension of this tradition of feminist revision, demonstrating anew the value of being alert to the intertextual context for our writing practice. To begin with, *Exploded View* evidences the vastness and diversity of what Lethem calls the *'public commons'* (66), that repository of stories we have to draw from when it comes to our creative interventions. The key intertext in *Exploded View* is not literary, not even a story. It is an automotive repair manual that features, among its various instructions and diagrams, 'exploded views' of engine components that show those parts separated in space as if they have been exploded into pieces. The car repair manual also includes photographs of male hands demonstrating how to manipulate parts. Tiffany uses this intertext – its scientific language, its mechanistic worldview – to structure her novel. Writer-readers might immediately be inspired to wonder: what other non-literary narratives might be available for creative repurposing? The novel also references more conventional intertexts, such as romance novels and US sitcoms, but the key intertext of the manual reminds us that stories are not just stories, providing entertainment or distraction. Texts effectively provide instructions about 'how the world works' – often in ways shaped by the hands of those in power. However, they can be blasted apart, dismantled into their constituent parts, and put back together differently. Intertextuality, as *Exploded View* reminds us, can give rise to a form of sabotage that is also a form of repair.

Exploding a conventional view of gender

Carrie Tiffany has consistently shown an attraction to non-literary and, more specifically, scientific intertexts as generative material for her fiction. In all three of her novels the cultural authority of those intertexts has also been undermined. *Everyman's Rules for Scientific Living*, a book set in rural Victoria, includes statistics about harvests, test results, advertisements and a lecture. Meanwhile, the plot works to subvert the authority of European agricultural science, which is exposed as a superficial body of knowledge unsuited to the Australian landscape. In *Mateship with Birds*, a character's fieldnotes about animal life are shown to be comically unscientific in the way they mistake the subjective for the objective – a confusion Tiffany exploits to unsettle the conventional separation of humans and animals. The intertextuality in *Exploded View* is more explicit and prolific than in these precursors, though a scientific text again provides the main intertext and target for sabotage.

The novel's first-person narrator is a lonely adolescent girl growing up in suburban Perth in the 1970s with her domineering stepfather, servile mother and hostile older brother. The stepfather is a mechanic who runs an unlicensed garage in their backyard and who – we come to understand – is sexually abusing the girl. The girl's mother loses herself in Mills & Boon novels; the girl and her brother watch US TV sitcoms such as *Hogan's Heroes* and *The Brady Bunch*; and the girl can recite passages from Ethel Turner's children's novel *Seven Little Australians* and the nonsense poem 'Jabberwocky' from Lewis Carroll's *Through the Looking-Glass, and What Alice Found There*. However, the key intertext is one called *Scientific Publications Holden Workshop Manual Series No. 51*. This is the title of a car manual the girl has stolen from her stepfather. The girl describes the book as 'something special' (27) and studies it in secret as if it is a sacred text that holds the key to ultimate knowledge and power – of the kind that her stepfather, who deadlocks the family into the house every night, seems to have harnessed for himself. On a road trip, during which the girl's family are effectively imprisoned in the man's car, the girl conceptualises her stepfather's control of the vehicle as central to his all-encompassing power: he 'has the road in his hands and the Holden that adheres to it and the stream of air it pushes against, and us strapped inside' (84). The girl, however, has seditious dreams: 'What people want is for their father to be dead so the road is all for them and they can go wherever they want' (124). The girl sees her stepfather's car repair manual as the key to usurping his power. She stows it among her personal items in the plastic bag she is permitted to bring on that journey. When she is stuck at home, the book is stashed beneath her bed.

The importance of the automotive manual as an intertext in *Exploded View* is signalled by the novel's title, which takes its name from a type of technical diagram in the workshop manual, as noted. The manual's influence, though, marks the entire novel – not just the title – as the girl's voice and her observations of her environment are conceptually and stylistically informed by this scientific intertext, which provides her with an authoritative schema for understanding her world.

Tiffany has described how she felt 'excited by the challenge of refining and concentrating' the intertextual technique she had used in previous work by 'using one governing text as a literal, figurative and analytical device' for *Exploded View* (76). That excitement and concentration are apparent in the novel, which takes on, as Tiffany herself documents, the automotive manual's 'language, its processes (assembly and disassembly), its visual style (the exploded view), and its function (technical mastery of a machine that represents freedom and independence)' (77). That level of appropriation is, importantly, entirely justified within the narrative because the car manual is, as Tiffany explains, 'presented as a generative force for the novel's narrator, a teenage girl who is estranged and silenced in the social world of a damaged family' (77). However, as Tiffany clarifies, 'the structuring role of the manual does not go unchallenged, given the ways in which this key intertext is gendered as distinctly masculine' (77) and given that *the girl* – as we know her – is identified as prototypically feminine.

From the very beginning of the novel, we see how the girl's worldview is shaped by the style and subject matter of the automotive manual. For example, the girl sees her family members – identified as 'father man', 'mother' and 'brother' – in peculiarly functional ways. She describes their roles in a mechanistic fashion and often in explicit relation to the mechanic's workshop. This is how she introduces us to father man:

> Here is a bonnet propped open. Dirty hands father man has under the metal lid, dirty hands pecking. Check the terminal connections at the battery for tightness and freedom from corrosion. Check the battery in its carrier for looseness. The electrolyte in each cell must be topped up with special laundry water that a mother uses in her iron. (13)

Each member of the family has a predetermined part to play – a part that is, notably, gendered. When it comes to the girl's brother, we read: 'Sport is work for boys' (14). The girl's mother has an office job, but the girl and her mother are also responsible for food shopping: 'It's what girls and women do' (23). Women are also tasked with cooking. The girl rationalises this gendered division of labour using the logic of the garage: 'Kitchen tools are called utensils, small tools suitable for women' (40). Women must also tend to their appearance. The girl's description of her mother's nightly beauty regimen effortlessly slides into a description of the rituals involved in caring for a car:

> My mother's preparations for the night take a long time. She puts on the radio. She has a hot shower. She shaves her legs. She dries herself with a pink towel and applies powders to her body. Then she sits at her dressing table on a spindly chair with curved metal legs, to tweeze her eyebrows and lotion her face and neck. When you are getting a vehicle ready for storage it's advisable to top off the petrol and the battery and lubricate the doors. (149)

The informational style of the instruction manual, when applied to human beings and their everyday behaviours, has a de-naturalising or defamiliarising effect. Defamiliarisation, a term invented by the Russian poet and literary theorist Viktor Shklovksy in 1917, is a trick more commonly associated with poetry, which employs unusual language to challenge our routinised habits of perception – our tendency, over time, to see without seeing. However, as Tiffany's novel demonstrates, defamiliarisation is also intrinsic to intertextuality, which involves setting a familiar text in an unfamiliar context to estranging effect. That sense of estrangement goes two ways. In the case of *Exploded View*, the form of the novel itself is rendered strange – exhilaratingly so – through appropriating the scientific aesthetic of the automotive manual. However, the automotive manual is also rendered strange by being incorporated into the dramatic setting of a novel. Indeed, the language of the car manual is transformed by Tiffany into a kind of poetry, which she exploits to hold up a carnival mirror to our world, illuminating anew the gender roles and rituals that we normally take for granted. It is in this context that the novel's reference to Carroll's poem

'Jabberwocky' resonates. The absurd language of that poem – discovered by Alice as she journeys through the parallel universe of Looking-Glass Land, much as the girl in *Exploded View* navigates her way through the masculine realm of machine logic – makes sense only when read as a mirror language. What we also see in both texts is a society of diametrical opposition – red and white in *Through the Looking-Glass, and What Alice Found There*, male and female in *Exploded View* – in which those two sides are literally or metaphorically at war.

Other significant intertexts referenced in Tiffany's novel are the Mills & Boon romance novels that the girl's mother obsessively reads. The mother's reading routine, like her other behaviours, is defamiliarised through the girl's understanding of them as akin to the repetitive, rule-bound operations of a machine:

> Tonight my mother is reading *Tangled Shadows*. Before that it was *Sweet Compulsion*; before that it was *Lure of Eagles*. Each book takes three days. She writes the titles down in a notebook in her red handbag so she doesn't get the same book from the library and read it twice. My mother is reading *The Tempestuous Flame*, *The Vital Spark*, *The Joyous Adventures*, *Stranger on the Beach* and *A Very Special Man*. My mother is full of romance. She carries it with her wherever she goes. (45)

The mother's romantic sensibility contrasts starkly with her programmatic consumption of the Mills & Boon novels. It also contrasts with the reality of her relationship with father man, who mostly ignores her. The girl describes her mother's and stepfather's arrangement thus: 'A car settles into a corner ... Father man has settled on my mother' (23–4). More importantly, the mother's romantic sensibility contrasts with her daughter's hyperrational and pragmatic one. While the mother fanatically seeks refuge in fantasy, in ways that prevent her from recognising the reality of her own (and her children's) victimhood, the girl is intent on seeing the world as clearly and powerfully as she can, following the scientific paradigm of the workshop manual.

Tiffany's novel thus sets into play a contrast between traditionally feminine and masculine texts – the romance genre and the automotive manual – but also the feminine and masculine identities – of passivity versus authority – they are conventionally seen to embody. Those traditional gender identities are starkly rendered by the girl when she pictures her family members as tools. The girl imagines her mother as a 'rag' (106), an item that calls to mind menstruation and abject servitude, while father man is 'a hammer' (106), an instrument of blunt strength.

The girl notably pictures herself as a 'knife' (106), a tool she associates with 'treachery' (107), suggesting how her refusal of victimhood requires a violent betrayal of both sexes, a queering of her identity. Her illicit appropriation of agency also requires her to betray the automotive manual, which she must reconceptualise, as Tiffany herself explains, as 'a space for deconstruction as well as reconstruction, a physical schema for the dynamic between sabotage and repair' (84). Using the ambiguous knowledge she acquires from the automotive manual – and inspired by the acts of sabotage committed by US prisoners in German camps in *Hogan's Heroes* on TV – the girl escapes through her bedroom window at night to loosen, damage, remove or bury parts of her stepfather's car or to impair those vehicles he is repairing. The girl also takes cars for secret night-time drives, revelling in the sense of autonomy she feels when controlling a vehicle. During one such excursion, she imagines 'taking my mother somewhere ... driving her away' (53), thus appropriating the role of the masculine saviour conventional in her mother's romance novels. It is during this trip that we hear the girl – whose silence is a powerful symbol of her powerlessness throughout the novel – first speak. Emboldened by her control over the car, she expresses a masculine sense of invincibility through a dramatic revision of John Paul Young's romantic song lyrics: 'Love is in the air. Touch me and I will kill you' (55).

The diagram of the exploded view, with its arrangement of parts separated in space, is what provides the girl with the inspiration for her subversive expressions of agency as the illustrations reveal not only 'how the parts fit together' (27) but also the possibility that they can be arranged 'in a different order' (28). Indeed, the girl's hope that she can 'save' (28) herself and perhaps even her mother is dependent on not only mastering but also modifying the worldview represented by the automotive manual in which a 'man's hands are in 13 of the 27 photographs' (81) and in which the feminine has no place:

> Nothing soft, nothing that bends, nothing that holds liquid, nothing that flows or splashes can be relied upon, in an engine. Over time a seal will always leak. The water will spill and be used up. There isn't much that's female in an engine. Oils and rubbers, acids and waters – these are the first places to look for faults. (14)

The girl, however, understands that she must locate herself somewhere in this masculine world of machines if she is not to be destroyed by it. The empty spaces apparent in the diagrams known as exploded views emerge as highly significant. The girl, who describes herself as 'invisible, of less interest than a dog' (76), not only identifies with these overlooked spaces but also insists that they are ones of Cinderella-like transformative potential:

> The air in between isn't nothing; it isn't blank. If you make yourself look for what's not there the empty spaces become parts themselves. The empty spaces become air parts, bordered by the metal and rubber. In *Exploded View of Water Pump Assembly* the air part around the fan looks like a design for a jigsaw puzzle of a windmill. Steerarma, hubner, suspenister. Why not? Why shouldn't the air parts have a name? If you cast only the air parts in steel and assembled them the engine would be peaceful, then. It would be beautiful. (27)

At the same time, however, the girl uses an embodied identification with machines to access a masculine experience of regulated, even dulled emotion. Her identification with the non-human involves a kind of dissociation that helps neutralise her pain. As the girl reports, 'When you put your mind in the engine some of what your body is saying ... can be turned down for a while' (146). Indeed, the girl intuits that an identification with machines underlies father man's power and his capacity for cruelty. This is apparent when she imagines her stepfather's own childhood experience of masculine brutality as the origin of his boyhood affinity with cars:

> Father man didn't say when he got prickles in his square boy's feet.
> He had some cut-down tools but he didn't have words or songs.
> His dad gave him a cigarette for his birthday. He might have been
> five. He might have been nine when the first car came but I imagine
> he always knew how to press his lips together wetly to make the
> sound of a motor, always knew how to hold his spittle to mimic the
> dead place in the gearbox between the gears. (42)

The girl similarly soothes herself with 'engine breathing' (40). However, when she looks at the automotive manual, she also reimagines forms of masculinity that are less machine-like, more human. Regarding the photographs of male hands that appear in the manual, for instance, she observes 'that sometimes a delicate touch is needed to manipulate small parts' (164), prompting her to reflect: 'There's no physical reason why hands that work an engine can't do soft tasks – plaiting a girl's hair, icing a sponge cake, patting a baby's back to make it burp. Engine hands must be strong, but they don't have to be cruel' (164). The girl even reinvents applications of the exploded view that might embody more nurturing, playful and celebratory expressions of masculine identity: '*Exploded View of Stroking of the Skin. Exploded View of Tickling. Exploded View of a Pair of Feet That Want to Dance*' (187). Thus, while Tiffany's novel may portray a world of men and women divided, the girl's reinterpretations of the scientific schema of gender repeatedly hold out hope that society might be imagined differently, that acts of imaginative sabotage might lead to repair.

*

The girl in Tiffany's novel, as we have seen, sneaks into the world of the automotive manual in order to loosen the metaphorical nuts and bolts of the patriarchal order that defines her world. In that way, her journey literalises the author's own – as well as those of other postmodern feminist writers who have explored patriarchal texts in order to explode them.

What does it mean, then, that *Exploded View* seems to end in tragedy rather than triumph? As vehicles tear down the highway, generating a relentless stream of road kill – 'Pain with feathers. Pain with fur. Pain with scales' (135) – and as father man continues his devastating abuse of the girl, we are at all times aware of her vulnerability. Her acts of subversion, as reviewer Fiona Wright describes, provide the girl with some sense of 'self-determination, in a family and a world in which she otherwise has none' ('When the manuals fail us'), but they are not enough to allow her to escape her stepfather's control. The girl watches US sitcoms in which families are happy and 'all the invisible laughers around them are happy too' (148), but such a world – as her alienated description of it suggests – is inconceivable to her. She is stuck in father man's story and in father man's world.

Tiffany's dramatic conclusion only leaves us, as writer-readers of her novel, with an even more powerful reminder of just how much our stories matter, how we all need to recognise a meaningful place for ourselves in the mirrors of our cultural environment, how intertextual sabotage provides a valuable weapon when – to revise the title of Wright's review of *Exploded View* – one of life's manuals fails us.

Structure, serpents and Serena McGarry: Kate Jennings' *Snake*

Debra Adelaide

June 25, 1997 [sic]

Dear Debra,
Can you do this one by Friday, July 12? (earlier if you like). About 700–800 words. I'm sorry it's only a proof copy – haven't had the finished book yet but it looks much the same.

It's wonderful having your reviews – hope you can do more.

Best wishes, Susan

I have the letter, handwritten, from the literary editor of the *Sydney Morning Herald*. I have the memory of reading *Snake* for the first time. And I have that proof copy still, although over the years I have acquired, and lost, at least two other copies of this book. I do not seem to have the review, though I would quite like to know what I wrote.

In my capacity as a freelance book reviewer I was often given books by Australian authors, but this was the first time I had read anything by

Kate Jennings since her 1988 collection of essays, *Save Me, Joe Louis*. In the middle of 1996 (not 1997, as dated mistakenly in the letter above), I was the mother of two small children, and I would have been anxious to do everything that came my way as quickly as possible. *Snake*, being fewer than 150 pages, and full of abbreviated chapters, was the ideal book to read and review.

Nineteen ninety-six seems such a long time ago. Minerva Press, which originally published *Snake*, no longer exists. The *Sydney Morning Herald* literary editorship has not only changed hands several times but the role has been reduced to just one Fairfax Media literary editor for the whole country, as opposed to one for each major newspaper. Reviewing from advance proof copies is now totally the norm. And no one writes handwritten letters any more, not even literary editors.

> Kate Jennings' style is as spare and compelling as the landscape of her native country. The reader can feel the heat and smell the disillusionment of this Australian rural scene captured in breathtaking detail.
>
> – Jill Ker Conway

I do recall being annoyed by this back cover comment. Jill Ker Conway was a friend of Jennings and the person who assisted her break into the world of corporate writing in Manhattan, well-paid work that saved her when her husband became ill and dependent, a story fictionalised in Jennings' award-winning 2002 novel *Moral Hazard*. But Ker Conway, it seemed to me, had entirely missed the point. *Snake* was not about the Australian landscape at all: it was far more interested in character, and in particular the long drought of personality, culture and spirit that so provokes its principal character, Irene. This was the book's extraordinary achievement and contribution as a distinctly Australian novel. Plenty of authors have written about the landscape, but not so many about the landscape of family within a rural setting. I was also really annoyed by that word 'breathtaking' – as if any book literally took your breath. Truly, I was an insufferable purist.

Since 1996 I have re-read *Snake* continually, and indeed could almost recite by heart some of its shorter 'chapters'. And I have been teaching it to postgraduate novel-writing students since the mid-2000s. It has so much to offer emerging writers about the possibilities of form, and demonstrates in particular how wonderfully elastic the novella can be. In this case, so elastic that it can almost be prose poetry. And so abbreviated, audaciously so. Now whenever I re-read certain scenes, paragraphs, and chapters I imagine Jennings sitting at a desk somewhere (or maybe in bed, maybe under the covers) cutting, cutting, cutting, peeling away all the unnecessary layers of detail to expose the essence of things. I imagine the pain of that, the courage, the ruthlessness. As a fundamentally digressive author, I can only admire this sort of dedication to craft.

Year after year for my creative writing subjects I set such texts, and every year in preparation for the class I tell myself I do not need to re-read this or that book, but I always do. These books (they include Kafka's *The Metamorphosis*, Gabriel Garcia Marquez's *Chronicle of a Death Foretold*, and another favourite, Muriel Spark's sublime and pitch-perfect *The Prime of Miss Jean Brodie*) always, but always, reveal something new to me each time.

I also set *Snake* for study in the hope that students will be inspired by its poetic brevity, its 'experimental' form, and its intriguing, sometimes maddening, allusions to and quotations from numerous literary and cultural references. For sheer practical purposes it is the perfect set text: it can easily be read in one night – the night before class in fact, if students leave it that late – and maintained in one's head in a way that few novels can be. But brevity does not mean simplicity: its complex themes ripple out and take their time before finally landing on the muddy shores of our imagination, long after Jennings has tossed the stone into the middle of the pond.

I sometimes say to students that one definition of a good short story is that it is like a hand grenade. The author lobs it through a window and then turns away, leaving the rest of us to pick up the pieces. *Snake*, while far from being a short story, has exactly that effect. But since I have now introduced two different metaphors far too close to each other I shall stop here and get back to basics.

Structure

Snake is the story of a rural family, and is set in the Riverina area of New South Wales where Jennings grew up. It introduces the character of Rex, a quiet, unassuming returned soldier, then Irene, an unpredictable and imaginative young woman. They marry in Sydney then depart to run a family property near a town called Progress (there is a great deal of irony in this novel). Rex and Irene have two children, Girlie and Boy – these names for me are simply heartbreaking. The novel ends with Irene's departure from her marriage when the children are older. Now alone, Rex allows the property to decline, and then drives himself into the river to drown. Part 4, the coda, is just three tiny chapters written in the second-person voice of Irene, post-flight. It is an ending both bitter and tender. Now I have thought about all this more carefully than back in 1996 I realise that Ker Conway was pretty much right: reading the entire novel is an exercise in breath-holding, partly because Irene is such a volatile character, but partly because the structure moves the reader along at a perfectly controlled pace. From the very start we know something awful will happen, but when, and to whom? It is exactly the sensation of encountering a snake: you pause, hold your breath, move cautiously.

At the time I first read *Snake* I had published one novel and was working on another, to be published eighteen months later. This first was an autobiographical novel – in that it was based on experiences I had working in a large country hotel – and it had poured out of me. I had no plot, no structure, and no idea of voice. I had nothing but scenes and characters, some invented, some lived, and I wrote that novel in a state of blissful ignorance. So innocent was I as a creative writer that I even had no idea I had written it in the present tense (a tense of which I am now often wary, especially in long-form fiction) and my draft versions were minimal, just two or three. When I reviewed the edits I was intrigued to see entire pages had passed by without a single markup. By that time I was also working as a freelance editor and knew this was odd: surely the manuscript of a first-time novelist needed a lot more editing? But, amazingly, it didn't: I had to re-read that novel for a second edition fourteen years after it was first published and, determined to edit it myself like it had never been edited, scrutinised the hard copy with a red pen poised to strike. However, I also found I needed to change very little. By that stage I had wrestled with a second difficult novel that had taken at least a dozen drafts, before I stopped counting them.

Many authors find their first novels work like this: the prose seems to flow onto the page like warm honey. And then the next and next books are where the real pain sets in. I will never recapture that time; I will never again experience writing without a single critic on my shoulder, without the faintest thought of publication, where I am writing as if in a gilded dream, and writing purely for myself alone. All my prose since then has undergone numerous drafts, and, especially, a lot of structural work: without intending to (indeed, consciously trying to avoid it) I cause myself a lot of complex problems, by writing multilayered stories that shift around in time and place.

The structure of my second novel was so maddeningly elusive that I finally printed the entire draft out, pushed all the living room furniture back to the walls, and placed the chapters out on the floor in a circle. Then I picked up whole or half chapters, slotted and sorted them into other chapters, into something approaching the structure I could feel was right but simply could not see. Then all that had to be transferred to the screen, another nightmare of shuffling around. After it was all over I swore I would never get into such a mess with a novel again. (I have got into worse messes.)

So here, therefore, is where I should say that reading *Snake* opened up my eyes to the possibilities of writing a novel that was straightforward yet clever in structure, that was stripped back to its narrative bones, and yet at the same time managed to be multilayered, dense, poetic and unforgettable. Yet, while I can see and admire and even aspire to all this, the problem is I do not seem to be able to do it. I have written for more than twenty-five years, I have thought about writing a great deal, taught it, written about it, but I remain convinced that writing is fundamentally a mystery, and that one of the worst things I can do when writing is to overthink it. When I have thought too hard about my writing, it has failed. I would love to approach a novel by happening upon a useful structure first and foremost, then building up the characters, then the scenes, and then arriving, fairly painlessly, at a decent first draft. I believe there are writers who work like this. I have read accounts by writers explaining how they work. I have tried several times to work this way myself but I simply cannot. I might as well expect to be able to play the bagpipes or to yodel. Instead, I have learned to embrace the baggy, cloudy thing that lies just out of my line of sight and grope around in the cold and the dark until something, anything, tangible emerges, sometimes just one short scene, but clear enough to help me keep going.

I have no idea how Jennings approached the writing of *Snake*, but I fantasise that she, being a more professional writer than I, indeed planned its four-part structure, and then wrote into it. While the whole story primarily belongs to the character of Irene, the structure is adaptable enough to represent the points of view of all the characters: Rex, Irene, Girlie and Boy. Because of this, the novel deftly delivers a portrait of an entire family. At the same time it offers a powerful sense of everyperson, beginning and ending with that second-person voice. But this structure does not institute a democratic process; it is not a committee, and not everyone gets the same amount of attention. The novel focuses first on Rex, moves through a number of alternative perspectives that are focused on Irene, and comes to rest upon her, with excursions into Girlie and, briefly, Boy, leaving us with Irene again at the end. Structure is connected to voice, which in turn is connected to point of view.

The second-person voice is hard to sustain over a long-form narrative – few novels manage to work using it alone (Jay McInerney's *Bright Lights, Big City* is one, Vendela Vida's *The Diver's Clothes Lie Empty* another) – and is thus best kept to the short story, or the poem. It offers a useful ambiguity and in its implicit address to the reader invites them to become that character. The great achievement of the second-person voice is that it manages to deliver both distance *and* intimacy. This is useful, but not necessarily desirable for much of the time. *Snake* commences with the second-person voice: 'Everybody likes you. A good man. Decent' (3). And Rex is very much a type, his fundamental quality of 'decency' capturing as much as condemning him from the very first line of the novella. Soon the reader is aware that Rex has no imagination, and his fate is to be married to a woman who abounds in it. This imagination and all that it entails – desire, aspiration, transcendence – is something Rex fears rather than embraces: 'What you have always found terrible is the region your heart inhabits, your imagination dwells' (11). Rex is neither stupid nor shallow but has been trained to be compliant, docile: 'If you could only concentrate long enough, you would have answers. Answers to what? That is part of the problem. The questions don't come easily either' (8).

Thus, while it is so tempting to condemn Rex, as his wife does, for being dull, or to feel alienation from him, as his children do ('foreigners', he calls them, (4)) we, the readers, cannot. The second-person voice has made us complicit, part of the character. We would condemn ourselves.

And similarly with Irene, whose second-person voice is not delivered to us until the very end. Part 4 is three pages, three short sections, basically just paragraphs, three short sharp bursts of gunfire, a final devastating volley after which a cloud of dust lingers for a long time. Until now Irene has been revealed via the third-person voice only. That original distance-intimacy connected to Rex turns out to have softened us up for the rather brutal experience of Irene, who is far from pleasant yet deeply engaging.

It is a long time since I felt inclined to scrutinise texts in that obsessive, blinkered Leavisite way we were encouraged to when I was an undergraduate, but over the years I have not been able to stop re-reading *Snake* and searching for ways to explain the superb rendition of Irene. The unlikable character in fiction fascinates me and Irene is remote, ruthless and selfish. Finally, I paid close attention to the structure, and that enabled me to see how despite its staccato delivery and disparate parts, the novel works as a compelling, seamless whole, and maintains its focus on Irene without alienating us from her.

Serpents

In the novel the chapter headings sometimes seem as meaningful as the chapters themselves, and several directly reference snakes. One of these is Chapter 10: 'In Sicily, the black, black snakes are innocent, the gold are venomous' (45).

DH Lawrence's poem 'Snake' (1920–1) was a set text in my first-year university English program and, along with his other poems, was reverently dissected in tutorials. I always found this example of Lawrence's poetry rather too prosy, too full of opinion, too didactical (when was Lawrence ever anything else?). But these lines, filleted from the poem and tossed into this novel, become small gems.

Journalist Erik Jensen observes that when Jennings was writing this novel she referred to a book called *Wicked Words* by Hugh Rawson. Jensen then lists the etymological examples of the word 'snake' provided by Rawson, reminding us of the many resonant phrases and terms this work invokes. *Snake in the grass, parlour snakes, snake medicine, snake pit, waking snakes, snake oil*, and so on (54–5). The single most resonant text in Australian literature is Henry Lawson's story 'The drover's wife', inspiration for many other stories by authors from Murray Bail, Barbara Jefferis, Anne Gambling and Frank Moorhouse, through to Claire Corbett, Ryan O'Neill, and most recently, Leah Purcell. First published in the *Bulletin* in 1892 and reprinted numerous times since, the story is iconic for many reasons but what endures is the appearance of the snake, vanquished by a resourceful, determined woman. The protagonist, alone with the children while her husband is away droving, and having failed to tempt the snake out from its hiding place with a saucer of milk, sits up all night with the dog, Alligator, her sewing, and a sturdy stick, waiting for the snake to emerge. As she sews she reflects on the biblical-scale and human catastrophes that she has grappled with alone: floods, fires, evil swagmen. Towards dawn the snake is dispatched and she burns it on the kitchen fire she has kept going all night. Unnamed, this character becomes an everywoman, every lonely but courageous woman the country over, struggling to cope. The snake is at once metaphorical and actual, both an archetypal source of evil, cause of the original fall of humankind, and a very real threat to vulnerable children, dogs and women.

You can, and plenty of people have, read a great deal into this lean realist story. You could go to town on the snake itself, on the milk, the stick, the husband's absence. But its heart lies in the universal fear of the serpent, that potent post-lapsarian symbol of all evil and danger. And every single association or reference, consciously or not, races through our minds as we read Jennings' novel, indeed before we even get past the front cover. *Snake*, I first thought when I received this book in the mail, *what a perfect title for an Australian novel.*

Throughout the novel snakes appear to support or undermine the characters: Irene likes snakes, regarding them a natural part of the world that she embraces via her gardening, the one pleasure she seems to extract from her otherwise arid life as a farmer's wife. Girlie is frightened by a snake, Boy tries unsuccessfully to kill one, and Rex despatches them efficiently. These encounters reinforce Irene's status as an outsider, Girlie's as a clumsy try-hard, Boy as a mere apprentice man, and Rex as the real man but the one we are meant to find wanting. Clearly though, Irene is also the serpent in this dusty garden of Eden, the one who will whisper treacherous things into the ears of the innocent and who will depart having caused eternal havoc. Except she does not slither away on her belly.

Scenes, sex and Serena McGarry

I still have not found the review I wrote of *Snake*, but Jensen confirms my quibble with that cover comment by Ker Conway I found so irritating ('Debra Adelaide spent much of her review quarrelling with the book's cover lines') and reminds me that I found in the novel a 'scrupulous clarity of purpose ... [and] the landscape, the characters, the events are at their most succinct and vivid' (88).

Scrupulous clarity still holds up. To demonstrate why this is such a brilliant novella and to see what can be learned about the craft from it, I could almost select chapters at random, but here is one that has stuck in my mind since the first time I read *Snake* back in the middle of 1996. It is such a part of my imagination that I feel I could have written it myself, or observed it, or even been part of it:

'Look at that lovely red canna.' They were driving by the War
Memorial Park. Irene braked, jumped out, the children trailing.
She bent to uproot some canna bulb.

'No, Mum, don't! You'll be arrested!' Girlie hopped from one foot
to the other.

'Oh shut up,' said Irene. A portion of bulb came suddenly free. She
staggered, regained her balance. (48)

This chapter is entitled 'For the term of her natural life'. In fewer than
70 words we are delivered so much. This includes Irene's admiration
for flowers and her devotion to gardening, along with her defiance
of authority, the ultimate representation of which should surely be
the war memorial builders of every country town – for there is always a
war memorial, and they always seem to be planted around with canna
lilies. It includes Girlie's timidity, her anxiety, her desire to conform and
obey the rules, and how totally different she is to her mother. From his
complete silence, we also infer Boy's lack of engagement with his family
and his immediate surrounds. We see Irene's sharp tongue, her readiness
to rebuke her daughter, her rudeness. And the brilliant final line reveals
Irene's vulnerability but also her resilience. She will stagger a few more
times in the novella but always regain her balance: it is pretty much the
story of her entire life. And after we understand all that, we return to the
title of this chapter: Irene is doing time, condemned to a life sentence as
a wife and mother in the country.

This is scrupulous clarity at its best. At its most devastating it occurs
again in another abbreviated scene towards the end of the novel:

Serena McGarry was the sort of woman who wore high heels with
slacks and her hair in a French twist, so when her husband, Ray,
who had been trying to make a go of it on the old Leonard place,

shot her and their two young children and then turned the gun on himself, no-one was surprised. Boy, who had noticed Serena clicking down the main street of Progress and been rewarded for his attention with a sunny smile, pestered his father for the reason. 'Debt,' said Rex. End of conversation. (116)

In fact, I almost lived an incident like this. In the mid-1980s I was working in that large country hotel that inspired my first novel, feeling trapped, bored and frustrated. One day the local newspaper splashed on the front page the shocking story of a publican in a neighbouring small country town who had been struggling financially, and had shot his wife and stepdaughter, before shooting himself. Locals had fetched the police when the hotel failed to open for business one Saturday morning. Upstairs, the wife and daughter were lying dead in a blood-spattered bedroom. The publican was just breathing, still holding a sawn-off shotgun and a hunting knife, and died later in hospital. During the 1980s interest rates were insanely high, unemployment in country towns was shocking, and random breath testing was killing a lot of the hotel trade.

But that is just my reading of this chapter and only part of the story. The takeaway from a scene like this is universal: perhaps younger readers might not get it, but I am just old enough to remember when the wearing of slacks out of the house for women was frowned upon, let alone the wearing of them with high heels, *and* your hair in a French twist. The exotic transgression of this character, who enters and exits the novel in fewer than 100 words, is underlined by her name, Serena, and then again when she smiles at Boy, who is of course only a boy. Just the first half of the first sentence of this scene is rich in implication, positioning Serena as an avatar for Irene (there is even some symmetry in their names) and as a warning of what might happen if her transgressions were to be matched by her husband's instability. Fortunately for Irene, Rex does not have the imagination for that.

Then there is the devastating closing-off of Boy's prurient, overheated mind: just in case he is thinking of Serena's possible extra-marital sexual life, Rex shoots him down with that one syllable, 'Debt'. But the 'End of conversation' is not, as it happens, the end of it because seven chapters later, we are told of Boy's own sexual adventures that have resulted in his girlfriend April's pregnancy. In part 3, chapter 58, 'Dipping his wick', Boy and April fly out of Progress to Sydney for an abortion. On the way back Boy feels 'as if he has been released from prison' (131).

Scenes such as these are marvellously condensed. They contain entire longer stories within them. You could write a full-length story – or even a novel – about Serena McGarry and her fate, or about Irene and her civic transgressions, and in fact this is something I have suggested to my students, taking details from 'For the term of her natural life', writing them up on a whiteboard and jotting down other ideas and possibilities that radiate from the spare details of the scene. What does Irene do with the canna lily root? Does it survive or die? Do Girlie and Boy bicker in the car on the way home? Where are they heading to in the first place? The questions and thus possibilities are endless, because this impeccably crafted scene, not one single syllable or comma misplaced or extraneous, is the work of a truly gifted writer.

Jensen claims that the reason for *Snake*'s 'failure' is that it was too small – 'Little books are pushed out into the world and then they die' (89) – but I cannot agree with this. *The Metamorphosis* is a little book. *Death in Venice* is a little book. *The Lover* is a little book. *The Children's Bach* is positively anorexic.

Snake might not have won the Booker Prize or had large sales but that does not make it a failure: it has been reprinted, several times, and offers readers an enormous amount to consider and reconsider. It is a novel that repays re-readings well out of proportion to its size. There is always something to learn from it. And, just for the record, playing the bagpipes or yodelling are skills I would love to have.

'Not crying now, but brilliant-eyed': Epiphany in Harrower's 'The fun of the fair'

Emily Maguire

Most fiction relies on a character arc – a transformation of the main character from the beginning to the end – for the resolution of its plot. In short-form fiction, the transformation often comes down to a single moment of clarity or realisation: an epiphany. But common as they are, epiphanies can be tricky to write. Phrases such as 'She suddenly realised' or 'The truth struck him like lightning' can sound clichéd and make the moment seem contrived. After all, how often, in real life, does someone stop in the middle of something and declare (to themselves or others) that they've had an epiphany?

So how can a writer show that a character has experienced a significant, maybe even life-changing, realisation without stating it outright? As with any aspect of writing craft, the best way to learn is from example. And when it comes to subtle but clear epiphanic moments, there are few better than in Elizabeth Harrower's 'The fun of the fair'.

*

The plot of 'The fun of the fair' is simple: on her tenth birthday, Janet goes to a fair with her reluctant Uncle Hector and his girlfriend Leila. When the couple wants some alone time, Janet is sent into a sideshow tent to see 'the giant'. She emerges visibly distressed, which bewilders her uncle.

In the last paragraph, Janet, who has spent most of the story chasing after and clinging to Hector and Leila, runs away from them – 'aimlessly, frantically' through the crowded fair. It's a surprising thing for a clingy little girl to do.

It might appear at first that she is throwing some kind of tantrum. After all, in the minutes before she takes off she has been crying; she has screamed that she doesn't love her family and won't go home. But the final words of the story suggest something else is going on. As Janet runs, we're told she is 'not crying now, but brilliant-eyed'.

'The fun of the fair' (as it appears in Harrower's 2016 collection *A Few Days in the Country: And other stories*) is fourteen pages long, and for thirteen pages Janet is a timid, needy child. Her transformation into a fearless, 'brilliant-eyed' girl seems to happen all at once in the last page, the result of a moment of epiphany.

*

The word 'epiphany' comes from a Greek word meaning 'manifestation' or 'appearance' and has long been used to describe a moment of spiritual or divine revelation. In the Western Christian tradition, for example, the Epiphany is the moment in which three wise men – the magi – see the Christ child. Epiphanies in the religious sense tend to be, like this one, supernatural and external. A god or other supernatural force provides a sign or insight that changes someone's understanding. The epiphany is experienced by the human, but created by the divine.

As a literary term, though, epiphany usually describes a different kind of realisation. It's the moment in *To Kill a Mockingbird* when Scout stands on Boo Radley's porch and finally understands what it means to walk in someone else's shoes. It's the moment in *Frozen* when Elsa realises true love is what she shares with her sister. It's when Dumbo realises it's not the feather that helped him fly.

Note that all of these moments are internal. There's no star in the sky that suddenly appears and leads the way, no curtain that falls open to reveal the killer, no mentor's voice intoning the truth. The epiphany comes as a shift *within* the character.

Another thing to notice is that these epiphanies are not the result of logic or conscious reasoning. If a character puts together clues or carefully thinks through previously discovered information, they may figure out the answer to a mystery, but an epiphany tends to come without conscious effort. It occurs seemingly out of the blue.

Seemingly out of the blue, but – and here's the tricky bit as a writer, and sometimes as a reader – an epiphany does come out of a character's experiences, thoughts and observations.

For a writer, the key to creating a character epiphany that is satisfying to the reader is in thinking at least as much about each of these moments leading up to the epiphany as you do about the epiphany itself.

For a reader, sometimes the epiphanic moment is obvious because it's announced outright with a phrase like 'She suddenly realised that' or 'In that moment he finally understood that'.

What this kind of signposting gives us in clarity it may take away in verisimilitude. In real life, a person may experience a powerful feeling or thought that, looking back later, they might call an epiphany. But in the moment itself, the person is probably so busy *experiencing* the insight or revelation that they don't pause to note its occurrence. They feel it, then surge forward, changed.

Accordingly, a realist writer like Harrower will not have her characters exclaim out loud that they've had an epiphany. She won't even have them consciously note that anything is different. What she will do is show us, the readers, that something has changed in the character and she'll do this by narrating the character's behaviour in the time before, during, and immediately after the epiphany.

Identifying the epiphany – and in many cases understanding the meaning of the story itself – is therefore a matter of close reading. How does this character feel and behave and when and how does this change?

*

'The fun of the fair' begins in a moment of crisis: 'And then, as if the lightning that ripped the sky apart wasn't enough, the lights round the edge of the swimming pool, and even the three big ones sunk into it on cement piles, went out' (1).

See that *and then*? It means the reader is running to catch up before we've even started. *And then* means there's been something before that. What? What's happened? Ah, lightning was the thing that happened first, the thing that would have been enough on its own. But now the lights have all gone out as well!

Let's try this a more conventional way, so we can see how this technique of plunging us in mid-event works: 'Lightning ripped the sky apart. Then the lights round the edge of the swimming pool, and even the three big ones sunk into it on cement piles, went out'.

Notice how even a very small change like this one gives a different energy to the writing. Harrower's choice immerses us in the drama, no warm-up. The reader is immediately aligned with Janet's inner state, which we're introduced to explicitly in the next paragraph: 'At once the solid blackness rang with shrieks and laughter; only Janet struck dumb to find that she had been obliterated. It was like nothing so much as that astronomical darkness into which she'd been plunged last year when they took out her tonsils' (1).

Obliterated – what a powerful word to describe what Janet is feeling. Others in the pool are laughing and joking around, but Janet is silent. This darkness – which is outside of her – feels like the darkness that was hers alone when she was under anaesthetic. We get so much information about this girl from these two sentences: if she is not seen by others, she fears she will cease to exist.

In the next paragraph Janet curls her toes into the sandy bottom of the pool 'so she wouldn't be washed away … The Pacific was just over there somewhere. Behind her' (1–2). Again, we're confronted with how small and vulnerable she feels in her invisibility, how alone, despite being literally surrounded by others.

Janet wants to call out to the adult who brought her here: Uncle Hector. But she remembers that he and his girlfriend, Leila, didn't want her to come in the first place and she promised her aunty – she 'crossed her heart' – that she'd be good. So this terrified child waits for 'ten minutes at least' alone in the darkness, before finally allowing herself to call his name, but even then it's only 'under her breath' (2).

The lights come on. Janet sees Hector and Leila, follows them from the pool, begs for acknowledgment that she was 'good'. But Hector and Leila are in a world of their own. Hector stands:

… hands on hips, feet apart. 'Listen you two, I'll meet you outside the dressing sheds in five minutes. Five minutes!'

'Bully!' said Leila, pressing her hand against her wet costume. 'You just wait.'

'What for?' He rocked back on his heels.

They stood looking at each other so long then, not seeming to notice that they blocked the path round the pool, that Janet, made reckless by the night, cried, 'For us! You've got to wait for us!'

'Oh shut up!' said Uncle Hector indifferently. (3–4)

Janet doesn't understand that she's witnessing flirtation. Leila's provocative 'Just you wait' is interpreted by Janet as 'wait for us' as if this grown woman is, like her, worried about being left behind.

Hector tells Janet to 'shut up' but, and this is important, he says it 'indifferently'. Let's think for a second about what that means. We've all, unfortunately, been told to 'shut up'. Most of us have probably said it to someone else at least once. What are the different ways we can say it?

It might be affectionate. Your best friend says, 'I can't believe how pretty you look. I'm actually embarrassed to stand near you, because you're so beautiful'. And you say, 'Shut up! You're the beautiful one!'

Or you might say it angrily: your brother has been pushing you to your limits all day, nagging and nagging and nagging for stuff and finally you snap: 'Shut up!'

But why would you say it 'indifferently'? Perhaps if the family dog who has been there as long as you can remember, who's become part of the furniture, almost, is yapping while you're lying in the backyard trying to talk to a friend. Then you might say, barely bothering to look in the dog's direction, 'Shut up'. You know the dog won't and you don't really care. He's not actually bothering you. You're focused on your friend the whole time.

It's not affectionate. It's not angry. It's just *meh*.

That's how Hector speaks to Janet. Not even bothered enough by her to be angry. She's a yapping family pet in the background and his focus is firmly on his girlfriend.

Hector and Leila make their way through the fair, stopping when they like, moving again when they like, and Janet chases after them 'wriggling in and out' of the crowd to keep up. After losing them for a minute she comes upon Hector looking at Leila and laughing 'in a way that astonished Janet'. She's never seen him like this: 'how lovely it was to see him laugh!' His happiness makes her feel she's having 'a marvellous birthday night!' (6).

A witnessed moment of someone else's happiness makes her feel her own birthday night is a success. That this is how she measures the marvellousness of an occasion meant for celebrating *her* suggests she is a child used to worrying about the pleasure of others over her own.

A bit later Hector and Leila go into the Tunnel of Love, and Janet is not invited. She's told to 'look at the giant' and though she feels 'deserted' she obediently buys her ticket to 'The greatest romance since Romeo and Juliet … the greatest giant in the world and his lovely little bride' (8).

In the tent, a very tall man and very short woman stare straight ahead, and then, 'with a simultaneous craning of necks' they acknowledge each other's presence. 'With an almost audible one, two, three' (10) they tell a story of meeting and falling in love.

It is immediately evident to Janet that they are performers with no feeling for each other at all and that the audience – 'shamefaced' – is in on the fakery. 'They didn't mean a word they said … And they don't care if we know it, she thought. They're saying all this and hating us. Love, they're saying' (11).

Janet is reluctantly pulled up on stage to show the audience the scale of the 'giant' and his 'bride', and she shakes both of their hands. Afterwards, she is upset, crying. She stares at her hand. Hector and Leila don't know what's wrong, and readers, too, may be a bit unsure. We know she found the show unpleasant and it upset her, but we haven't had much of an explanation about why.

And then we have this moment as Leila and Hector are wondering what to do with this distressed child: 'Janet drew a little away from them. Amazed, she looked at the sky, and the fair, and her uncle and Leila. She looked at the people who passed. Roughly she wiped her eyes and took a backward step' (14). And then she runs, and shouts 'I don't love any of you.' Our last image of her is 'not crying but brilliant-eyed' (14).

The epiphany has happened, but when? What was it?

*

Early in the story we learn that Janet does not live with her parents. There's no explanation as to why, or if they are in her life at all, only the information that she lives with her aunty, who finds her 'a trial'. 'Indeed, she was so far from ideal, in spite of her intentions, that it was suggested in her defence that she'd been born rather badly behaved' (4). This is what she's been told and it's what she believes, but actually, as readers, we don't see any evidence of this. Janet doesn't behave badly at all in this story. In the pool, for example, when the lights go out and she feels *obliterated* and terrified of being washed out to the ocean, she doesn't even call out, so as not to bother Hector.

When the three of them enter the fair Janet notices a 'middle-aged man, neat and sedate in his navy-blue suit' going around on a 'flying-horse' ride. It is obvious to her that he is not doing this 'for his own pleasure'. Perhaps, she thinks, he is doing it 'to please that girl with blonde curls beside him' (4–5).

It's a passing moment; one of several descriptions of the colour and movement of the fair in this section of the story, but it's an important one. It represents the possibility that an adult might do something for the sake of a child's happiness, and not the other way around.

Several times she rushes past things she's interested in, because she must keep up with Hector and Leila. They are experiencing the fair the way they want to and all she can do is chase behind and try not to lose them. They, the adults, are the ones to go on a ride while she has to mind the bag and wait.

And does she feel, as many children might, that it should be her up there on the ride? If she does, there's no indication of it. Instead, her impulse is to let other people know that she is related to two of the people on the ride, as though reassuring herself that she is not alone, she is connected. And she wants to share the important facts of her life: she is ten today. She went for a swim. Like her sense of obliteration in the pool, there's a sense that her birthday happiness is not real if it's not known by others.

And then, still doing all she can to please the adults, she goes into the tent when she's told to and stays in there even though she feels uncomfortable. Here is where the change in her begins to build, though. She realises that the performers 'didn't mean a word they said ... And they don't care if we know it' (11).

This is a revelation to her. When she entered the tent she believed that this was actually going to be, as advertised, 'The greatest romance since Romeo and Juliet'. She's shocked – we know this from her thoughts and her blinking – that these two are just pretending and don't seem to even care that everyone knows it. And the audience is in on it: the people in the tent seem to know it's not real but go along as if it is.

Then she has her encounter on the stage and leaves, and then looks at her hand. She holds it out, away from her. She looks at it again. We know something has changed. Something has happened to her when she shook the hands of those performers. Hector thinks she's upset because the giant scared her, but it's something else. What can it be?

If we read those passages we see the contrast between the performance that she herself puts on and her feelings:

'Well, now may we both shake you by the hand, and wish you the very best of luck? We'd like you to accept our hearty thanks for your kindness in assisting at this demonstration for the benefit of our patrons.'

The giant bowed and shook her hand. Janet said, 'How do you do?' (12)

She shakes the woman's hand and although the woman's eyes are saying to her, 'Nothing nice. Nothing good', Janet still says, 'How do you do? Thank you. Good night' (12).

Janet touched these people, went along with the pretence that they were who they pretended to be. All of them performing love or politeness or belief, all of them knowing it's a performance, and now here she is outside and the hand that took part in that performance is here, part of her and only her.

This all leads us to the moment of epiphany. While Leila and Hector stare at each other, wondering what to do with this crying child, 'Janet drew a little away from them. Amazed, she looked at the sky, and the fair, and her uncle and Leila. She looked at the people who passed. Roughly she wiped her eyes and took a backward step'.

The big clues here are in her movement – she draws away from the adults and then takes a further backward step – and in this one word, 'amazed'.

Think of the very first moment when she feels 'obliterated' by not being seen, and not seeing others. Think of the way she chases after her uncle and his girlfriend, the way she yearns to speak to bystanders and assert her connection to others. But now, look, she has noticed something amazing: her individuality. She physically moves away from the adults. She can do that. She can stand alone.

Those performers are treated as though their height or lack of it is all they are, the only interesting thing about them; Janet through her physical interaction with them has seen they are full human beings just like her. She sees that they have allowed others' ideas of who they are to place them there, like that. It is horrifying to her to see this display of two people resigning themselves to someone else's story about who they are. Worse than resigning: collaborating, encouraging.

She will not do that. She will not allow this view of others, their narrative about who and what she is, to become her own narrative.

Janet is ten years old and experiencing an extreme surge of emotion, so she wouldn't, and doesn't, stop to articulate this. But the feeling is: I am not what others say I am. I do not accept the narrative being imposed on me. I will not comply.

Although it is, like many epiphanies, distressing at first (hence the sobbing), in the end it's a gloriously hopeful moment. Remember earlier when Janet notices the middle-aged man riding the flying-horse for the pleasure of the girl by his side? Janet has accepted she won't ever have that. The adults she's stuck with aren't up to it. But there was someone she saw, right before the man and the girl. A boy on the same ride, shrieking and 'waving an arm to no-one in particular' (4–5).

We have the sense that this post-epiphany Janet, 'not crying now, but brilliant-eyed' will take herself on all the rides (literal and metaphorical) she likes, and she will shriek and wave, whether there's someone in particular to see her, or not.

How to build a glass church: Peter Carey's *Oscar and Lucinda*

Belinda Castles

Sydney Harbour had a silver skin. A cormorant broke the surface, like an improbable idea tearing the membrane between dreams and life. – Peter Carey, *Oscar and Lucinda*, 363

In *30 Days in Sydney*, Peter Carey tells us of how his friend the architect sees his world, the way he watches 'the pink Pacific light illuminate a sandstone cliff, or the water at the end of a mangrove creek turn copper as the tide recedes'. After a dreamily vivid account he writes, 'He can see like no one else I know' (29).

When I was a very young writer, missing Sydney in the interesting and wet northern city in England in which I was trying to write my first novel, I dreamed of seeing like Carey. I read *Oscar and Lucinda*, and to absorb his glinting, expansive, crushing novel of colonial Sydney was to be given a distinctive vision of a place I so wanted to see again. My reading of the novel was infused with longing: to be immersed in the air and light and smells of a place that was not yet my home, and to be a writer. I was reaching towards something as I wrote my own small novel of Sydney. I saw and felt the world with a vivid intensity and wished to find the language through which to express these perceptions.

As we grow into adults, reading can take on a new bewitchment. We seek access to other worlds and selves expressed through fresh forms of language, in order to enlarge our own yearning selves. And for those of us setting out to try and make something with words, we begin to ask of the authors we admire: what are you doing, and how are you doing it?

On rereading this novel now in middle age, having lived in Sydney on and off for over twenty years, Carey's vision re-presents this city to me in all the splendour of its light and water, its days of gentleness and lashing hostility, its layers of physical history tracing the brutal injustice of its invasion and settlement. And I remember too that it is not just the way he sees that illuminates the world, but his rendering of sensation: 'the shrieks and tearing beaks' of the cockatoos on Cockatoo Island (338), or a buttoned-up housekeeper walking along the streets of Balmain, who 'occupied that thin strip of dry shadow when all the rest of the street was wet with sunshine' (340).

Sydney is particularly well suited to a writer attuned to the power of the senses. Delia Falconer writes in her memoir of the city: 'The material constantly intrudes – even as I write, a pulpy smell of iodine from the over-warm February harbour comes through the window – and this freights every one of its books, paintings and conversations' (5). It is a city to be touched, smelled, heard, to be experienced as more than a modern, urban place of business, play and culture; its physical nature, weather and past want to make themselves felt too.

To familiarise, or refamiliarise, you with this novel, *Oscar and Lucinda* is a story of two gamblers from opposite sides of the world, of risk, of appalling crimes against the Aboriginal people of this country, of love, ambition and the building of monuments to these. It is a big novel, in length and scope, published in the year of Australia's bicentenary, in which the country found itself reckoning with its two centuries of colonial history. My memories of this novel are a flickering slide show of images: a house on a windy promontory above the water at Balmain. A factory looming over the seething oily sheen of Darling Harbour. A proud, reckless woman with her arms in a huge jar of pickles. A glass church on a river, filled with bats and a thin, wretched Englishman.

The images and events are stored now in my most vivid reading memories, because aside from anything else *Oscar and Lucinda* is a gripping, larger-than-life story – and language is a key feature of that vividness. Language, along with shrieking cockatoos and streets wet with sunshine, is one of the materials of our sensory world. Carey's writing is bound up with the stuff of life, its endlessly fascinating textures, and his sentences are somehow made of similar materials: silky or rhythmic or airy, violent, or shimmering with memory. Language tells of the elements of which our world is made, and of how they are perceived by the characters in a story but, marvellously, language is itself material; its textures and shapes are assimilated by the reader as sensory and tangible. Written language shapes the worlds it makes: the sentences and their arrangement matter.

Here is a sentence that makes me linger over it, to live for a little while in its tangibility, emotional resonance and dreaminess. Oscar's father Theophilus has come to say goodbye on the ship that will take his estranged son from England to New South Wales. With great feeling, he gives Oscar the caul taken from his head when he was born, as a talisman against drowning. 'He was remembering a child and wife in a Devon lane – myrtles, perfumed hedges, luscious red mud, which caked so thickly on their boots that their feet became as heavy and padded as creatures in a dream' (217). The imagery of beloved, lost people amid the landscape of home at this moment of farewell is sensory, textured, sticky and real, until the moment it lifts off into something lighter and stranger. The claggy earth weighs down their feet and turns them into something other than their daily selves. The movement of this sentence, from the lively particulars of dear people amid the vibrancy of nature as they move into another realm, clumping softly into dream memory, shifts from the tangible to the ethereal, in the way of a memory coloured by feeling. It is a sentence shaped around loss: vividness and connection evaporate into beings beyond his grasp. The textures of the language itself trace the passage of the real and present into memory. The quick, sensory list that conjures the place in which they were together – myrtles, perfumed hedges, the onomatopoeic caking of luscious red mud – drift into softer sounds of V and D, *heavy and padded*, and long, slow internal rhymes: *creatures in a dream* – that soft close of the sentence. And here in the ship, in the present moment that Theophilus must live through, the child, now a young man, will leave forever.

That red Devon mud gives rise to the most brilliant greenery; it spills onto tracks and roads as well as boots and into houses, its rusty dust lives for years in the corner of the shed. When you have lived in Devon, or I expect when you have not, that fertile red clay inhabits the inner vision. It appears from Salman Rushdie's memoir, *Joseph Anton*, that Carey spent only a day, with Rushdie, physically researching a Devon beach on which to base Oscar's home village of Hennacombe, and a treasure from that day's haul is this red mud (119). Its sensory vividness, its ability to conjure associations and memories, for Oscar's grieving father, and for the reader, is an example of what James Wood, in *How Fiction Works*, calls 'thisness'.

'Thisness' is one of those words that seems to perform its own meaning. Saying it involves concentrated activity in the teeth and tongue, an encounter with its wettish textures. Wood tells us that the medieval theologian Duns Scotus coined it for 'individuating form', and that it was later taken up by the poet Gerald Manley Hopkins (Wood, 54). 'By thisness', Wood writes, 'I mean any detail that draws abstraction towards itself and seems to kill that abstraction with a puff of palpability, any detail that centres our attention with its concretion' (54). He gives an example from Shakespeare: 'I mean the precise brand of greenness –

"Kendal green" – that Falstaff swears, in *Henry IV Part 1*, clothed the men who attacked him' (55). That the specificity of this green turns out to be a fiction (it was dark) does not undermine its resonance, the way it glows in the imagination; even though what Kendal green actually is must be invented in the modern audience's eye as it is spoken, even though it is a lie.

Palpability of detail does not constrain meaning to the merely literal. If anything, it immerses the reader so fully in the worlds of sense, memory, perception, that they are more readily primed to examine and feel the complexities of motivation and emotion of the perceiving character, to enter their dream world. The sticky red mud of Devon clings to the boots of an austere preacher's wife and child, but only now in his interior vision. The people whose love defines Theophilus are moving further and further into his past, beyond a boundary that is about to close. I feel the sting of their loss because there was once sticky red mud on their boots, remembered by a thinking, feeling person, and because these details are set like a gem into a finely wrought, emotively constructed sentence.

There is an abundance of such detail in this novel, of Sydney and the landscapes of Devon and New South Wales, and also of closed worlds, filled with arcane particulars: the cell-like bareness of Oscar's Oriel College room, the 'carving, scrollwork, plush' (207) of the ship *Leviathan*, wasted on Oscar, hiding in his cabin from any glimpse of the terrifying ocean, the miraculous, dangerous processes of Lucinda's glass factory, with its hissing and steaming, its 'snake of red elastic glass' made 'into a question mark ... by a whiskered Falstaff with a fat belly and a grubby singlet' (370). Such places in fiction, workplaces in particular, have a strange allure. They speak of unknown worlds, specialist knowledges. The textures of their 'thisness' seem particularly convincing and immersive. The details of such places and their animating characters nudge open a door, give us access.

Lucinda's factory, though, is more than a lovely bit of worldbuilding;

it is a node in a larger network of images. The novel is strung through with images of tautness and tension, like this one, when Oscar has news for his friend Wardley-Fish: that he is to take up a mission in New South Wales. 'You could feel [Oscar's] quivering energy in the floor and table. It felt like a trout feels on the end of a line – all the energy of a life forcing its patterns onto inert matter.' (185–6) The quotation from *Oscar and Lucinda* that opens this essay, in which a cormorant breaks the silver skin of Sydney Harbour, manages to describe the entire novel – one glittering state holding, holding, until an unstoppable force breaks through. But this imagery of something poised, about to change, to break free or be destroyed, is most dramatically configured and sustained in the metaphor of glass. Lucinda as a child in Parramatta witnesses the conundrum of a Prince Rupert's drop, a long-tailed glass bead, an accident of manufacture. It remains intact when her father throws it against the wall of the Church Street magistrate's court, and then 'sprayed like brown sugar' when nipped between the blade and handle of his pocket knife (134). She is fated to bewitchment from this moment on.

Nowadays, you can find video online of these glass droplets exploding; I have just watched one. The bead is the shape of a tadpole, or sperm, and the presenter takes a hammer to it, with no luck, and then uses pliers on its tail – success. The filmmaker slows the frames down and the glittering explosion moves up the tail to the head as though energy is being shot through it. It is incredible! And witnessing it calls to mind the itching temptation for Lucinda of these 'very more-ish' little objects:

Fireworks made of glass. An explosion of dew, Crescendo. Diminuendo. Silence.

There are drugs that work the same, and while I am not suggesting that our founder purchased the glassworks to get more drops, it is clear that she had the seed planted, not once, but twice, and knew already the lovely contradictory nature of glass ... a joyous and paradoxical thing, as good a material as any to build a life from. (135)

And so Carey shapes a metaphorical landscape through glass, whose properties can express the tensions of the novel: the fragility of fortune, gambling, adventure, ambition, faith and love. In this novel to be fully alive is to take preposterous risks, and this is what brings our gamblers together. They play cards on the ship to New South Wales, and are reunited in a gambling parlour on George Street. For both of them it is not just money they risk but, as a single woman and a priest in a harshly judgmental society, their reputations. They live in a house together, held apart by the fiction that Lucinda loves the priest Dennis Hassett, recently transferred to Boat Harbour (Bellingen). Eventually, they make a great wager, all or nothing, resting on the delivery by Oscar of a glass cathedral to this priest. The tiny bead of explosive potential has found its apotheosis in this mad venture.

> The bet had a life. They contained it ... it was this bee in the box, the Big Bet, the glass bet, which gave the days their excruciating tension, their lovely current, the nights their lightness, their expectation. They did not kiss or hold hands. The bet gave them a future they stretched towards. (395)

Carey is a writer who corrals the elements of his metaphors to give distinctive textures to his worlds. For comparison, venturing forwards briefly to his later novel, *The True History of the Kelly Gang* (2000), we find a world made of different sensory surfaces, constructed through a new landscape of metaphor. Both novels are set in the mid-nineteenth century in colonial Australia, but here the figurative language is of the organic world of rural Victoria where Ned Kelly is raised. His is a childhood and young adulthood of brutality and police antagonism, but it is also characterised by the plants, animals and country that make his universe, in the way that the manufacture of glass characterises Lucinda's in industrial Sydney. Here, we learn of Ned's feelings as Sergeant O'Neil implies that Kelly senior was a murderer and betrayer of his accomplices back in Ireland: 'The memory of the policeman's words lay inside me like the egg of a liver fluke and while I went about my growing up this slander wormed deeper and deeper into my heart and there grew fat' (11). We discover that his favourite sister Maggie was 'as true and steady as a red gum plank' (16). About the things his father taught him Ned tells us:

> In the bush he taught the knots I use to tie my blanket to my saddle
> Ds also the way I stand to use a carpenter's plane and the trick of
> catching fish with a bush fly and a strip of greenhide these things
> are like the dark marks made in the rings of great trees locked
> forever in my daily self. (19)

Ned's family history is embodied in him in ways that in turn embed him in his hardscrabble life on the land. This is a life far from Lucinda's world of glass, and expressed in a much looser grammatical structure and rhythm, modelled in part on the real Ned Kelly's 'Jerilderie Letter', a justification of his actions written towards the end of his short life. Carey explained the influences on the voice of *True History* in an interview:

> The Jerilderie Letter is a howl of pain ... there is this original voice
> – uneducated but intelligent, funny and then angry, and with a
> line of invective that would have made Paul Keating envious. His
> language came in a great, furious rush that could not but remind
> you of far more literary Irish writers ... it was Kelly's language
> that drew me to this story. In those eccentric sentences was my
> character's DNA ... What I finally wrote grew not just from the

Jerilderie Letter but from the first 10 years of life which I spent in the very small town of Bacchus Marsh. I once knew people who spoke more or less as Ned does in this novel. I could inhabit his voice like an old, familiar shoe. (in McCrum, 7 January 2001)

It's a voice you have to get used to as a reader, but this happens surprisingly quickly – your mind punctuates the sentences so easily that it must be that the ease has been built into their structure, that he is inventing sentences that show you how to read them, as all distinctive fictive voices do, to the point where you go about thinking in their rhythms for some time after the book is set back on the shelf.

Voice is a slippery subject. It is rare perhaps to know in the way Carey articulates here where a voice comes from; he said in an interview about the voice of *Oscar and Lucinda*, 'It really is totally intuitive ... I just kept on writing until it felt right' (Grenville & Woolfe, 38). Reading Carey gives us access to one of the fascinating conundrums of voice: that a writer can employ deliberate effects in their choices about sentence structure, rhythm and figurative range that differ for each new book, but still sound like themselves. 'Voice' is itself a metaphor for a number of selections, conscious and less so, that the author makes. In the case of Carey it is a particularly apt one; if we think of an actor well known to us, the way they use voice, we recognise the distinctive timbre, pitch and tone of this one distinctive human being of the eight billion in the world, even as they convince us that they are someone new with each appearance, from a different place, perhaps, with a different accent and history, a different way of being in the world. You would hear them on the radio and know it was them. When I open a new Carey novel, I think: Ah, there he is, and I am back in the sentences that make this new world in a new way, but in which I can hear a specific writer, whose voice I know.

In *Oscar and Lucinda*, the voice has a more staccato rhythm than Kelly's rolling vernacular of the later novel. Angela Carter wrote in her review at the time of publication that Carey 'constructs his narrative out of short, or shortish, sentences, often of an off-beat, ferocious elegance … These sharp, highly coloured splinters are assembled into very many short, or shortish, chapters' ('Oscar for envy'). The allusion to glass here is, you would imagine, no accident, even if the shaping of his novel through an assembly of shards was not a conscious decision on Carey's part. Here is an example of the technique and effect Carter describes – Oscar's first impressions of Sydney:

> Sydney was a blinding place. It made him squint. The stories of the
> gospel lay across the harsh landscape like sheets of newspaper on
> a polished floor. They slid, slipped, did not connect to anything
> beneath them. It was a place without moss or lichen, and the people
> scrabbling to make a place like troops caught under fire on hard
> soil. St John's at Randwick was built from red brick with very white
> mortar. The fine clay dust that overlay everything, even the cypress
> hedge beside the vicarage, could not soften the feeling of the place.
> It was all harsh edges like facets of convict-broken rock. (307)

It is important that the stories of the gospel can find no purchase here, that they are made of the wrong stuff, but for now let's look at the structure and arrangement of these sentences. Splinters, Carter called them. Like the real and figurative convict-broken rock of Oscar's Sydney, these sentences have sharp edges. Grammatically, this is because they tend to be paratactical, that is, the sentences are not linked by conjunctions (while, because, until etc) that might smooth out the flow.

Here I have added conjunctions within and between sentences as well as some small linking phrases to see what happens to the rhythm:

> Sydney was a blinding place, **so much so that** it made him squint.
> **It seemed as well that** the stories of the gospel lay across the harsh
> landscape like sheets of newspaper on a polished floor, **and that**

they slid and slipped and did not connect to anything beneath them. **Perhaps it was because** it was a place without moss or lichen, and the people scrabbling to make a place like troops caught under fire on hard soil. **For example,** St John's at Randwick was built from red brick with very white mortar **and** the fine clay dust that overlay everything, even the cypress hedge beside the vicarage, could not soften the feeling of the place, which was all harsh edges like facets of convict-broken rock.

You will see that I have almost ruined it, deadened that dramatic choppy rhythm, muted some of the drama of the details with my tinkering. I say 'almost', because the tangibility of those details, gospel stories like sheets of newspaper, people scrabbling like troops under fire, resist my efforts to remove their spiky energy. Still, I have dulled the power emanating from those pauses between sentences and clauses, that energy conjured in part by the reader, who experiences these spaces, that rhythm and drama, as inextricable elements of reading this novel.

Back to the content of this paragraph, in particular the Bible stories that cannot be attached to this landscape, different as it is to the continually watered fields and hedges of Devon where Oscar learned the gospels at his father's knee. He should have listened to his own forebodings before he tried to transport Lucinda's church across such country. In taking on this task he marries his ambitions to those – darker, more brutal – of expedition leader Mr Jeffris, whose vision of their voyage with the glass is that 'These sheets would cut a new path in history' (441). Oscar instigates and participates in this devastating, slicing path across the country, retreating into laudanum dreams of horror, but also a persistent dream-vision of a 'glass-house shaped like a seamless teardrop; the teardrop suspended in a wire net; the net held by cast-iron rods out from a cliff above the sea' (465). More tension, embodied by glass: the real, heavy, fragile load being carted by soldiers into this country, and its dream form, the sheets transformed into a building, and for now aloft, defying gravity.

The glass church must make the last stage of its journey, constructed, by river towards Boat Harbour. There are of course already stories in this land; the church is a house of alien teachings disconnected from Country, ignorant of it, violent towards it in the hands in which it arrives. The narrator tells us that Oscar:

> drifted up the Bellinger River like a blind man up the central aisle
> of Notre Dame. He saw nothing. The country was thick with
> sacred stories more ancient than the ones he carried in his sweat-
> slippery Bible. He did not even imagine their presence ... In this
> landscape every rock had a name, and most names had spirits,
> ghosts, meanings. (492)

The point of view shifts fluidly in this three-page chapter, from Oscar to a local Aboriginal boy, Kumbaingiri Billy, to the insects inside the church that Oscar tries to bat away, who 'did not understand what glass was ... For one hundred thousand years their progenitors had inhabited that valley without once encountering glass. Suddenly the air was hard where it should be soft' (494). Glass changes the very nature of the air, bringing this invisible boundary, made of industrial magic, into a place where the country and people and stories are all part of the same world.

Let's leave Oscar here, in his glass church on the Bellinger River, caught in an encounter between a hard, lovely material – strong but vulnerable to counterforces – and the continual movement and pressure of water. I suggested earlier that we read as writers by asking: what are you doing? Now, then: how are you doing it? We can identify elements of technique, but how does a person manufacture a 500-page novel and hold it all together without it cracking apart? Did Carey sit down to write amid visions of glass, light and violence and make his hands on the keyboard available until the dazzling shaft of inspiration found its way onto the page?

In the early 1990s, novelists Kate Grenville and Sue Woolfe put together an ingenious book about writing: *Making Stories*, in which they interviewed Australian novelists, including Carey, about the process of writing particular novels and included small sections of those novels in progress. It is an artefact of an age that was almost over even when it was published in 1993, in which writers typed their novels on a typewriter and made amendments on the physical page. Writers still type, and they still print their work out, and annotate those print-outs, but there are countless decisions lost to the record; where once there would be a trail a literary detective might follow to see the development of, say, 'Newspeak' in George Orwell's *1984* (Rubin), now that information is lost the moment a writer hits 'delete' and types a new word. In their introduction, Grenville and Woolfe say that they 'wanted to erode the idea that the writer is someone unlike other people, someone to whom the Muse has simply dictated a masterpiece (xi)'. This is perhaps the single most important thing I have learned about the work of writing, and it is amply illustrated in this gift of a book. Anyone who hopes to improve at their own writing has an interest here. If we are given evidence of the process, we begin to see that the ugly duckling of our frustrating false starts, poorly fleshed-out characters and clumsy phrasing can shed its fluffy feathers and become a sleek and powerful animal. *How are you doing it?* Or, as Grenville and Woolfe put it: 'How did Peter Carey control the enormous fabrication of *Oscar and Lucinda*?' (xii). And then, via their method of interview and presentation of select fragments of the draft, they extract illuminating answers.

Among these are two elements of method I want to think about. Aptly, one of them is a process taken from the language of engineering: 'cantilevering'. The other, just as apt in its sticky thisness, is 'porridge'. Cantilevering is how Carey describes his method of beginning a section, then stopping it and starting it again, extending this time, a little further, and so on, as a bridge supported at one end stretches out above the dizzying empty space below. It is clearly illustrated in one of the manuscript extracts he provides. On the page you see a very short block of paragraph – the beginnings of a character study on Oscar's Oxford friend Percy Wardley-Fish – ending mid-sentence, then a block about three times the size, and then a passage of several paragraphs extending over the page (Grenville and Woolfe, 55–6). What Carey says about it speaks to the uncertainties and strange, intricate labour of making a story:

> PC: I don't know what I'm writing about, it's inauthentic. Somehow it's lying, somehow it's not true. So I go back and start again.
>
> INT: Do you visualise it more clearly, or ...
>
> PC: Yes, it becomes more fully imagined. It's like this thin bit of wire that you want to encrust ... so maybe that's all it is, just building it up so I can see it, believe it. (39)

This is not the only way to progress with a piece of writing – some favour the white-hot dash through a draft for editing later – but it is a useful method to consider, and it is how I have written this essay, over several weeks of COVID-19 disruption, with a full household, and learning how to teach through a screen. It allows you to lay down foundations, and slowly watch your bridge extend over the river.

During this part of the conversation between Carey and his interviewers, in which they discuss recreating nineteenth-century Oxford, we also come to the 'porridge' part of his method:

> PC: The big question for a writer is, how can you know this? In what corner of yourself can you find what you need to write truthfully about things of which, objectively, you'd have no knowledge?

INT: So did you find such a thing here, for instance? Is perhaps something of your old school, Geelong Grammar, in here?

PC: Yes. When I was at Oxford with Robert McCrum, I needed to look at a room, a room that Oscar has […] So we looked at this guy's room, and I made some notes.

I said to Robert, well I think I can do Oxford, I'll use Geelong Grammar in some way. He looked at me rather doubtfully but that's why I thought I could do it. And the other thing is there's a whole lot of this that's just part of our imaginative life from literature as well, and that's part of the porridge. (40)

In the way that he conjures Ned Kelly's voice from an amalgam of his letter, the Irish greats of literature and the voices of his childhood in Bacchus Marsh, a knowledge is available to Carey that can be drawn upon if he sets himself patiently to the task of building this world. You and I have these kinds of knowledge too, the voices of memory and artefact, our experience in the world and what we seek out through research, our attentive reading and observation – our porridge.

It is heartening to hear a Booker Prize–winning author talk about the process of writing and remembering and discovering himself into believing in his own characters and worlds – about finding faith in his own imaginings through an incremental process. It is a gift to us, not because we need other writers to be cut down to size, but because it is hugely encouraging to our ambitions to know that those we admire begin with scraps and intuitions and must do the work of craft to turn them into something that communicates their vision to the reader.

What does that mean for us? Well, we may not be geniuses, but we have the weird dreamy fragments in our brains, and we can work.

A metaphysical meeting place:
Sixty Lights by Gail Jones

Irini Savvides

> Reading was this metaphysical meeting space – peculiar, specific,
> ardent, unusual – in which black words neatly spaced on a
> rectangular page persuaded her that hypothetical people were as
> real as she, that not diversion, but knowing, was the gift story gave
> her. – Gail Jones, *Sixty Lights*, 114

18 April 2020

Dear Reader,

These are strange times, unlikely and uncanny. These are three adjectives I have always loved, but which at this time have taken on a new meaning. This is a moment that calls to us to find comfort in things that are known. Tomorrow it is Easter Sunday for us Greek Orthodox. Usually at midnight tonight I would be holding a taper candle of beeswax, following one of the wizened old women who would shepherd me outside through the multitudes at St John's Parish in Parramatta, and we would call out over and over again: *Christos Anestis!* I would be looking among the thousands of people for my family, searching through the crowd to spot my beloved tall twin nephews and the rest of my people standing with them, not as tall as they. The light would be passed from candle to candle, a sea of flame bringing joy to the depth of the darkest night. In its flickering and sparks we transfer light to light and the shadows disperse, if momentarily. At the resurrection I would remember my father winding my long dark hair around his left hand to stop it going up in flames when I was but a child. Instead tonight I will sit alone at the desk and watch the livestream service, mourning the empty church and longing for my people.

The truth is I know a great deal about longing for my people. Perhaps like every fictional character, and maybe every person, I have spent my life looking for my kinfolk. As a child my father wrote to my grandmother, whose name I have: a letter she famously kept under her pillow. On that fragile blue airmail paper he wrote about his daughter, who did not seem to be much interested in real people, but spent her time with her nose in a book, or writing. He prophesied that I would be a *paramythou* (taleteller/storyteller) when I grew up. Written and spoken words have such power. This is one of the things I have come to know. Was it a blessing or a curse, I wonder now, those words he penned? To be the teller of tales.

It is true that books are often my favourite company. When the world is too much I have been known to reread *Jane Eyre* all weekend to find my moorings. I do have some actual friends, nonetheless. I have a real friend named Pip, who is doing a PhD on Victorian literature. This is unlikely, but true. We both have this passion for *Jane Eyre*, the famous heroine. At first I was somewhat put out having to share; Jane was mine. We all have those books, do we not, that give us the kin we have been searching for? I love Jane because she never seems to fit in her world, but keeps seeking the world she will fit into. Because she knows her folk when she finds them, even if the world tells her that this is impossible – her heart knows her folk. When Rochester asks her if she has been sitting at the stile waiting for her people the first time they meet she says that they all left England long ago. But some of them did not, and we know she has now met one of them from the folk tale, recalled from Bessie, that frames the scene.

Jane is my people because she is plain, because she is smart and because no one wants her, for so very long. Because when she loves she *loves*. Jane is my people because her art gives her the first taste of happiness she knows when she is creating it, regardless of what her audience takes from it.

The plight of another fictional orphan, Pip, in Dickens' *Great Expectations*, has also been a reading 'home' I return to again and again. It was not just the discovery that Jane was my folk I collected from this era, but that Pip too, like Jane, has an impossible, eternal love ... for Estella. The young Pip, when we first see him, in the opening pages of *Great Expectations*, is an orphan sitting forlornly in that graveyard trying to find his parents in the chiselled letters on the headstone. There are words and phrases that haunt us. Orphans – in all three of these texts. There is a time in our lives where this word becomes a skin we inhabit, rather than just a word. A favourite moment of irony in Gail Jones' *Sixty Lights*: 'How fiction predicts' (102). When I found a text that wove two orphans through it, what could I do but fall in love with this strange, unlikely, uncanny gift?

It is not straightforward for me to tell you what this novel, and Gail Jones, have taught me about writing. During my PhD study I learnt that I am more interested in weaving thread than in writing straight lines. I think of my Cypriot grandmother weaving silk at the *woofa*, the hard-edged wooden frame that she coiled the fabric in and out of. A thread at a time. An image. A way to see anew. What *Sixty Lights* has given me is the ability to look again at what writing can be. A tapestry of threads, woven through time. Pleated.

So I am loath to tell you my story straight. I am much more interested in telling it slant, like the famous poet who wore the white dress. Let's start there then, shall we. On the cover of *Sixty Lights*, there is a picture of a woman in a white Victorian dress. She is holding a photo of a gilded frame, a daguerreotype. This novel, stitched into three parts, and sixty lights, speaks out metaphorical images through storytelling. The sixty lights are snapshots, finely crafted vignettes giving us images threaded through time and space to savour. Across worlds and woven throughout time.

The woman on the cover herself is ghostly, the dress slightly out of focus. I have looked at the collar over the years wondering if it is lace. I am the grandchild of the seamstress Philomela, both she and her mother Panayiota were dressmakers so as I look, I know in my core that it is not lace, but just a frill. The fabric is self-striped, with flowers embossed on the skirt, perhaps calico or damask? I wish that deft craftswoman, my great-grandmother Panayiota, was here to ask. She would know. Lines of women past, passing knowing through threads of silk.

In the image Lucy holds a frame with a picture of a stately-looking gentleman, suited, bow-tied, moustached – typical Victorian fare – his face half-hidden by a shadow. She herself, the woman doing the holding, has no face. It is the image that matters. The fabric she wears is translucent like her skin, gossamer. Her pale arms almost merge into the folds of the cloth – *ghostly* comes to mind. *Dissolve* comes to mind too, an apparition. I have wondered if the author liked the cover, knowing something about the process that is writing a novel and then having another select the image that may sell it. The word that haunts me when I look at the cover is *strange*.

Strangeness seems to seek me out, as in the history of one of my own book covers. Long ago I spoke as one of the *Sydney Morning Herald*'s Best Young Novelists about my first novel, *Willow Tree and Olive*. Like all those I have written after, it was a fragmented narrative told by a person who sits at the margins and watches. Story weaves her back together. Poetry and place and travelling to a world she has never visited before, yet which still knows her somehow. As I spoke, I was a little unnerved by a woman with a knowing gaze at the back of the packed room and the eerie familiarity she possessed. Was she a cousin, a relative long lost that I should, but did not remember? Her ethereal cyan eyes were strangely familiar. She came and introduced herself after the talk, putting out her hand. 'Hallo', she said. 'I'm your book cover. I am Olive.' It may have been an old picture of her, but the gaze was unmistakable. Yes, I thought. Knowing.

It is the idea of finally knowing, albeit in a different way, what reading can bring to us as writers, that has held me in the thrall of this novel for well over a decade now. The bind for me is in finding my own voice to give words to this, a bind thrice laden: by my appreciation for what this text does, then for Professor Jones as my PhD supervisor and finally for her as an Australian writer and thinker who has given so much to us as a nation. This is made more poignant in the belated recognition given to her latest novel, *The Death of Noah Glass*, which has recently won the Prime Minister's Literary Award. I know she does not write for awards, but this recognition was overdue. *Syncharitiria.* Congratulations. It is a much more beautiful word in Greek, is it not? There are many Greek words that sing to me as I read her books; three in particular come immediately to mind: *ekphrasis* (I speak out), *ana khronos* (against time) and of course the verb *hyphainein* (to weave). I know that this word is also used to refer to giving counsel and weaving wiles.

I started this letter earlier in the year. At that point in the Orthodox calendar, it was *Fota* (Epiphany) and in Cyprus that is the day we give our gifts. It may help, reader, if I think of this almost as a letter to you both, to you and for Gail, a small one in thanks for the literary illuminations. I hope, reader, you will not mind if it is not only for you. For as I have said my people are many, and found in unlikely places.

Another Greek word comes to mind as I write: *makarios* (blessing). I can only read as an Australian writer through my own lens. My reading is infused with the traces of walnut *glyko* and dark treacle-syrupy coffee.

My words will never be as lyrical as those in *Sixty Lights*, but surely that is what teachers are: guides to motivate us to be better writers, partly by a careful reading of their work. Then putting what we learn on the page. Some days placing anything on the page.

Since I cannot talk to you of all that I have in me about this novel, let me do something simple and tell you of three of the kinfolk I have found in it. One of the most precious moments in my reading life was to encounter one of its main characters, Honoria, on the stagecoach. She is heading towards Melbourne when destiny upturns the carriage she is travelling in, literally and metaphorically. Just before the accident she is reading *Jane Eyre* and seeking love, while remaining wholly herself. I have read *Sixty Lights* many times, sometimes for permission to revel in the snapshots, to revisit favourite lines and turn them over in my mind, wondering what I think of them. Sometimes I read it because I want again to have Honoria contemplate this next line. 'She travelled *Jane Eyre*' (12).

Honoria travels *Jane Eyre*, and later so too does her daughter Lucy. Those of you familiar with *Sixty Lights* could well have been reading my description of Jane earlier in this essay, asking, could you not, was I talking of Jane or Lucy? Lucy Strange is perhaps my second favourite character in the book. Not fitting in, seeking her folk, plain, smart, a woman to whom art gives flashes of joy. Whose heart knows her folk. The *flaneur*.

Lucy has the adventures that Honoria longs for. Both are orphans, both fall into unlikely loves. One reader does marry him and one does not. There is a moment in the text where the playfulness delights me and I laugh aloud. When 'Lucy knew herself double' (83) I could not help but think how the characters over two generations play out different parts of Brontë's heroine. One falls for a hero who is not quite Byronic, but more ironic anti-hero. Rather than being intrigued by her mind, William, her first love, cannot really see her. Lucy is a creature before her time and more in keeping with our time, 'entirely modern, a woman of the future' (141). Has she inherited the story in the womb and carried it across time and place? Do we *all* inherit stories and carry them across time and place? But in *Sixty Lights* it is not in love but in friendship that Lucy's mind first meets a better match. Her unlikely soulmate, Isaac Newton. What pleasure is there in the naming of these characters? It is always a good reminder to me to have a little personal fun when I write.

One of Lucy's adventures takes her to Bombay, as a possible bride to Isaac, the man in the gilded frame. Yet Lucy, on her voyage over, falls for the man who knows about words, and one of his words entrances Lucy: 'bioluminescence' (110). It is a word well worth falling in love with after all, unlike William, who says it. But Lucy learns many languages on the ship across.

Perhaps there is a moment of epiphany for readers at the midpoint of the novel when Lucy is in-between worlds: literally, on the voyage from London, and figuratively, between youth and adulthood. Lucy is reading novels in the library onboard the ship going to new worlds. We are reading her reading novels and the meta-fiction asks us to consider this: 'She thought for the first time what it meant to read a novel? What process is this? What self-complication?' (114).

If you wish to write, I guess you too will need to ask such questions. In a moment of candour, Lucy tells Isaac that she feels imprisoned. I cannot help but think of Jane pacing back and forwards along the corridors and of course Bertha physically restrained above her. They know there is a world of different hues out there. Brighter ones. Confined to a world that does not understand either of them, Jane and Lucy learn to speak, one literally and one through her images. It strikes me that it is the intellectual companionship Lucy finds with Isaac that gives birth to the realisation in the novel that she has always been a photographer. What has Lucy given me as a writer? Questions. 'How, she wondered silently, to attest to it all? All the lights, all the darks, all the blotted cloudings in between' (147).

Is it a hard thing, reader, to be told that reading this text has helped me to write because it has made me sit with these enigmatic questions? These very questions engrossed me as I tried to decide what part of Cypriot history my PhD novel would tell. The lights – the wife of a freedom fighter against the British refusing to give up his whereabouts despite a British gun being held to her temples, the darks – my father's back being broken in the same battle against the British in the 1950s, the blotted cloudings: that fighting for independence two decades later brought invasion. In the end, I found that if as a writer you sit long enough in silence, and for me, stare long enough at the photographs of another time and place, you will find the story hiding behind them.

Reader, you must excuse the fact that I do not tell you the plot of *Sixty Lights*. Or about the skies as the boats sail. Or about the shifts from Australia to London or to Bombay. I want instead to tell you about Molly, she whom I ache for the most. It is she who cleans up after death visits time and again, she who knows the names of the flowers, who has so much stolen from her, so yes, maybe she is my favourite kin in the text. Or maybe what I like best in this novel is the way she is described: 'the wine-dark Molly Minchin' (52). I adore that phrase. It is one of my favourite translations. Fancy turning Homer's epithet from *The Odyssey* to mark a character, with the trope harking back to another possible translation: wine-*faced* sea. Ah, the weavings of myth and the women who tell them.

Reader, come and eavesdrop on a real moment of time. If this letter was for the author and not you, this is what I might say. Dear Gail, as one of my PhD supervisors, you know well my predilection for the Mediterranean. Especially a small divided country at the crossroad of three continents. When it came to needing to give myself permission to write in the interweaving way I favour, I admit, I felt that like Arthur, who is driving the carriage that overturns with his future in it: 'Honoria Brady was the accident he had given up hoping for' (15). I came into my postgraduate study anxious to learn how to produce a chronological narrative, which as we both know is not my style at all, nor how I see the world. I thank you, because in reading your books I have learnt as you told me once that *a novel can be anything it likes*. Anything you like. You make me sit with questions. The haunting question for me is still, '[w]hat shall Lucy do with her inheritance of story?' (73).

The inheritance I seem to have taken from this text is about weaving. Time and again I see how your structure is the loom and how other stories are rewoven through it repeatedly. Again, we have spiralled back to supervision. Reader, can I tell you of a moment where in reading: 'A single sentence had reorganised the presences of the world' (55)? It was from another Australian author, the Melbourne-based Greek Cypriot poet Angela Costi. It was the moment where I found the voice I would give to the exegesis. The moment where I said I was interested in how writing was like making lace, having found her poem that formed around the trope:

> thread weave through out and in,
> our skin an embroidery of old maps and new. (66)

In response to this idea, Professor Jones handed me a reading list. On it was *A Penelopean Poetics* by Barbara Clayton, who proposes that we can examine literary texts using Penelope as a model of a 'potential bardic figure, a weaver of song, and the implications that her *metis* [twisting of the plot] is predicated upon its own undoing' (23). This idea of writing as Penelope weaves, threading an idea by day and erasing it at night, leaving only a ghostly trace, is evident in *Sixty Lights*. Talking of Wilkie Collins and a woman in white (one may smile, thinking of the cover), Lucy comments about how this encounter is the end rather than the beginning of the story. 'But in her mind now, the novel unplaited and reversed' (243). This process of weaving in and out of time and across texts, gathering shadow-like traces, enabled me to both write my exegesis on Cypriot women's poems as a form of mediation about the

Turkish invasion in 1974, and my accompanying novel *Images of the Missing* – and then to read texts anew. By examining both the process of how Penelope weaves, and what her unweaving and reweaving added to the story, Clayton suggests we may establish an alternative way to read a text. As a reader, I revel in how *Sixty Lights* weaves and reweaves aspects of *Jane Eyre*, *Great Expectations* and many other tales, both literally and figuratively, as the stories replay generation after generation. I loved the trope of the accidental reworked, when Jane meets Rochester when his horse slips on ice, and Honoria meets Arthur when the carriage tips over.

What I relish about this novel is the way it reworks ideas and images from different angles, unsettling concepts across the arc of time. If I was to bring the author a real gift it would be a Liberty handkerchief from a favourite store of mine, Beautiful Things. I would make sure it was crumpled, not ironed, in keeping with the novel's concept of time. Well, maybe not crumpled, but pleated. Then I would tell her how much I treasured the lightning stories, most particularly when Arthur, asked by his new wife Honoria for his stories, cannot tell the one that haunts him most. As a child he and his mother have just avoided death and it is of such importance that it becomes, often like the moments that truly mark us, *untellable*. I have been spellbound by the moment in the text when Arthur's mother carries a burnt-out umbrella after this. It is described as 'a Florentine halo, through which, in dazzling mauve, shone spokes of storm-swept sky' (50). What this moment teaches me is what language and image can be. Impossibly beautiful. I make my students draw images from text all the time. I want to see what they see. I am always humbled by the visions of the next generation. Here is a true story, it is not yet a few days old.

This story begins with a drawing. It starts anew with an image drawn by one of my former high-school students, Natasha. Unbeknownst to her, it was a birthday gift to the dead. This student (thrice gifted – a national Australian swimmer, a stupendous artist and fine mind) had sketched a portrait of my father, who had died in the previous year, when I was teaching her *Hamlet*. She sent it to me as a gift this Easter, two days before what would have been his eightieth birthday. And as I tried to find my own words to thank her and realised they were inadequate, I turned back to *Sixty Lights*. I sent these words: 'I will speak to her of all ... my yearning to create an artwork that summons one, just one, sure and precise memory, immediate as a photograph' (215–6).

Ekphrasis has fascinated me as a writing tool for decades now. So many threads in Gail Jones' work speak out texts across time. The inheritance of stories in this text allows the next generation to bring a transformed telling: 'Looking at photos cracked open time. / Lucy Strange saw both the past and the future' (233). I too have lived this. A moment when a photograph ruptures time. My PhD novel *Images of the Missing* started as a love story, but I wrote myself out of this idea and I knew that it was not the real tale I wanted to tell. Sometimes walking the labyrinth is the only way to find the thread, so early one morning when I was in Cyprus to research, in the old city of Lefkosia, I did just that. I started asking questions of strangers and finally it led me to MAM bookshop. Mentors come in all shapes; mine that day was white-haired and immaculately dressed, and sized me up before answering my questions. Once satisfied with my intention: 'I want to know about the stories no one else has told about the women refugees in 1974', she told me to wait upstairs while she descended into the caverns beneath her store to bring up the riches. The pile of books were water stained. She had kept them three decades. Slowly, she opened one and flicked the pages until she saw the image she wanted, then started talking about the shot.

It was a photo I was familiar with. It was of a mother and her four children, I assumed, running from the invaders with terrified looks on their faces. I asked her about the family. 'Look more closely', the old woman told me. 'They are not related by blood, those children were orphans.' She knew the young woman in the image, who took the brood by the hand and ran. Which got me thinking about women's hands, about what they do in war. About how photos can both be true and yet our readings of can them be fabricated – simultaneously. How they can open up and shut down ideas.

Which brings me to mystery. Reading Ramona Koval's *Books and Writing* interview with Jones, I was strangely affirmed to hear her discuss an improbable moment around her writing process. She discussed the fact that one of the inheritances of her familial stories was the suicide of her great-grandfather after the death of his wife, leaving his children 'doubly orphaned' (6). This was a connection she had not made when writing the text that uses this very phrase, about children who live this loss. When we write it seems at times things we have lived and read come back to us involuntarily. Mysteriously.

Which brings me to the Greek word *mimeisthai* (to imitate). Years after writing *Images of the Missing* I realised how integral *Sixty Lights* had been to my craft. In my own book these were the threads: my mute photographer, my snapshots of the refugee camps, the gift of *Special Things Seen* (86). There was me using *ekphrasis* in ways only a reader of contemporary Cypriot women's poetry may notice. There was me playing with the loops of time, with repetition and then and then and then and then. But most strongly there were the improbable friendships between unlikely characters. None of these decisions were entirely conscious as I wrote it then, but looking back, almost a decade later, all are evident.

I would never for a moment assume I have succeeded in any of these undertakings. Nevertheless, *Sixty Lights* gave me the courage to write moments, to weave and reweave. Which brings us to time and its circles. I love the ironies of the writing life. In my study, I wanted so much to learn how to write a tightly crafted chronological narrative. Instead, I learnt from reading this novel that each of us has a different vision of time, and mine is more in keeping with Penelope's – a weaving, an unweaving. How to end? Simply.

Dear Gail,
I thank you because your novel has allowed me my peculiarity
as a writer.
'I photograph you in my mind,
Your affectionate friend' (202),
IS.

Lines of sight:
Living images in
the short fiction
of Gerald Murnane

Stephanie Bishop

For some years I circled Gerald Murnane's fiction without finding an entry point. It was like being stuck on some troublesome link road where I couldn't find the turn-off that would take me deeper into the surrounding landscape: grassy, flat. Fields of wheat maybe, or perhaps something wilder. Easy to recognise and yet somehow impossible to get into. The repetitive nature of this travelling started to irritate. So many people said there was an experience there to be had, that it was worth the journey, only how did I find my way to it? Occasionally I would make progress, only to discover that my attention, so carefully focused and steady to begin with had shot off somewhere – a stone skimming over the smooth surface of the prose – and vanished. Over and over again I read a few pages, then closed the book.

*

It is easy to read anticipating a familiar set of experiences. To read with the assumption that the expectations we, as readers, have been trained to hold will once again be met, and that once this happens we'll be free to mark this or that piece of fiction as a 'good story'. These readerly expectations are often to do with character and form – we anticipate the rising structure of a story, the presence of dialogue and exposition, each taking turns to move us swiftly along, deeper into the drama of human lives. Some description here and there to set the scene, although not so much as to delay our progress.

But there are certain kinds of work which, in refuting these expectations, also refute that mode of reading. They have a kind of fizz to their edges, like an electromagnetic field that the mind is caught or repelled by. There is a charge to them. I'm not sure that 'write what you know' is useful advice, but I'm even more wary of any suggestion that one should *read* what one knows, or rather, that one should read for what one knows, or that one should read in order to find, reaffirmed on the page, what one thinks one already knows, but maybe doesn't. 'I can relate to this', my students say in response to certain works, pleased to discover this, to be able to say this, to assert literary judgment on the basis of such recognition. There is nothing wrong – and often something profoundly important – in seeing your experiences magnified and rearranged in the pages of someone else's fiction, in that deepening of understanding, that camaraderie of shared feeling. It is a form of human communion. But this attitude, if too rigid, if fixed too hard on the idea of identification, can also be a dangerous limit and mark a premature closing-down of the possibilities for experience.

*

One goes to art for the adventure. To feel those very same borders blur and undo themselves. This is a process, and one that sometimes requires a chaperone or provocateur. In this context refusal or dislike is still a response, a lead, signs that some button has been pushed. 'Nope, I thought it was just boring – I couldn't finish it', my students are sometimes known to say. Or they stare at the table, pick at the hole in the knee of their jeans. I have seen a T-shirt emblazoned with the phrase *I Am the Anticlimax*. Very often they don't know what it was that bored them, or when, exactly, the boredom started, or why they couldn't find a way into the piece of writing. The experience of boredom itself doesn't necessarily warrant their attention. They can say, blithely, again, 'I don't know. I just couldn't relate. It just wasn't relatable', suggesting that the work didn't step up enough to meet them on their own terms, or that it failed to reaffirm life as they knew it, as they recognised it. They needed, as we often do, a point of connection to start from. Connection, though, is different from a mirror. What they were perhaps missing – as I have also missed, returning to certain books over and over again, in the hope that maybe this time the words would unlock themselves – is that they haven't yet figured out how to meet the work at its own level, to meet it where it is, to read it as it is asking to be read, as it stands, for the experience it contains. I think of that grassy field in the distance, the road I couldn't find. The years spent wandering. With the exception of a bold few, this is what they often tell me when I give them Murnane's work to read, in the early days of their studies. They collectively stare intently at their screens, hoping I do not pick them out to speak, to elaborate. Only when I say, 'I agree with you, I used to feel like that too', do they look up, curious.

I read, and re-read, and read again alongside them. Out loud, and to each other, and to ourselves, breaking it down. Sometimes sentence by sentence. Then paragraph by paragraph. For me, this is where the teaching becomes interesting. There are a few significant junctures where the act of reading and the act of writing begin to double up and overlap, and the sense of readerly muddlement is one of these; because such reading works in both directions, across both activities, and investigations in one area lead readily to discoveries in the other. Most of the time, when I look over a draft of my own fiction, there are two warring versions present. The first is the idea of the work that I started with: the thing I'd like to think I have written, and that I have been trying to write. The second version is what is actually there on the page, which is often a mess of scraps, half-chapters, fragments that appear in the wrong place. The pattern isn't clear. The very problem of the work is obscure. Too many things are wrong to know which loose thread to pull at. Which to weave back in. There is both too much and not enough going on: the mess is repellent, too difficult. If I knew what the biggest problem was I might be able to fix it. I have to find a way in. If I could just read the work well enough, and closely enough, with sufficient critical nous and practical know-how. Half the challenge, or maybe all of it, is just trying to understand what is there, to see it for what it is. This is how my students must also face their work. We might read our drafts in search of the ideal version that we began with, hoping to find this confirmed. But if this is the mode of reading that we rely on, we will completely fail to recognise what has in fact been written, which may not only be radically different from the ideal, but work by different rules, proceed according to a different logic. I ask them to put their expectations on hold in order to see what exists on the page and, perhaps more importantly, to sustain a kind of attention that is not about the comprehension of something complete and entire, a kind of attention that cannot cherry-pick for argument's sake, that is not concerned with forming an opinion. A kind of attention that can tolerate a maximum of uncertainty and instability. An attention that is both loose and sharp, curious, probing, exploratory, alert to uneasy sensations and contradictions, able to sit in the midst of this difficulty, refusing quick conclusions. One that does not read for meaning or attempt to reduce the work to a summary, but can stand back a little and just look at what is there. I ask them to be both patient and stubborn. Be patient stubbornly. The room falls silent. When they start to speak it is in fragments, half-thoughts, flashes of words, they begin to finish each other's sentences.

I once heard a gardener say that he learned how to garden only by killing a great many plants. The same might be said of writing, and reading fiction: the lesson is one of observation, and the refinement of this. The conditions for plant life are often mysterious, and complex in their variations over time, noticed only through the repetitive tasks carried out by the gardener over the passage of months, years, the seasons. Over a similar period of time I repeatedly encountered what I thought of as the opaquer sections of Murnane – the bits over which my attention skimmed and where the mind would not take root – with enough frequency that these sections started to form a pattern in my mind. What I first thought was erroneous, and ill-fitting, was actually what the work was doing on its own terms. Once I could see it as a pattern, I began to attend to it, dig around a little. I started to see it for what it was, and as it is. Look closer: the more frequently I encountered what I had thought of as weedy and errant passages, the stronger the pattern, and the greater the attention I gave to it. Over time, the sections that at first seemed obscure to me began to unfold, and to expand, to make a network of my attention across a number of disparate fictions; 'Stream system', 'First love', 'In far fields', 'Pink lining', 'Emerald blue', on and on across the body of Murnane's work as a whole.

I ask my students to apply the same question to the things they are reading as to their own work, and to also apply this question to the life or experience that they might be writing about, or drawing on or responding to in some way: what do you notice?

*

First impressions can be accurate, and, at the same time, establish expectations that are misleading. In the opening paragraphs of Murnane's short fiction there is the presence, very often, of numbers; '[p]age 66A of Edition 18', 1964 compared to 1957, '[d]uring the last two hours of the Saturday and the first two hours of the Sunday', '1 to 100' (Murnane 25, 105, 145, 217). I notice this because I don't really understand numbers. They scare me a little. They put me off. I sometimes write them back to front. In Murnane's short fiction, there are often two numbers present in the opening, which form first points of orientation, and mark a difference between multiple states or times, setting up a tentative frame in which the story will move. The numbers allow the narrator to shift back and forth between different moments of history or experience: compare and contrast. But this understanding is slow in coming. Initially, at least, the presence of numbers, combined with a certain formality of diction, a general absence of adverbs and a complete absence of contractions, suggests an attitude of glassy, slightly eerie, precision; 'On the day before I began to write this piece of fiction, I received in the post two items from a man who was born when I was already eleven years of age' (418). Time splays: we go backwards (the day before), then forwards (the day of writing), then very far backwards again (the man born) then forwards a bit (the eleven-year-old), which is still backwards in time relative to the opening.

*

The apparent logicality that is suggested by numbers is something of a ruse: a join-the-dots activity that ends with an abstract configuration and not the horse and rider you expect. In Murnane's fiction, the starting point is rarely where you think it is. One is quickly disorientated; the opening scene – the scene suggested in the first paragraph – is often not pursued or at least not immediately, and never by way of a direct route. Instead, Murnane's narrators and protagonists take this moment of beginning as a springboard off which to leap back into the prehistory of that same scene. The prehistory is often abstract, visual, and comes before the story proper starts, or before the story deepens, because to say it progresses or proceeds is not quite accurate. Or else the numerical presence is summoned in order to draw attention to an experience of simultaneity – the train of thought that was occurring while the last paragraph was being written. More often than not this ulterior thought process (the previous and the simultaneous) is concerned with an image that has appeared, unbidden, in the mind of the writer, and that seems to have caught them unawares, as if to say: this is what I noticed.

Murnane is a writer of vision over and above any of the other senses. Each fiction traces the way in which two or more images overlap in the mind, in relation to the two or more timeframes set out in the opening. There are many ways of reading his work. But the overwhelming centrality of images has long struck me as one of the most significant and magical properties of his fiction. The initial numerical precision can mislead, suggesting logicality, when what tends to ensue is a strange and roving matrix of associations: images that slowly accumulate history through a web of connections. The strong contrast between the visual image and the numbered states puts the reader off the scent. It is easy to miss the turn-off, to attend too closely to the false order, to hunt the initial suggestion of numerical logic down to the end and not find the thing one went looking for.

*

More often than not, when I ask my students what they notice, this is a question to do with sensation. What are they alive to in the passage of their own life? When I ask what they notice in the reading of another's work, this too is a question to do with some experience of feeling: bewilderment, curiosity, an unclear burgeoning of affection, delight, sometimes things as strong as love or suffering or repulsion or disgust, however inexplicable these responses might at first seem. They are not allowed to explain or justify their responses with the word 'like': I did/ didn't like it. Or rather, they are not permitted to end them there. We try to trace these back, whatever feelings we may have, whatever lawless sensations, to their origin in the formalities of the work – the language, the patterning, the tone. I'm trying to avoid the question of 'What does the work mean?' – a question that easily bores me, or that seems secondary and dependent on the initial experience of their impressions. To repurpose Emerson, what is their original relation to that work? And what is the work's relationship to its own moving parts? What conversation does it have with itself? What opens up inside of you as a result of the work, and then: what happens in the textual surface of the work, in its various formalities, that unlocks this foreign vein of feeling? Run it forwards. Play it back. Try the two tracks at the same time.

*

Murnane's two (or more) timeframes are always proximate, the narrative tracing the difference between the past and the nearer present, coming close to the present but never inhabiting it exactly or for long. The attention to images allows these timeframes to syncopate. Sometimes the images refer to the same place at different times, sometimes to different times within the same place. They establish a set of co-ordinates within which the narrative can oscillate rather than progress. 'Stream system', for example, opens with the physical presence of 'two bodies of yellow brown water' compared to 'two bodies of pale blue, each with a distinctive outline' as they appear in the street directory map, the difference in time being between the near present 'this morning' and, roughly, 1943, when the narrator was a child, a point from which we move forwards, towards the contemporary (25). The image on the map that designates the stream system establishes, in the mind of the narrator, a series of further images associated with that body of water, images found in his own history and that are somehow like that body of water on the map or that remind him of that outline, and that take him closer, each time, to the real creek water that he has just walked by and knew as a child. The images of the bodies of water and their outline loop through his past: the outline of a piece of jewellery seen in a catalogue in 1946, or the outline of the stream 'seen' in the shape 'of a pair of female lips boldly marked with lipstick', or in the drooping moustache of his grandfather (33). The fiction traces these associations as we shift backwards and forwards in time, developing, through deviation, the original or primary image; the bodies of water. In this fiction, as in many others, any unpredictable move of visual association is mediated by numbers and dates that mark in time the point of an image's reappearance: 'At some time during his ninth year, when he was trying to remove from his mind the image of the face of one or another schoolgirl' (308), '[d]uring the years 1961 and 1962 the man who had seen in his mind at Hepburn Springs in 1987 a young woman' (185). While the images seem, in themselves, to be random, the narrative impetus is to trace the precise order of these images as they occur in the associating consciousness of the narrator: to trace the logical development of this wayward visual experience.

*

Always, in every story, there is such an image, a key image that triggers the beginning of an associative web: the image of a cloud, a box of books, a man in the grass. The image is present, the narrative circles it, the image develops in complexity in line with its growing associations. It is almost impossible to reduce these stories to a summary of the plot, to explain what it is that 'happens' in them. A man looks at a map. Another man, or maybe the same one, recounts the way he takes stock of his bookshelves. Another imagines living in a house painted cream and dark green. We readily think of 'fiction' as meaning 'story', but this can be an unhelpful constraint. A story implies a particular way of shaping a narrative. Whereas fiction suggests a mode of practice, or attitude towards the material, and is at heart chameleonic; a fiction can adopt any shape or form it chooses. Murnane's short fiction claims this flexibility: these are not so often stories as maps, constellations, networks. In Murnane's short fiction the very idea of what we commonly think of as a story is inverted and given to us inside out. We do not know what the central image of any given fiction means. The narrator or protagonist does not seem to know exactly what this image means, and they pursue its development, and trace its presence not for this reason – not to uncover its meaning, but in order to understand its origin and the web of associations in which it lives in the image system of their own history, in the dense fusion of layered time. One memory image undergoes variations over time, shifting a little each time it is revisited in the mind. But what kind of images are these? What are the qualities that mark them out, what are their special powers? How do they have the force to hold the narrative together, to be both vital organ and connective tissue?

*

I often ask my students to consider the poetics of a piece of work; to consider the features or laws that govern the development of any given piece of work, on its own terms. This too is what they must come to understand when considering their own writing and assessing what they have written, without yet perhaps understanding exactly what it is. What are its habits, its rules, its preferences, its way of moving? Murnane is an interesting writer to examine on this front because his fiction seems to confound any preordained ideas about narrative logic, rejecting any prefab model of 'the short story'. At certain points in his fiction Murnane himself offers a kind of meta-fictional gloss on how this logic works in his own writing processes:

> I would then explain to my student that the sentence was a report of a detail of an image in my mind. I would explain further that the image was not an image that I had seen in my mind recently for the first time or an image that I saw in my mind only at long intervals but an image that I saw often in my mind. I would explain that the image I had begun to write about was connected by strong feelings to other images in my mind.

> I would then go on to tell my students that my mind consisted only of images and feelings; that I had studied my mind for many years and had found in it nothing but images and feelings; that a diagram of my mind would resemble a vast and intricate map with images for its small towns and with feelings for the roads through the grassy countryside between the towns. Whenever I had seen in my mind the image that I had begun to write about just then, so I would say to my student, I had felt the strong feelings leading from that image far out into the grassy countryside of my mind towards other images, even though I might not yet have seen any of those other images. (218)

The self here is not a coherent character pursuing their desires, but a subject wholly composed of images that embody, or are infused by, states of feeling. It is a sentiment that recurs almost verbatim across the short fictions:

> He had come to believe he was made up mostly of images. He was
> aware only of images and feelings. The feelings connected him to
> the images and the images to one another. The connected images
> made up a vast network. He was never able to imagine this network
> as having a boundary in any direction. He called the network, for
> convenience, his mind. (295)

This network comprises dynamic and not descriptive images: images prone to change, progress, rippling with mobile energy. Often these are images of landscapes in which human life unfolds. Sometimes they are remembered landscapes, while at others they are fantasies, hypotheticals. The images mean first one thing then something else, they signal one connection then another, they become a nexus for multiple states of feeling. These are not the 'dead images' that come to us 'from cameras' or 'the contrived images that might come by way of cinema screens or television sets': foreign and unsustaining images that the narrator imagines expelling from the mind as one might pass something through the digestive system – 'pebbles or buttons that I might have swallowed' (241–3). Rather, these images – febrile, mobile, fraying with associations – are what Murnane describes as 'living image[s]', images that originate within the grassy landscape of one's own mind (294). Although they are not the mechanical images of the camera, they are experienced as cinematic; 'I have seen [them] as though on a screen in a cinema in my mind' (254).

*

Over and over again what the narrator or protagonist of Murnane's short fiction wants to know is why a certain image appears and lodges itself in his mind in this way. '[H]ow that image ha[s] come to be there' (295), what is its emotional origin, what is its relationship to his own lived history, how might he understand his history in relation to the patterning of this image, its myriad associations, what is the cause of its repetition and longevity? The short fictions trace the development of this epiphanic knowledge. Such knowledge is not much concerned with the meaning of the image, which is never glossed, never para-phrased, the instrumental understanding of an image never extrapolated from the vision. The epiphany is reached when the cause of the image's endurance and repetition is located in time, when the image and the number at last come together, the emotional and historical significance drawn to the surface of the image, infusing it entirely. The image holds locked inside itself the long history of its own associations and reappearances; the journey of the fiction is to excavate this history until we find within it the origin of the image. Murnane's visual epiphany tilts the focus towards the internal life, shifting our attention towards the development of understanding, rather than the development of external action. The magical trick within these moments that are often positioned as conclusions is that this final feat of location is itself also an image: a vision of a field of grass concludes with the final variant of that field of grass, the *ur* version of that field of grass, the grass to begin and end all grass, the field of grass that explains the presence of the field of grass.

*

These images have a kind of transmigratory power: they are seen first in association with one body; and later, without us knowing why, they are seen in association with another body, belonging first to one person, then another, moving through a series of different states before the narrator finalises the constellation. If the conventional narrative form relies on a principle of causation (what happens, and why, and what state of change does this bring about?), Murnane's fiction flips this. The mystery of the images is preserved through the refusal to gloss, extrapolate, or provide a summarised understanding. This refusal makes the images more complex, rather than less. It honours the power of the image's recurrence, its aliveness. Both the source of the image and its repetitions are observed, allowing the image to become multidimensional. These living images, Murnane writes, are the receptacles of 'precious knowledge ... knowledge being ... always something visible' (294). To de-visualise the image by translating it into a verbal insight of the sort that can often mark the epiphany (*and she finally understood, saw him for what he was, recognised that ...*), would be to reduce the form of knowledge that Murnane's fictions seek to map. I don't know what the field of grass 'means' in any simple way. But the less I understand it, the less I need to. The greater the density of its associations the more robust its power, the better its capacity to endure, the more vibrant its resonance. Each fiction is less a story than a genealogy of these living images: the box of books, the stream, the 'house painted cream and dark green' (113), the 'water-filled ruts that had been in his mind for thirty-three years before he began to understand how that image had come to be there' (295).

An obsidian mirror: David Malouf's *Ransom*

A.S. Patrić

The book is a mirror. Not like the one you find on a bathroom wall. More the kind you find in volcanic glass, in which you see yourself with the distortions that lava left beneath the surface. Gone cold now but that living, molten heat is still there in what a book shows you. Perhaps you've seen obsidian. That's what comes to *my* mind, at least. Obsidian often looks much like the unlit screen of your phone. The Aztecs and Mayans used obsidian to find their reflections. They also used sharpened pieces of this volcanic glass to cut the hearts out of sacrificial victims in their religious ceremonies. Writers have used paper, and now more often use an illuminated screen, for our own forms of sacrifice. We cut reflections out of an erupting world. Afterwards, it appears to be inert – a file to click on or dry paper bundled up into a book.

When I began writing this essay the mirror I had in hand was the clearer kind, glass with a sheet of silver behind it. Every detail could be reflected spotlessly. I was going to look at David Malouf and offer you pristine portraits; the way he rendered aspects of himself, what I saw of myself, and perhaps the kinds of reflections you might find as well. Then the fires began to burn across our country at the end of 2019 and went on for the entire summer. Satellite photos showed us the whole continent billowing smoke, drifting out across the azure Pacific Ocean. A pall of ash-grey air drifted across our towns and cities. I began to lose sight of Malouf, the prospective reader of my essay and most of the reflections I had of myself. It would clear eventually, I thought. The mirror would be useful once again but then the pandemic arrived – a fire of the blood that cannot be stamped out and billowing fear like smoke, this time across the entire planet. The world and all our masked faces became almost unrecognisable. What use are reflections (literary or otherwise) now?

If I still had that clear glass, bathroom-mirror-perfect, I'd write about the plot of *Ransom* and the way Malouf is searching for himself in two different figures from the world of the Ancient Greeks, one the rampaging hero of the Trojan war, Achilles, and the other, the old king about to be destroyed, Priam. Reflections returned to the eye from obsidian however are not the same. Similar details remain, but now, I also see the image of a falling man. He wore a white shirt over black pants and he died in New York City at precisely 9:41 am, 11 September 2001.

Near the opening of *Ransom* we read: 'He had entered the rough world of men, where a man's acts follow him wherever he goes in the form of a story. A world of pain, loss, dependancy, bursts of violence and elation; of fatality and fatal contradictions, breathless leaps into the unknown; at last of death – a hero's death out there in the full sunlight under the gaze of gods and men' (6).

It was in 2001 that Malouf began developing what would become *Ransom*, a piece of writing for himself rather than for an audience. Malouf has said that writing *Ransom* was a way to process the attack on the World Trade Center and after he finished it, the manuscript sat in a drawer for years without thought of a publisher (Ashcroft, 2010).

The trauma of seeing those two immense towers tumbling down into the heart of the archetypal modern metropolis did not belong only to Malouf. The Falling Man, captured on film in the clear light of a bright morning, almost floating down in a gentle tumble from the top of one of those immense glass and metal towers – that image was a dark piece of volcanic glass, sharp enough to cut out anyone's heart. It would have taken, in reality, four or five seconds. Plummeting. No floating. It might have been an accident. The flames were raging right up through the building and people had broken through the windows to get air and to move further from those incinerating flames. So perhaps he simply went too far out onto a ledge, and slipped. He might have been pushed in the general panic. And then there's the possibility that he made a decision. To not choke and burn. To step out into the open air and to fall. The only certainty: this was not suicide. And the camera could not have caught this particular descent if it were a single instance. The photographer, Richard Drew, took many photos and had a chance to steady his camera. To set perfect focus in the mirror of his viewfinder. It's estimated that more than 400 people fell that day from those burning towers.

Trauma doesn't only present as pain. For me, the whole experience was unreal and numbing, more like watching a documentary turn into a thriller or horror – dazzling Hollywood special effects but with disappointing B-grade scripts handed impromptu to amateur actors. The grand spectacle confused the narrative we had accepted as reality and I simply didn't want to stick around for the denouement. Leaving the new global drama wasn't a choice and yet the thought of writing about it, going deeper into the experience, didn't cross my mind. As an Australian, it didn't feel like it was a story for me to tell. Americans would have to live directly in that unfolding narrative, as would those in the Middle East in the many years of US vengeance.

I didn't see the photo in 2001. Some people tried to ban the image, and others merely found it too painful to look at. I don't know if David Malouf saw the Falling Man then or since. He didn't *need* to see the image. The event had already struck him deeply enough to require a response. I did need the image though, for myself. One man falling 'out there in the full sunlight' made me feel the impact in my own body for the first time after the attack. Almost two decades have now passed since the Falling Man died and we still don't know his name for sure. The names of most of the 2977 who died because of the attacks on 11 September 2001 are known, first attributed to bodies and then carved into tombstones, but they have become to the general public even more anonymous than this one person falling some 90 floors to the concrete below. It's odd then to consider the fact that we remember the name of a man who fought in a war some 4000 years ago near the Aegean Sea (are barely able to discern fact from fiction, history from myth) and that a part of each of us is named after this man, Achilles.

Writers can now see with greater clarity the impact of those attacks and the world that stumbled out of that Manhattan rubble. Any number of narratives might be built on the new landscape that opened up for an author's mind since that day. In 2001, though, everyone knew that the world had become unrecognisable. That's true again for all of us living in 2020. Here again is an experience that is unreal and numbing, the doco that turns into a disaster flick with amateurish scripts and bad actors; this time without the Hollywood spectacle.

For some writers, as with David Malouf, looking to a point in the past that resembles the current moment will offer potent narrative options in which we can find reflections that can come alive in our writing. This essay is in itself a failure to deal with the tumult of an ongoing crisis and yet for me it also holds an obsidian-tinged hope that a previous global upheaval might show us how we can begin to gather up our courage to write again.

A second quote, this one not from the perspective of Achilles but the other narrative half of *Ransom*. King Priam reflects:

> 'There are things,' he says, almost under his breath, 'that once we
> have touched them, once they have touched us, we can never throw
> off, however much we scrub away at ourselves, however high the
> gods set us. In our nostrils, the stench is still there, the old filth

sticks. The smell of those others – which was my smell too, the smell of the slave's life I was being dragged away to – I can never rub off' (69).

It's easy to imagine people wearing masks, keeping a social distance from Priam as he speaks those words. Malouf had no conception of the world created by COVID-19 contagion but for writers who find themselves in this global panic, *Ransom* offers at least one method to struggle against things that cannot be thrown off. There is an endless array of potential narratives that are responsive to hope and imagination than the current crisis affords any of us. Not merely a flight of fancy ad infinitum, history has the literary benefit of being our larger reality.

All of history is who we were, perhaps via the direct route of DNA or reincarnation, but certainly the cultural legacy that informs not only our literature, but is the calibration of every word we speak. A writer who sets a story in the past can find that their fiction is given dimension simply through taking a deeper route through a broader reality beyond the contemporary drama, and allows a reader to come into direct contact with a more profound literary and spiritual self.

A direct parallel might yield fertile narratives for writers wondering which stories are reflective of the current moment. *Year of Wonders*, arguably a literary masterpiece, by another Australian writer, Geraldine Brooks, is a story set in an English village in 1666 as the bubonic plague rose again in different parts of Europe to decimate entire populations. The village chose to quarantine itself so that the disease might not spread further across England. Published in 2001, *Year of Wonders* was a response to the AIDS epidemic that had resulted in millions of deaths in the two decades prior. Writers need not restrict themselves to such direct parallel narratives. All that's necessary for any literary work to come alive is a deeper connection within the author. What this means is finding a narrative which can reflect the essential experience and core identity; it means using an obsidian mirror instead of simple representation or direct correlation, so as to grant the reader unexpected perspectives and insights otherwise impossible to find.

David Malouf recalled in 2001 what it felt like to be under attack, growing up in Brisbane during the Second World War (Ashcroft, 2010). The relentless Imperial Japanese military coming closer day by day, with brutal, seemingly unstoppable progress. A young boy at the time, he read a children's version of the Trojan War. As an old man, he considered the moment in Homer's epic poem where the raging Achilles brutally drags behind his chariot the corpse of his greatest opponent, Prince Hector. When Malouf developed King Priam as a character through the pages of *Ransom* he presented a father mourning not only the loss of a son and heir, but a king wanting to find another response to violence. Not surrender and not retribution. Malouf was looking for a deeper connection to humanity, both in the writing of the book, and between deeply embittered and entrenched enemies.

> Quietly, as they ate together, he and Achilles had discovered a kind of intimacy; wary at first, though also respectful, and at last quite easy, though Priam had to continually remind himself who it was he was breaking bread with, and what lay out there wrapped in a sheet and waiting to be reclaimed. (198)

Malouf started his career by writing poetry and the discipline such a concentrated craft developed can be found at the level of sentences, in his choice of words. There's never a lazy expression or flat sentence. That poetic sensibility can be seen in the subjective, felt experience in which each character has a deep presence within every passing moment of the story, as well as a strong focus on the perennial, central themes in life. Malouf's prose rarely affects the flowery or pompous elements that might arise when a poet writes novels.

This poetic sensibility not only makes for shorter novels with more driven narratives, it has given him an ear for the music in a word and the way it begins to sound when sentences beat with a rhythm. *Ransom* is read at *andante* tempo, where the reader enters the story and continues to move at a steady walking pace. When a writer can really lock into a steady rhythm, prose becomes hypnotic and the reader falls deeper into the fictive illusion of a novel. Malouf writes with superb tonal control and taut prose in which nothing is extraneous. His best narratives have a feeling of spaciousness, a surprising feature given that he always retains extreme thematic focus.

An example of this can be found if we contrast his narrative with other literary treatments of *The Iliad*. The modern psychological treatment given to Achilles has focused on his relationship with Patroclus, the man Hector killed in battle, and the reason for the horrific revenge. Titillating narratives tell us that Achilles and Patroclus were in love, and therefore the loss was not only of a comrade fighting on Achilles' behalf while he was absent from the fray, but also the heartbreaking loss of a lover. Instead of relying on pop-song rationale, Malouf draws a portrait of childhood friends growing up together, after Patroclus loses his father at an early age. Malouf increases the emphasis on these childhood reflections by having Achilles think of his own son, growing up without him, back in Greece, as the war with Troy drags on for years. When Priam finally reaches Achilles at the end of Malouf's book, he is not so much King Priam, full of wrath over the death of Prince Hector; he is simply a father who has lost his son. It's only through this connection that these warring foes can negotiate a successful ransom.

Malouf also brings an Australian tone to Homer's characters, without going so far as investing them with our accent. An American tone might drive these great ancient figures to proclaim their ambitions and fury in speeches. An English tone would perhaps be more sober, but there would be the double-bind of self-effacement which yet illuminates a deeper nobility. Each nation might bring its own unique perspective to such characters, but Malouf turns these epic heroes into regular people who all stand on the same ground, looking at each other on the same level. King Priam's companion as he crosses the battle lines is Somax, a character entirely of Malouf's making. There's no separation of high and low, king and peasant, as the Crown and a carter talk to each other, eat homemade pikelets or dip their bare feet in a cool stream. Somax is a bloke who owns a couple of mules and a cart, grinding out a living in the city of Troy. He could just as easily be from colonial Parramatta.

Writing in a historical context gives writers at any point of the geopolitical map a way of joining the largest global conversation there's ever been. Australian writing is often self-referential to the point of being hermetically sealed. It can feel like a breath of fresh air to open up to a far broader geography and historical context than can be found on this continent alone. David Malouf did this significantly with *An Imaginary Life* near the beginning of his career and now nearer the end with *Ransom*. In both instances he set his narrative in the ancient world, first of the Romans and then the Greeks. In these two books Malouf is in dialogue with, respectively, Ovid and Homer, literary immortals, grand voices that have spoken to generations for hundreds of years. A bit presumptuous in 1978 for an Aussie writer from literary backwater Brisbane, except that this has always been the way literature has worked, no matter who you are or where you came from. That was, at least, the galvanising realisation I had when I first read *An Imaginary Life* as a young poet in the eighties wondering at the possibility of a life as a writer.

With *Ransom*, Malouf enters a point in history in which an individual could become so significant that they would be deemed a hero, so invested with importance that they were thought to be inspired by the divine. Some of them were worshipped as gods after their deaths in a process called apotheosis. Our present cultural moment offers far fewer heroes. Perhaps actors and athletes can briefly become heroes, but even they are easily brought back down to earth. This might tell us something about the world we're living in now, but it also poses a new challenge for a writer creating fiction in the present moment.

The reason a hero arises in a narrative is because the author has a desire to address one of the great themes of history and life – what's worth living for and, conversely, what's worth dying for? Which is very much the focus of *The Iliad*. Every one of the many characters of Homer's epic addresses this theme in one way or another. Malouf chooses two characters, and both of them are heroes, because he too wants to ask that essential question. A hero need not be a soldier fighting a war, but the reader (and the writer) needs an extreme situation to be able to bring to life that essential question. Otherwise fiction falls into the general malaise of modern literature, in which characters are not defined by their personal sacrifice or willingness to accept extreme individual hardship to achieve a larger social good. The problem, as we've seen in 2020, is that the world beyond the page goes on demanding a response to the question of life and death.

When *Ransom* was published in 2009, it received a rapturous response both in Australia and internationally. It could easily have fallen into the category of historical fiction; been entertaining but ultimately forgettable. Certainly, the quality of Malouf's prose was a factor in *Ransom*'s success, yet he has brought that same care and focus to all of his many works. Malouf stands as an author who exemplifies the writer as artist. Such noble ambition can of course lead writers to produce philosophical, abstract novels that are beautiful bubbles floating in the air, bursting at the slightest touch of the actual world. *Ransom* stands as Malouf's great work because it was able to use an ancient historical narrative to reveal the constant elements within human life. The novel's success was primarily based on its relevance to who we are now.

Homer might have offered us the heroic paradigm to understand the struggles we each might face to bring meaning into our existence, but *The Iliad* also presents an entire, coherent cosmology. In the world of *Ransom*, the religion and cultural perspective of another society is not ignorantly dismissed as being idiotic or worthless. The god Hermes appears as a young boy by a river to escort Priam and Somax through the battle lines of the Trojan and Greek armies – otherwise an impossible action for two fellows on a cart drawn by a couple of black mules. Were sentinels really so lax, imagine the kind of havoc assassins and commandos could do in enemy camps while soldiers and generals were at their ease or sleeping. Malouf negotiates the miracle in his narrative in a kind of whisper of divine power: 'The captain and his companions stood as if spellbound, the hands on their half-drawn swords too heavy to lift, the tongues in their open mouths also stopped, and their feet, their breath' (163).

The divine not only exists in every aspect of the ancient Greek world, it permeates every moment – it guides, or even interferes, with our decisions as humans. The modern mind now only allows the gods to be seen as comic-book personifications. Malouf makes space in his novel for one of these divinities to playfully enter and depart, and in doing so he allows us a glimpse of another order of reality.

In Homer's *Iliad*, the many gods are in full view. Divinity is a constant factor, and the gods are features of the landscape that must be navigated and who often demand extreme forms of negotiation. Our cultural prejudice easily explains all this away as so much superstitious nonsense. Scientific materialism has arguably already reached the limits of its cosmological framework. We need only take a sober look at the state of the modern world, our environmental existentialism, warring political divisions, crushing cultural ennui, to see a general helplessness in navigating a viable future.

A fundamental reason why a modern writer might want to enter another historical context now is to find a subtle, sophisticated paradigm that is yet able to provide literary metaphors apt for investigating our ongoing chaos. In reading writers like Homer or, indeed, Sappho, Plato, Aristotle, Ovid, Epictetus, Seneca et al. we realise that we have never superseded philosophically any of these minds or the subtle, perceptive, profound worldview they shared, and invested with their entire lives. As were the lives of millions of others who might have no names now, yet all committed to helping the world evolve through the miraculous act of creating a clear reflection of humanity on a piece of paper. One might ask whether it is even possible for us to understand ourselves if the only reference point is our own generation.

As writers we are a part of a long sequence of communication. We might understand literature as a process of remembering, and that outside of our sphere of words, there is a great forgetting.

Ten thoughts on fiction that slays: Reading Julie Koh's satire in a post-truth pandemic

Beth Yahp

1.

In a year of fire, flood and plague, followed by forced immobility – birdsong filling our suburban skies instead of aeroplanes – the yearning for movement grows in me. I look out the window at the stunted cabbage tree and potted jade plants in the corner of the balcony where a fledgling butcherbird holds court, eyeing me through the window's glass, its only subject. It's brown-tinged, fluffy as a puppy, but with a fierce jet eye as murderous as the hook that will sharpen on the end of its upper bill. I know the grown butcherbird is lethal and what's more, impales its prey on sticks or hangs it in the forks of trees. Its cocked head is slightly mocking, its pointed gaze daring me to exit my glass cage. 'C'mon, let's tussle.'

Looking out past my two screens, in between Zoom classes and meetings, I think of Julie Koh's *Portable Curiosities*, both the title of her 2016 book and a travelling exhibition of 'crazy old mimes' in one of her stories. These Portable Curiosities are the very last of their kind, dressed only in nappies as they continue to passionately perform their almost extinct humanist or artistic professions – historian, glass artist – in black boxes with peepholes for the curious. Koh's stories are described as satirical, as well as 'absurdist, bleak and blackly comic' and Koh the author as 'not pulling any punches, weaving elements of the mysterious and the grotesque with the all-too-real' (Sophia Barnes in the *Sydney Review of Books*, 2016). The Portable Curiosities in her story 'Satirist rising' are billed as a public warning against irrelevance.

Alarmingly, Koh's story foretells the nose-diving trajectory of our already diminished state of the arts and humanities in Australia in 2020 – the arts, like universities and other precarity-fuelled industries, riven not just by a pandemic but by a government's ideological agenda, under cover of a pandemic.

The butcherbird's call, when it comes, is enchanting and musical, interspersed with harsher notes.

2.

I'm having trouble reading these days. I'm having trouble teaching, trying to inspire my writing students in their own reading and writing when all I see of them are their mostly blacked-out boxes in my Zoom window. I'm never sure if they're actually there. It goes without saying that I'm having trouble writing myself, but I know by now this is something perennial, coming and going like the seasons, like the baby butcherbirds and rosellas, and the occasional kookaburra that goes off like an alarm clock at 5 am.

Yet, in 2020, even the seasons seem unreliable.

Is the challenge to do with trying to read and write, in this year of disruption of biblical proportions; or is it trying to do so at a time when writers and readers, like artists and universities, have been officially designated 'non-essential' – no emergency JobKeeper to keep us in our jobs? Instead, we get a one-two punch to the gut of a massive fee hike for our arts and humanities students – future readers and writers, translators, lawyers, glass and performance artists, historians.

My brain can't take in the scale of 3 billion terrestrial vertebrates wiped out in the recent Black Summer fires that now seem so long ago, or the 2.2 million humans dead worldwide from COVID-19 and counting. After months of hand-washing, mask-wearing and hunkering down in the home office (aka bedroom), it feels like time itself is infected and scale gone wonky its symptom: everything seems simultaneously too fast and too slow, too big and too small, with no rabbit hole, magic potion or looking-glass needed to enter into this space of entrapment and excitation.

3.

The students who turn on their cameras look anxious over Zoom. I'm trying to impress upon them Julie Koh's use of precise concrete and sensory detail to evoke place and setting in her stories, her immaculate worldbuilding through bursts of thick description. I point out the almost dryly ethnographic documentation that freezes on the page an ethos, a zeitgeist, through the accumulation of ordinary objects and mundane atmospherics that we may notice in life but not note.

We read of the satirist in her story 'Satirist rising':

Her hotel room is very 2015. There is something consoling about it. A regular double bed with crisp white sheets, a bolster and two rows of pillows. A desk with a Curiosity Inn writing pad and a cheap plastic pen.

...

The window's fauxview is set so the room looks out over a
historically accurate city street and, in the distance, a motorway.
Above the motorway are green road signs bearing white arrows
and the names of unfamiliar – perhaps now obsolete – roads.
(30–31)

The overabundance of over-ordinary details grounds us in strict realist
mode, that straight man of fiction, suspending our disbelief even as
her characters may throw us hilarious asides and their situations and
predicaments leapfrog us into the absurd. Then their worlds, we realise
too late, have already tipped us into the most unfunny of extremes – still
laughing. It's a heady combination.

Some of my students' faces fill their own boxes as they lean in to
listen or speak, zooming in closer than I'd get to see them in our on-
campus classroom; others are blacked out, of course, though sometimes,
if they've forgotten to mute their mikes, we can hear their other devices
bleep or pling, or someone munching, or breathing.

We read about the black boxes with peepholes the satirist peers into
at the Curiosity Inn:

Under a spotlight, an elderly man in a nappy sits on a rotating
golden disc. His skin is a sickly white, his muscles wasted ... With
both hands, he seems to be twirling an invisible stick on its axis,
keeping it horizontal at all times.

In the second box, an old Asian lady ... She sits wide-eyed on her
rotating disc, watching her right hand move slowly through the air,
twisting and turning, fingers separating and coming together. It is
as if she has never seen a hand before.

In the third box, a black man with a white beard, his nappy
discarded on the floor, has stepped off his circular platform and

is pacing his box ... He pauses occasionally to shake a finger at an imaginary audience. (33)

Some of my own audience are almost miniaturised on my screen, attending class from way over on the couch or in bed, vague outlines in dimly lit rooms; other students' on-screen presence is even smaller, even further away when they're outside, hanging out their washing.

'Charlie! We can see you!'

I feel I should offer him extra marks for taking his laptop along, and the classroom with him, making everyone laugh for a bright, fleeting moment. The sky is blue and it's sunny out in the backyard. The Hills Hoist spins its colourful burden.

Usually, I don't move out of my chair or room.

I feel my mind, like my body, skewered, in lockdown.

4.

How to describe it? It's a bit like a giant butcherbird is poised above me, hooked bill grown and waiting, a scenario one could well imagine in a Julie Koh story or essay. In them, before you know it, time glitches; ordinary worlds morph in scale or substance:

A fat (Asian) girl who feels small in a world that rewards thin women ('peony-like' women, if Asian) grows into a monster-sized goddess of mercy, squashing her human supplicants ('The fat girl in history', 207–26); or:

A writer, searching for authenticity – and publication – transforms herself through meditation and training; her inner cockroach develops into a human-sized roach, in an act of literary mimicry that is her final authenticity ('C is for cockroach' in *Sydney Review of Books*); or:

Time stands still for an instant as a two-dimensional yellow man steps out of his no-dialogue role in a third-rate action movie, smack into a shocked viewer's popcorn in three-dimensional Sydney ('The three-dimensional yellow man', 97–108).

Along with the satirist in 'Satirist rising' – once the most dangerous individual in the world, now 'a festival of deformities, all gathered in one little old lady' – these are Koh's people, her brilliant but often fatally flawed protagonists, her outsiders who usually come to fictionally satisfying but no-good ends. Along the way, they react to 'inciting incidents', try things out or resist things, as protagonists do, and they laugh, eat, talk, watch TV, argue with their mothers, go swimming, cry, dream of being chased by faceless men, are hunted and murdered in the woods for orchestrating musical disturbance, work menial and/or boring jobs, get massages, avoid eating lethal ice-cream, write, talk about writing and how to get famous, visit cat cafes and literary festivals, try to date vampires, et cetera, and suffer or cause suffering, as protagonists do in ways little or large, as their plot journeys unwind.

Koh herself says that hers are plot-centric stories, even offering readers a selfie of the tips of her leopard-print ballet flats nudging at a grid of scrawled-upon and rearranged pages of a draft story laid out on the floor. It's a good way to work out structure, she advises and I echo: look at your own work from a distance, like an omniscient narrator, like the gods of old, classical, imperial or colonial, and the new gods of politics, finance, industry and now technology must do, seeing the whole as moveable parts. Plot-driven these stories may be, but as Ursula Le Guin, a mistress of plot, advises in *Steering the Craft*, 'The story is not in the plot but in the telling. It is the telling that moves' (loc. 1561).

5.

In Koh's stories, the movement is both inner and outer transformation of mind and/or body (from girl to goddess in 'The fat girl in history', from woman to cockroach in 'C for cockroach', from celluloid to flesh in 'The three-dimensional yellow man', from satirist to tragic joke in 'Satirist rising'), yet the socio-political and cultural webs that her characters are entangled in hardly budge.

The giant Asian woman capable of squashing every Aussie in sight is a reminder of the 'yellow hordes' that were so feared and reviled for potentially overrunning Australia in the nineteenth and twentieth centuries, a useful fear to pop up every now and then, currently in the guise of carriers of the 'China virus' (aka Chinese-looking people, like one of my students, who writes of a day in quarantine in Sydney and an Asian woman being punched for wearing a mask and another Asian woman being punched for not wearing a mask).

The newly three-dimensional yellow man, a writer and scholar of Russian literature as well as a martial arts whiz, is forced to finally admit that in Australia his expertise will never exceed his yellowness.

To learn how to become a human-cockroach, the writer goes to China – to an expat-run 'Harbourage' for wellness and soul-seeking foreigners where a 'darling' old Asian lady artfully scatters garbage and brings a 'carefully curated feast of paper, glue, eyelashes, leather, faeces, banana skins, and three beautifully arranged charcuterie boards covered in cling wrap' ('C is for cockroach').

(Koh is an adept of the list, the deployment of objects strung on a line of commas, little interruptions to their assertions of worldly presence and thingness, each bumping delicately up against another – 'eyelashes, leather, faeces, banana skins' – like a mantra, like jewels on a necklace, or themed items in a cabinet of curiosities, curated for the reader.)

Her characters change; the worlds they inhabit, not so much.

Even so, there's a certain grandiosity of scale in operation in Koh's stories, produced from a wild and decidedly wicked imagination that bestows her characters with extravagant gestures to suit their over-reaching aspirations (to be a writer, to be taken seriously, to be desired), even if they're doomed to mostly fail. Here they get to be protagonists, rather than sidekicks, to bask in our spotlight, command our eyes and ears for the time it takes us to read them. I read these stories as literary wish fulfilment or revenge tales for the abject or deluded, who are trapped in worlds that might be bleak, absurd or preposterous but are nonetheless recognisable, even plausible. The power of these worlds is that they are speculative in Margaret Atwood's sense, 'employing elements that already exist in some form' in the capitalist utopias (perfect) or dystopias (nightmare societies) that we already inhabit. Atwood has coined the term 'ustopia' to describe these spaces and societies, like Koh's, that straddle the collapsing differences between the two (2011). Ustopia, according to Atwood, is both a place: 'a mappable location', and a 'state of mind' (2011). In her own 'ustopic' spaces, Koh deftly suspends our disbelief in their more outlandish aspects, like a juggler of bright suns and black holes, like the early explorers and anthropologists who wielded their artefacts, maps and magic lanterns to enthral 19th-century audiences of the Royal Geographical or Ethnological Societies of London with their tales of faraway signs and wonders. The specimens they brought home.

We peer into the cabinets of curiosities laid out before us for our knowledge and entertainment. We await what happens next, even if we know or think we know what it might be.

6.

In an interview for *Books+Publishing* in 2016, Julie Koh describes her stories as lethal. 'I write what amuses me', Koh says, 'and – unfortunately for my karmic record – what amuses me is fiction that slays. Strong satire cuts through the noise because it pinpoints what is so absurd about contemporary society. Wit and desolation are a lethal combination'. The absurd provokes both laughter and despair, the delicious discomfort of feeling two things at once, as the satirist 'leads you, laughing, into the abyss' (*Kill Your Darlings*).

The lethal effect of Koh's fiction cuts both ways, outwards towards readers, towards society, as satire intends, but also inwards, as Koh perceptively explores in 'Satirist rising'. Here the ageing satirist observes, 'My work is a special kind of demon. When I point out ugliness, I too grow ugly. When I cripple with my words, I, too, become lame' (35).

7.

Why read or write satire in a time of 'post-satire' and 'post-truth', when the world already satirises itself so well, and feelings and beliefs (the domain of fiction) trump facts, and the times themselves are already life-threatening? 'Post-truth' becomes Oxford Dictionary's Word of the Year in 2016, its use increasing 2000 per cent that year alone when Donald Trump wins the elections in the US, while in Australia things chug along as usual: 72 children, including 33 babies born in Australia, are returned to detention on Nauru; greyhound racing is banned for its systemic cruelty and culling, then unbanned in time for a by-election; the Minister for Immigration, now the Minister for Home Affairs, is forced to apologise for referring to a female reporter as a 'mad f—ing witch'.

To satirist Tom Walker (aka fictional British political correspondent Jonathan Pie, who has over 81 million views on YouTube), 'Satire is just about looking at something from a different angle, shining a mirror on something' (2018). In his character's case it's the 'in-between' moments that he brings to light, though his are angry rather than the usual funny or cute blooper out-takes excised from the news. I'm a fan of Pie's mixed metaphors, often delivered with the male rage meter topping its scale. His apoplectic lack of power in the face of political and social dynamics beyond his control is relatable as well as side-splitting. It's because he *cares,* and we do too. Sometimes, 'You get things wrong, you use hyperbole, you go over the top', Walker says, insisting however that satire can never go too far (2018).

The real world goes or has already gone further. Even before Brexit, Trumpworld or the pandemic, the 'monstrous discourses' have floated as freely among us as the acts that accompany them – imprisoning children, debasing women, enabling cruelty and killing for profit or political gain. Our quotidian is just a few steps back up the path from the eating of babies, as Jonathan Swift satirically suggested in *A Modest Proposal* of 1729. Even so, the outrage generated is deeply felt, more deeply perhaps in our time than Swift's when his savage solution, recognised as satire, was mostly ignored. In our time, satirists like Pie are attacked for unscrupulous 'free speech', while QAnon's conspiracy theories, operating in the same speculative realm, aren't recognised by many as such. QAnon supplies all the ingredients of a thriller and spreads like wildfire through social media worldwide and out into the streets, even here in Australia.

Satire pricks, people awaken. This is how it works.

Part of its pleasure is surely trickery of the innocent or ignorant as well as in-jokes for the wise; part of its justification is 'an intent to inspire social reform' (literary scholar Robert Elliott, 1998). For Julie Koh, satire is an act of consolation: rather than wound for laughs or teaching moments, her lethal acts of fiction are 'to console people who already agree with me' (2017). She's not alone in this, as the steep rise in millions of Colbert and Seth Myers fans since 2016 demonstrates – their *Late Night* rants punching up at the most powerful, making the unbearable world somehow more bearable, including for me. These lockdown days I provoke my own anxiety levels by doomscrolling, Macquarie Dictionary's Word of the Year for 2020, then I salve my angst with satire. I remind myself that laughing is a micro-workout: it burns calories, uses muscles, releases endorphins, strengthens the immune system and reduces blood pressure. And it's as contagious as a virus. A good kind.

Koh's remark about the consolation of satire is intended to sound flippant, and like most of her words on the page, or out in the world, it both is and isn't. The satirist wants to have it both ways.

8.

In 'Satirist rising', the wheelchair-bound satirist is decomposing. After a lifetime of growing 'uglier by the second' due to practising and refining her art, she has some years ago achieved her artistic pinnacle with the publication of her book *The Self-Fulfilling Prophecy*, a 'satirical future history' that is coming to pass. Now 'she unwinds her bandages. She peels the sheet of green gel protectant off her chest and stares at the spreading, gaping sore under it, which refuses to heal' (31). The astrological prophecy of misfortune uttered at her long-ago birth, for being born with 'Satirist rising' instead of 'Sagittarius rising', sets her life's course as the creator of the greatest satire ever written and prophet of her own undignified but poetically just demise. As an artist, now the last of her kind, she knows that artists, in order to produce their art, must overcome their dignity. She 'notices a new tumour forming on her neck, expanding by the second' (31).

The satirist is enticed out of hiding to participate in 'The End Game Leadership Series' at the Curiosity Inn. The inn's motto 'Where Curiosity Will Get the Best of You' is also a kind of prophecy, for here the satirist encounters her own future in the exhibition of the 50-odd Portable Curiosities, the last of their kinds, whose fates she has also prophesied.

Dressed only in nappies, they have nothing to distract them from practising their artforms, freed from any kind of instrumentalist professionalism or economic rationalism – surely the dream come true of every artist and every deep thinker, talker and writer? They're no longer dependent on the 'teat' of the state (aka grants, fellowships, bursaries, contracts and the like). Now in the hands of a private collector, they have been returned to a more innocent state of freedom and agency than the failing utopia of the artist-as-professional/consultant/small-business-owner model of the long 20th century's late capitalism and its ardent advocates, particularly in government. This is a happy solution, less violent or controversial than Swift's *Modest Proposal*, or the equally murderous endings for artists in two of Koh's other stories:

'The level playing field', published in *The Best Australian Stories 2015* and also Koh's first collection *Capital Misfits*, in which generations of performance artists, who have no money because no one likes their art, sign contracts to live and work themselves to death in the sewers under the stadium, while competing to rise up to the 'Level Playing Field' where everyone has the opportunity to play, and:

'Inquiry regarding recent goings-on in the woods', from *Portable Curiosities*, in which an exiled 'guerrilla orchestra' is found to be the cause of auditory disruptions and therefore picked off one by one by outraged villagers until the last, a second but defiant violinist, has his violin broken, his ears cut off, his voice box taken out, his arms severed, his legs crushed, and what's left of his body strung up with his own violin strings.

In 'Satirist rising', a fire alarm offers the Portable Curiosities a chance to escape their nappies and black boxes, but they are unwilling to leave. The last historian explains:

> 'We're perfectly content in our cells. There aren't any locks.
> We're no longer dangers to society, just a collective warning
> about wayward irrelevance. No one bothers us. We're fed and
> clothed. In the back panels of our boxes, we each have a mat for
> sleeping, a hose for washing, and a hole for shitting. In exchange
> for participating in our own public ridicule, we can practise our
> respective disciplines.' (42)

'Satirist rising' offers a tantalising tweak to the model for private rather than public support for the arts and humanities that our government has pursued through relentless funding cuts and even the removal of the word 'arts' from its major arts funding body. Rather than seeking patrons or draining state resources by insisting on the universal value of the arts and artists, the humanities and humans, especially in times of crisis – climate change bushfires, a pandemic – artists and humanists should instead offer themselves up for collection to mega-rich specialist collectors. It's a neat solution, easy on the balance sheet, and more than easily justified and spun. For their value to interest such high-end collectors though, all artists would need to be wiped out, bar one of each. It's an endgame that offers a 50 per cent saving on Noah's Ark for maintenance and feed.

Even the satirist finally understands this and, after a last supper, offers herself up for collection.

9.

It's no accident that the satirist Julie Koh describes herself as 'the fictional Julie Koh'. Both in cyberspace and in life (that is, on her author website, in interviews, essays, speeches and perhaps even at dinner parties), Koh wears the fictional Julie Koh like a mask and a weapon – then expresses surprise – and worry – when punters and friends alike are taken in. The satirist's art, after all, is to take us in. In her fiction, Koh wields the techniques of autofiction – her autobiographical self deployed as a character mishmashed with other real, dead or made-up people. In her non-fiction, she invents texts and references, confesses to murders she hasn't committed, recommends favourite books that don't exist.

In this way, Koh makes the page, and the world, equally unreliable, speculative spaces quivering with both threat and possibility – the threat that nothing can be trusted; the possibility that what we take for granted isn't set in stone. That absolutes can move and change. Koh plays this edge for all it's worth: 'I write faux non-fiction now', she says. 'I've started to use myself as a character, a very narcissistic writer ... writing pieces which publishers are expecting to be non-fiction but are actually just made-up shit. I like being post-truth in that way.' (*Sisteria*, 2017)

Unfortunately, Koh isn't the only one.

In an essay titled 'The end of satire', Justin Smith, a philosophy professor and author who lived in Paris when the mass killings of the satirical magazine *Charlie Hebdo*'s cartoonists and journalists were carried out, writes, 'Satire is a species of humour that works through impersonation: taking on the voices of others, saying the sort of things they would say, using one's own voice while not speaking in one's own name'. The danger of satire, he goes on to say, is that 'it has become impossible to separate [satire] cleanly from the toxic disinformation that defines our era' (2019). Satire's flipside includes the conspiracy theorists and online trolls whose own fictions have proliferated at a pace with that of conventional satirists and perhaps more widely in our post-truth era.

In lockdown, I read about Joshua Goldberg (aka Australi Witness, a 20-year-old suburban nerd still living with his parents in Florida in 2015). In the guise of an Australian Islamic State mujahid, he convinces two Muslim men to attack with 'weapons, bombs or with knifes' [sic] an exhibition showing pictures of the Prophet in Texas. The men are killed by police and praised by Australi Witness as martyrs. His other guises have included a neo-Nazi and a 'fictional Australian left-wing anti-free speech activist' as well as various accounts set up using real people's names (*Sydney Morning Herald*, 2015). He plays social media like a novelist might their fictional world, creating characters, setting them loose, seeing what happens – delighting in suspending his readers' disbelief.

There's nothing in the definition of satire that stipulates what its intended 'reform' should be, if any, or who gets to bleed life into fiction and fiction into life. We live in Atwood's Ustopia, where the story spaces of fiction and non-fiction now effectively bleed into each other. In a post-truth world, what can we trust? I get a headache thinking about how much I am amused and consoled by Julie Koh's cutting, often self-deprecating satirical fiction. It is surprisingly empathetic given the psychological and actual violence inflicted upon her characters by the systems that govern their worlds. Koh describes this violence with devastating detail, yet it is clear that her satire targets systems rather than the characters caught up in them. It is the system that maims and murders, with or without its victims' collusion. My headache gets worse when I think about the trolls, gaslighters and conspiracy theorists like QAnon and Australi Witness, or Donald Trump and other copycat leaders closer to home, who know how story works and can deploy its craft and techniques, like Julie Koh, to suspend disbelief and amplify dramatic tension. Their fictions spread more fiercely and efficiently than a virus, filling potential spaces of amusement and consolation with outward-facing hostility; with humour that stokes hatred and fear.

In these lockdown times I'm uncertain about most things: the weather, the seasons, my job, my writing, whether I'll be able to go out tomorrow or shake hands, when I'll see my family again. But, having worked with thousands of new or experienced writers and readers, the latest via Zoom, I know one thing for certain: that the challenge is ethical. It's about having the capacity to make an ethical call, one founded in care and deliberation. It's not about writers or satirists or even trolls needing to be censored, cancelled, imprisoned, stowed away in black boxes as warnings, or killed. Instead, it's about readers reading in ways that aren't instrumentalist or unassailably aligned. It's about readers being able to think and feel two things at once, as fiction encourages, without acting rashly upon those thoughts and feelings. It's about risk and movement. As Maria Tumarkin writes about writers like Julie Koh, 'to think is to keep moving and doubting. To risk rolling down a hill. In other words, for the writers on the outside who keep on moving, the risks (personal, professional) are *always* profound' (2018). The challenge is to become readers who are prepared to take profound risks too. It's readers, young or new readers especially, being given the space, support and capacity to read uphill, against their own feelings and beliefs. It's what the arts and the humanities equip us to do; and it's why, in our era, they are so feared, reviled and attacked by those in power (aka the state and its friends).

10.

Outside my window it's now late spring, a coolish day of coastal winds hinged between yesterday's 40°+ and tomorrow's thankfully only 30°+ Sydney temperatures. The ferocity of last summer's fires seems closer now. It's been long months since the fledgling butcherbird first came to visit on my balcony, making a bid for some new territory buzzing with insects and even a little shiny black skink or two. It hangs around for a few weeks, growing sleeker and even a little acrobatic in its swooping, the hook on its beak sharpening nicely, or so I imagine as it stares in at me, at my desk, on the other side of the glass. I can hear the other members of its family, though I only see them as grey-brown flashes through the foliage of the neighbour's blue quandong and jacaranda – unless, I also imagine, I am being fooled by a pair of butcherbird twins, or even triplets, and can't tell the difference. *Teehee-hu-hu-hu*, they sing, swooping past with secret signals about whose turn it is. I discover that sometimes butcherbird young, once fledged, stick around for a year or two and even help with feeding younger generations of siblings.

In the easing of the lockdown, time still goes slow, and fast, and the world, or just me, still feels both too large and too small, too near and too distant; I know these things happen when I'm stuck. When my desire to move is both impossible and ever-present. When this happens, one of the Portable Curiosities in 'Satirist rising' offers some words of consolation:

> 'One doesn't always receive the type of freedom one expects,'
> says the glass artist. 'The Prophecy I spoke of predicted our freak
> show, but what it didn't foresee was that the landscapes of our
> minds would continue to flourish. Mighty glass oceans, darting
> glass clownfish, swaying glass sea anemones. A glass ship that sails
> forever towards the horizon.' (42)

I stop there. I resist the last glass artist's last five words – 'My prison is my patron'. Because however 'just up the road' we are, however close we've come to the satirist's prophecy, we're not quite there yet.

A manual for writers:
Elizabeth Costello

Nicholas Jose

I

What sort of book is this? *Elizabeth Costello* (2003) by JM Coetzee parades its defiance of category with a teasing insouciance. It is a novel in parts, 'eight lessons' and a postscript, some of which appeared separately as essays, including two in book form as *The Lives of Animals* (1999), a work that might be classed as philosophical non-fiction. Elizabeth Costello herself is pure invention – a fictional Australian novelist who strays into the roles of occasional lecturer and public intellectual as she struts the world stage. She is improbable: there is no female Australian writer in her generation (born 1928) like her, nor could there easily have been, for reasons to do with Australia's cultural history as a distant British dominion. Africa, on the other hand, produced two white literary giants from this cohort: Doris Lessing (born 1919) and Nadine Gordimer (born 1923), both Nobel literary laureates like *Elizabeth Costello*'s author and, unlike him, female. Yet, as a made-up character Elizabeth Costello proves irrepressible, popping up in Coetzee's next novel, *Slow Man* (2005), set in Adelaide, and in later short stories, with an unruly life of her own (2004; 2017), as if she won't let her creator go.

The date of the work matters because *Elizabeth Costello* marks Coetzee's move from South Africa to Australia in 2002. It is a threshold text in that sense. Africa pulls and pushes Elizabeth in the book, while Australia is there as reference point, the 'far edges' she comes from and to which she returns (15). The book is transitional in theme and approach too. It moves away from the author's concern with his country of birth, demonstrated at its most explicit in the preceding novel, *Disgrace* (1999), which won the Booker Prize and was later made into a movie. It also moves away from the readily accessible realism of the autobiographical works that come before, *Boyhood* (1997) and *Youth* (2002). By contrast, *Elizabeth Costello* has puzzled readers, some of whom identify it as the start of a regrettably frustrating, metafictional late phase in Coetzee's writing. Two novels prior to *Disgrace*, *Foe* (1986) and *The Master of Petersburg* (1994), also depart from Africa, but in the more familiar mode of rewriting a classic author or work, respectively Defoe and Dostoevsky, two of Coetzee's 'more severe' masters (to use Wallace Stevens's phrase from 'An ordinary evening in New Haven'). The imaginary Elizabeth Costello, best known for her rewriting of James Joyce's *Ulysses*, takes us further into this hall of mirrors.

The opening of *Elizabeth Costello* is breathtaking. I gasp at its boldness every time. Let me quote it in full:

> There is first of all the problem of the opening, namely, how to get us from where we are, which is, as yet, nowhere, to the far bank. It is a simple bridging problem, a problem of knocking together a bridge. People solve such problems every day. They solve them, and having solved them push on.
>
> Let us assume that, however it may have been done, it is done. Let us take it that the bridge is built and crossed, that we can put it out

of our mind. We have left behind the territory in which we were. We are in the far territory, where we want to be. (1)

These two short paragraphs dispense briskly with the niceties of novel writing. Setting is taken as given rather than carefully built up. Voice is communal rather than individuated, including 'us', the reader, in the enterprise of authorship, without any scrutinising 'outsider's eye' (18). Here is the impatience of 'the old trouper' (207), who will turn out to be Elizabeth Costello, cranking up another performance. There is no time or energy for trivial things. It's a version of late style that takes the form of plain speaking, with blunt verbs that do the job: 'knocking together a bridge' so as to 'push on'. An abstract problem is literalised. The locatedness of the fiction – always a question for Coetzee as he seeks to escape the fate of being a provincial or national writer – is skipped over: 'we are in the far territory', metaphorically, entering the space and time of story. Once upon a time ... Yet the metaphor suggests a campaign of some sort, military, colonising perhaps, with some urgency, as we occupy territory under pressure, filling the space with our imagination, from where Elizabeth Costello appears in the next sentence as an imposing presence.

This is far from the 'Realism' that the title of the first lesson promises. As writers we are learning other lessons: how to strip our prose of adjectives, adverbs and other extraneous material, how to suggest irony, anxiety and scepticism through the simple and commonplace, how to raise questions and move on. 'People solve such problems every day.' The technique creates narrative by omission, generating a forward impulse into time and the world. Very quickly the paraphernalia of a 'moderate realism' (4) works its magic and we are transported to places that are recognisably part of the contemporary scene: an airport, a hotel room, a car, an auditorium – ordinary places, realistically generic, real enough as sites of transition.

'Supply the particulars, allow the significations to emerge of themselves. A procedure pioneered by Daniel Defoe ... No large words, no despair, just hats and caps and shoes' (4). Show don't tell. Though of course there is plenty of telling going on here. Still, the fiction has kicked in and pulls us off course, away from Elizabeth as the focal point to her son John, whose emotions arouse empathy. He is the human here, ambivalently filial, sad and alone as he looks after his admired mother without always understanding her – she who is in touch with the divine. His body acts when he sleeps with Susan Moebius, the literary scholar who interrogates his mother. As the name suggests, this loops back into the double nature of Elizabeth Costello as human animal and what she will later call, straining for language, 'secretary of the invisible' (199, a phrase from poet Czeslaw Milosz). She considers herself a voice for the gods. There is for John a double engendering, bodily and spiritual: 'the same being that engendered *Eccles Street* [Elizabeth Costello's famous book] engendered him' (11). He has come out of his mother as have her books and we feel for him in this, even as we are in awe of her, with an admixture of niggling disbelief.

The drama progresses through the staging of scenes that are created by disruptions, interventions, actions and responses that are mostly left unresolved. Again this is part of the forward momentum. The technique we learn as writers in this first lesson, 'Realism', is how to skip. The word is repeated: 'We skip. They have reached Williamstown and have been conveyed to their hotel' (2); 'It is not a good idea to interrupt the narrative too often ... Breaking into the dream draws attention to the constructedness of the story, and plays havoc with the realist illusion. However, unless certain scenes are skipped we will be here all afternoon' (16); 'We skip ahead again, a skip this time in the text rather than in the performance' (24). The verb 'skip' indicates the movement the method creates. Like 'knock' and 'push' and 'jolt' and 'shake', it suggests the physical effect that language can have, the corporeal sensation that accompanies it, playful, rousing, the animal dimension. That is central to this book, where animal imagery is pervasive and animal awareness is everywhere. Try listing the examples: seal, duck, shark, cat, mouse, goldfish, whale, cockatoo, bee, ape, flea, parrot, dog, monkey, gorilla, elephant, python, from lesson one alone – the list is endless. It is another way of embedding the fiction in the real, as against the 'heady abstractions' that will push in on Elizabeth Costello when she is questioned, finally, at another departure gate in Lesson Eight. That gate is where she must account for her life as a writer before an ultimate panel of judges, a last test before she can pass, in every sense.

The story so far constructs gender as a theme. The mother writer is a woman. 'Whatever she does, she does as a woman', the critic Moebius claims (23). There's a question about whether her significance as a writer is *because* of her gender. John defends her capacity to 'think her way ... into other existences' (22): 'She has also been a dog'. But the conversation quickly moves from literary discussion of sexual difference to its enactment in the narrative as John and Susan Moebius become lovers. There's irony here in the perennial argument about gender difference being staged by another John, Coetzee the author, who, if what the critic suggests is true, can only do what he does as a man. This destabilising reminder ripples through the text. Later Elizabeth remembers how Renoir said he painted his voluptuous nudes with his penis (148). Is the author writing with his penis when his text challenges the limitations of a male writer when it comes to thinking about female experience, and vice versa? 'Have you considered the possibility that my mother may have got beyond the man-woman thing?' John asks Susan (25). Is such a thing possible? The tease is all part of the work's appealing comedy.

II

Elizabeth Costello is a book about writing and the writing life. In particular it is about being a writer from Australia in an age when writers are expected to speak as well as write, to offer opinions and wage campaigns from the platforms their books have given them. I find the fictional Elizabeth easiest to identify with when she is fatigued in a foreign hotel, donning the practical clothes she takes on tour, her hair still greasy despite a quick wash. This is the incarnate human being who performs the roles assigned to her and she will be familiar to anyone who has been on the promotional circuit. Coming from distant Australia to the metropolitan centres of intellectual life makes it harder not to misstep. She transgresses, as the comedy darkens and the debate becomes more combative, in Massachusetts in lessons three and four and in Amsterdam in lesson six, 'The problem of evil'. She compares the mass killing of animals for meat to the mass slaughter of Jews in the death camps of the Holocaust, both examples instancing a failure of sympathy for other beings. She is challenged on this: 'If Jews were treated as cattle, it does not follow that cattle are treated like Jews. The inversion insults the memory of the dead' (94). Philosophically it is a category mistake. She might defend herself as speaking rhetorically, for effect, as a novelist rather than a philosopher, but that justification gets slippery when she suggests that another writer is 'obscene' for rendering Nazi evil with sensational impact (177). *Obscene*: that which should be kept offstage, which takes evil further when it is imaginatively communicated.

The Australia that Elizabeth Costello comes from is not only a place of drought and flood and the extermination of Indigenous people, it is a society that in her generation offered a humanistic education to its young. She can reference Aristotle, Aquinas and Descartes and she is at home with the Western canon from the Greeks to Jonathan Swift and the poet Rilke. But she is a novelist and the question of what a novel can do in the world nags at her. Her sister, Bridget, is a nun doing good work in Africa. Bridget says, repudiating her sister's vocation in favour of her own, that she does not need to consult novels to know the possibility of human transformation (128). Elizabeth can only respond in circular fashion: 'The humanities teach us humanity' (151). The more urgent question – how to live? – remains unanswered.

The discussion of these weighty matters is presented in the novel as dinner-table conversation, conference Q&A and academic exchange. These are sophomoric seminar topics, time-honoured questions, old chestnuts: philosophy versus poetry, believers against unbelievers. 'Are we being serious?' asks Sister Bridget (128). It's hard to be certain. Metaphysical argument disrupts the social surface only to be displaced in its turn by the exigencies of the mundane. A faculty dinner to celebrate the distinguished author, for example, goes bad when Elizabeth names 'disgust' as a reason for her vegetarianism, even as the guests are eating their choice of snapper or fettucine. 'Much food for thought,' concludes the university president awkwardly (87, 90). The shuffling of register and scale makes for a sly comedy of its own. That is one lesson of this writer's life. The mismatch between the immediate context and the grand reach of the work makes things unstable. 'UNIVERSE EVIL, OPINES COSTELLO' is the flip headline she imagines in the Melbourne *Age*: a travesty of the severe inwardness of her dialogue with herself (160).

III

She then turns away from ideas to the erotic life with its compulsions and raptures, when it seems that gods commune with mortals and the breast gives succour. She tests her words against experience itself. At last she finds herself 'At the gate', required to write a statement of what she believes. By lesson eight the 'moderate realism' of the opening has given way to a simulation more literary than life-like, 'a purgatory of clichés ... straight out of Kafka' (206, 209). The demand for a statement of belief again challenges the value of her profession as a novelist, someone who makes things up, a speculator: '*I maintain beliefs only provisionally*' (195). Does she believe in art? The only thing left that she does not need to invent is herself, the body that she 'somehow *is*' (210). Yet she manages to come up with something else, recollected from the extremes of her Australian country childhood. When rain comes after drought, tiny frogs awaken in their thousands from the dried mud of the river where she grew up: 'the resurrection of the dead' (217). That's how it happens, regardless of her belief in it. They exist. As she exists.

The river is specified as the Dulgannon in Victoria. It is fictional, of course, but who's to know. It's off the map. The frogs are part of a non-human Australia, a wordless Australia, a pre-verbal child's memory. They exist with their life cycle beyond this stagey court of last things. Although it fails to convince the judges, it works for the reader. The frogs lodge in the memory. Reading these pages, as an Australian, I cherish the natural phenomenon that Elizabeth Costello describes so eloquently, 'the chorus of joyous belling', at the full stretch of her powers. 'It is the thing itself, the only thing' (217). That is what Australia provides in this strange novel: an exceptional answer.

IV

Another version of Elizabeth Costello writes the postscript where she identifies her confused husband and herself as '*extreme souls*', for whom everything in the world means something, even as verbal language fails (228). The frogs would be an example of that, had words not conjured them up. The experience that the couple channel as it envelops them takes on a religious quality, where self dissolves. 'We interpenetrate and are interpenetrated by fellow creatures by the thousand', so this last letter insists (229). That may be true of the imaginative writer too, the poet at the extreme, 'a vessel of revelation' that comes from somewhere else (229).

Is this a 'mad' book? As a manual for writers it teaches us that the novel can be anything. That's sane enough. The question of the boundary between non-fiction and fiction became a widespread cultural preoccupation around the time *Elizabeth Costello* was published as many writers, ranging from VS Naipaul to Helen Garner and including Coetzee himself, seemed to lose faith with fiction. As it works that boundary, *Elizabeth Costello* subtly shows that the novelist cannot write a sentence that is not also, to some degree, a hypothesis, an untruth. As it bounces between abstract ideas and a central human presence who feels the pull of earth's gravity, this book wonders about the mediating efficacy of language, the medium in which the novel lives.

The passage about the frogs appeared in the *Macquarie PEN Anthology of Australian Literature* in 2009, where the inclusion of JM Coetzee raised some eyebrows. Having moved to Australia and become an Australian citizen in 2006, and having written, in the figure of Elizabeth Costello, a literary work about Australian life 'in any of its phases' (to quote Miles Franklin's criterion for the award for Australian literature that she endowed), Coetzee is surely eligible for inclusion in an anthology of Australian literature. He is a migrant writer, if you like, continuing the migration and mobility that are among the formative themes of writing from Australia. More than that, it matters that the frogs in the Dulgannon come from the south of the world, as a hemisphere regarded as remote and even mute gives voice to itself. Meg Samuelson, a fellow migrant from South Africa to Australia, speaks of Coetzee's 'southern comparativism': 'one might think that Coetzee has invented the character [of Elizabeth Costello] in order to test what it might feel like to be an Australian novelist' ('An "international author"').

Elizabeth Costello is an idiosyncratic novel, an eccentric *sui generis* production. In that respect it can take its place in a line of Australian fiction. Like *The Fortunes of Richard Mahony* by Henry Handel Richardson it voyages between hemispheres, between male and female, between pessimism and optimism, in an unresolved odyssey of transformation. Like *The Aunt's Story* by Patrick White, it is a male writer's imagining of a questing woman's inwardness. Like *An Imaginary*

Life by David Malouf, it reaches beyond the limits of language and culture. It is outlandish, cynical, worldly, like Christina Stead at times. It is as much a do-it-yourself performance as Joseph Furphy's *Such Is Life*, with its insistent vernacular philosophising, or, a century later, the fiction of Gerald Murnane. The frogs of the drolly named Dulgannon come from Henry Lawson's 'In a dry season', as it were, the opening of which is as briskly knocked together as the bridge at the start of 'Realism', lesson one:

> Draw a wire fence and a few ragged gums, and add some scattered sheep running away from the train. Then you'll have the bush all along the New South Wales western line from Bathurst on. (253)

And there is more. The shared idiosyncrasy is a consequence of creating a literature from scratch, in English, from unwieldy and recalcitrant materials, in a country that had no literature in the alphabetic Greco-Roman and Judaeo-Christian sense until it was colonised. The idea of Australian literature has sometimes seemed like a joke, a category mistake in itself. It has been that way ever since Barron Field's ode to the 'anomalous' kangaroo in 1819. Anomaly comes with the territory. Exceptionalism would be too grand, too doctrinaire a term. This is more like the add-on that calls the rest into question. Coetzee knew about Australian literature before he came to Australia. He was taught literature in Cape Town by an Australian, RG Howarth, and taught Patrick White himself later (Kannemeyer, 91–96, 229). For all these reasons it is relevant and rewarding to read Coetzee here, like an Australian writer. *Elizabeth Costello* is its author's work of arrival, with Australia as a source of hope, in sight over a long period of time.

Nearly two decades later Coetzee would write of Australia on the basis of more sustained acquaintance, having deepened his understanding of the divisions in Australian society, the racism that has operated 'ever since British colonists established themselves on the continent' and the recurrent re-emergence of the victimhood that came with the exile of colonisation and later migration. In 'Australia's shame', an essay on Australia's regime of offshore detention for asylum seekers, Coetzee is pained by the entitlement asserted in refusing the appeals of others at the gate. 'What is ... a mystery is why so many Australians wish refugees ill' (2019). There proves to be a burden of conscience to arrival, as well as a mystery.

Elizabeth Costello is a sunnier vision, for all its questions. Its most fantastic invention is Elizabeth herself. In the years since then, though, Australia has outdone even her. There is now a great female Australian novelist appearing on the world stage. Her name is Alexis Wright and she is real. Her heritage is Waanyi from the lower Gulf of Carpentaria. In her world humans, animals, birds, fish and spirit beings are one and she tells those stories in another reinvention of what the novel can be in extreme times. *Carpentaria* (2006), *The Swan Book* (2013) and more, as the cycle of life goes on in the river's flow. A ninth lesson wraps around the eight lessons in a crackling, commanding voice that tells of a new future for the planet from this old land. I imagine Elizabeth Costello would be surprised and pleased by this development.

Everywhen in everything: Reading *Carpentaria* like an Aboriginal writer

Mykaela Saunders

The best books are those you revisit over the years and build a relationship with – with each visit you learn new things about yourself and about the story, deepening your understanding of both each time. Alexis Wright's Miles Franklin award-winning epic *Carpentaria* has been my favourite book since I first read it in 2008. I have admired and puzzled over it during every reading since, and I've learnt so much from this fantastic story as a reader and as a writer.

I began writing fiction and poetry in 2017 as part of my Doctor of Arts degree. In the same year, I learned about reading like a writer – how to do it, and how important it is when learning to write.[1] I like to begin with my gut: identifying what I love and hate about a story, then figuring out what the writer did to produce this effect. In this way I've learnt how to break stories down into their constituent parts to see what they are and how they work together.

---

1   Two of my teachers, Fiona and Beth – who I am stoked to be in this book with – both
     taught me something about reading like a writer.

The first time I read *Carpentaria* I was not yet a writer and had no idea about craft or any of the things I'll discuss in this essay. I just knew that I loved the story. When I started writing creatively, I re-read *Carpentaria* to see if I could demystify some of its magic and learn from it. The first time I read this novel like a writer, what stood out to me were the cultural aspects of the craft techniques, and it got me thinking about how I might use these in my own work.

Carpentaria is a wonderful example of a text that centres our ways of what Indigenous knowledge systems scholar Veronica Arbon describes as 'being-knowing-doing' (2009) – not least the way it renders time, and the way this speaks back to the time it was written in. I am interested in writing about intergenerational memory and sovereignty, so I am enamoured of how Wright incorporates 'all times' into her story.

Wright observes of the way Aboriginal people tell stories: 'they will bring all the stories of the past, from ancient times and to the stories of the last 200 years (that have also created enormous stories for Indigenous people), and also stories happening now. It is hard to understand, but *all times are important*' (quoted in O'Brien, 2007). This speaks to my own worldview and my goals in writing.

At 500 pages, there is a lot to unpack in this novel. In the years since it was first published in 2006, scholars and critics have dedicated countless words to its content and context. Instead of going over old ground, I want to introduce the concept of *everywhen*, or all-times, as the deep structure of this novel. Various craft techniques are deployed to condense *everywhen* and weave all times into *Carpentaria*'s narrative present. I'll focus on *Carpentaria*'s structural and linguistic organisation, and Wright's interrogation and interweaving of Aboriginal and Western time and cultures. Then we'll look at imagery of time and how this is used in characterisation.

Let's first discuss *everywhen* in its cultural context, and the differences between Aboriginal and Western conceptions of time so we can elaborate on the deep implications these differences have for the narration and relationships within the novel.

*

So, a brief note about the novel's context and when it was written. *Carpentaria* was conceived of and written throughout the Howard years. The Howard government repealed many of the legal rights and self-determination advancements that grassroots community had won in the 1990s (and had fought for long before that). Howard refused to apologise to the Stolen Generations on behalf of the government for past wrongdoing, and he oversaw the disbanding of ATSIC, which was the closest we've come to meaningful Aboriginal governance since before we were invaded.

Along with John Howard, the One Nation politician Pauline Hanson also pushed back against any acknowledgment, let alone celebration, of Australia's black history. Through her political party One Nation, Hanson pushed an agenda of a 'united' Australia, yet in the same breath would single out and demonise Aboriginal people (and Asian-Australians).

Both Howard and Hanson were ostensibly assimilationist in that they wanted to mainstream blackfellas into all aspects of Australian life – but they were spectacularly hypocritical about it. On one hand they denied our unique status in this country as First Peoples, and they minimised our very real differences to non-Indigenous Australians, and so professed to deny us any 'special treatment'. Yet on the other hand they singled us out repeatedly, most famously in 2003's Northern Territory intervention, where whole communities were stripped of their basic human and legal rights under accusations of paedophilia and alcoholism. And so in this way a whole group of people were pathologised and criminalised.

*

The way Australia classifies its own time as precolonial, colonial and postcolonial serves to divide a continuum of time into dissimilar units relative to non-Indigenous occupation. Of course, many Aboriginal people will say that we are not yet postcolonial.

This way of divvying up time in relation to Australian occupation speaks to Western obsessions with naming and defining eras in order to distance contemporary life from the past and privilege new, improved versions of civilisation. We see this with the classification of society into movements: for example, pre-literate, New Age, postmodernist, New World Order. Defining eras also creates psychic, not actual, distance from the past and declares 'more advanced' versions of humanity and intellect.

Western 'rationalism' attempts to divorce its contemporary knowledge from ancestral memory; contemporary knowledge is always presented as the most up-to-date and most correct, yet it refuses the wisdom of all knowledges from all times. In Western culture, there are statutes of limitations in law, and scientific knowledge often becomes outdated and inaccurate as time goes by. In contrast, Aboriginal Law remains the same throughout all times.

Indigenous Law is a living, integrated body of knowledge that environmental activist David Suzuki says 'has built up over millennia and that will never be duplicated by [Western] science because it is acquired from a profoundly different basis'. If we think about time in a Western, linear sense, then non-Indigenous occupations of our lands might be figured as a 2.5-centimetre length of string in comparison to a 1-metre length of string representing Indigenous occupation; imagine a tiny inchworm dwarfed by a massive eastern brown snake. Even in a linear reckoning of time like this, our ancestral memory is far longer than any other on earth. Still, the enormity of *everywhen* must be understood beyond the sense of eras or epochs.

Let's unpack the concept of *everywhen*, which is an analogy of an Aboriginal conceptualisation of time, first put forth by WEH Stanner in his seminal translations of Aboriginal culture for the Western world.

Time is understood differently across cultures, and in the Aboriginal mode of temporality, all things that have happened are still happening now. It is difficult to render this idea precisely in English. However, one way we already do talk about this is by using the verb *Dreaming* rather than the noun *Dreamtime*. *Dreamtime* denotes a discrete event with a beginning and an end, located in the past; by contrast, *Dreaming* is ever-imminent and emergent.

In 1953 Stanner said: 'I have never been able to discover any Aboriginal word for "time" as an abstract concept. And the sense of "history" is wholly alien here' (23). He translated Aboriginal dimensional spirituality – commonly known as Dreaming – for a non-Indigenous audience: 'it was, and is, *everywhen*' (24).

Everywhen embodies the laws and patternings of culture that are formulated from the creation of Country in the Dreaming. These laws do not change, and they are the framework for all possible events to unfold within. In the *everywhen* framework, all times are compressed, and nested inside Country, and all times are known through our unbroken ancestral memory. The past is not just 'events that happened before now', because this implies a linear continuum of time. In the *everywhen* paradigm, the past is still alive in the eternal present, and it is the framework within which all potential and possible events can unfold at any time.

In a cultural sense, Aboriginal songs and stories all demonstrate this, as they all come from the land and they all contain information from the past while remaining relevant for us today and onward. The only way we can make sense of ourselves is in the context of our kinship and histories. The past is also stacked inside us; we are all embodiments of family through DNA, through epigenetics, and we are embodiments of our communities through culture and through our transgenerational traumas and strengths.

The deep structure of *Carpentaria* is patterned on *everywhen*. This is an apt frame of reference for the way the novel has the ancient, land-based, Aboriginal mode of time engulf the shallow scratchings of colonial time, as seen in Wright's masterful patterning of *everywhen* in structure, voice and imagery.

In the novel, all times – including the Dreaming, BC times (before Cook) and colonial history – all bleed into *Carpentaria*'s narrative present. The narrative present is concerned with the sagas of the Pricklebush mob in relation to each other, to Uptown, and to the mine. Wright uses historical events to pattern contemporary social relations inside and across communities. Country is also conscious, in accordance with Aboriginal beliefs and, as it has always been, Country is affected by Aboriginal relationships with it and by the colonial relationship with it and with us. In the novel, there is a deep excavation of Country and community, of ecosystems and ghosts, their relationships and their hauntings.

There is no quick reading of this story, and this is intentional. On page 2, we read 'To catch this breath in the river you need the patience of one who can spend days doing nothing'. I think a similar patience is required to tap into the rhythm of this novel. The densely packed and often convoluted sentences are rhythmic and hypnotic, and long sentences need absorbing, slowing the reading pace. Even the lack of white space on the page helps create this effect. Poetry, for example, often with sparing use of words and lots of white space on the page, allows the reader to enter the page with their own thoughts. In *Carpentaria*'s dense walls of text, the reader's mind is caught and absorbed into the page.

*

Now let's discuss the narrator, then examine the serpentine shape of the story through its beginning and ending: how the narrative voice swims in and out of time to give this structure temporal dimension – and a cyclonic shape.

Carpentaria's 'intrusive narrator' is a Dorry: someone who is overly concerned with other people's business. The narrator is intimate with Pricklebush ways and is concerned with the wellbeing of Country and community while practising a detached curiosity with Uptown. And as the voice mostly centres the Aboriginal characters and explores cross-cultural social relations through their worldviews, the narrator is an explicitly Aboriginal consciousness who is talking to a decidedly Aboriginal audience (but allowing a white audience to listen in).

The narrative voice reproduces Aboriginal orality; it has the same inflections, interjections and cultural dialect as Aboriginal storytellers – it is suited to be spoken. The narrator's generous voice provides near and far historical context for everything. Using long, rambling sentences that move through time, the narrator puzzles, delights, educates and entertains. This is modelled on the techniques of Dreaming stories, which are also texts of entertainment and education, of religion and law, seasonal calendars, moral compasses, histories, genealogies, and models of kinship patterning.

Most Aboriginal people have got at least one old aunty or uncle, god love 'em, who yarns like this. The meandering way they'll tell a story is by providing detailed context and background information on everyone and how they're all related. I grew up listening to old people and working-poor people telling wild stories that were never confined to one time or place. They were long stories with long journeys and broad contexts. Because to tell a story about a person properly, you need to tell the story about where they're from, who they belong to, and then locate all of this in the context of their family and other relationships in community – and then to locate a community, you need to locate it in the context of all history. Much like the way blackfellas introduce ourselves by who and where we belong to, to establish our connections in order to figure out how best to relate to each other, *Carpentaria's* narrator does this with characters in the novel too.

The narrator takes interest in a few characters and these characters function as anchors to the narrative present. The narration cycles in and out of characters' heads and the town itself, to offer broad historical contexts as well as social-relational contexts to the story at hand. The narrator will hover and give a wide view of a scene, then dart into a character's head and speak through ventriloquy, and swim around different spheres of consciousness to show events from different perspectives. Sometimes they penetrate deeply into a character's psyche. Layers of consciousness are woven around characters, using imagery and exposition to provide historical context for social conflict. This vocal plenitude is intoxicating and seductive.

The narrator mostly uses a third-person point of view – except for a brief section of chapter 11, 'The mine'. Here, the narrator briefly becomes a 'we', seemingly spoken by some of the fellas from Fishman's convoy who destroy the mine and rescue Will. Apart from this section, the narrator is divested of any self-reference and doesn't explicitly acknowledge themselves as a consciousness with a stake in the story, so they are a consciousness without being a character that other characters interact with.

In this style, third-person narrators often attempt to make their voice invisible, so that the reader's mind can seamlessly merge with the story. Not this narrator! They have an opinion on everything and everyone. They're aware of when tales become too tall, they feel sympathy and outrage, and they don't shy away from brutal situations, but also don't bash readers over the head with how we are supposed to feel.

The voice belongs to the Gulf. It circles around Desperance, sometimes visiting other parts of the continent, but only in relation to a journey from a character. As the assumed voice of Country and community, the narrator has all the authority of a knowledgeable local. This is not an ancient archaic voice from long ago, with some romanticised precolonial utopian mindset, but an up-to-date voice who encompasses all times, even the hard ones. And as *Carpentaria's* narrator is both ancestral and contemporary, we should consider it the *everywhen* voice of Country, because for Aboriginal people, Country is a consciousness.

*

The first chapter of *Carpentaria*, 'From time immemorial', contains a narrative frame that sits outside the embedded story. This opening frame begins with church bells pealing – the embodiment of Uptown time – loud, precise and demanding. These few sentences are the only part of the novel to use the present tense. As *Carpentaria* is a novel encompassing all times it needs to begin from the most current, most present vantage point possible. This opening paragraph then declares that 'Armageddon begins here' (1), and so, paradoxically, the novel proper begins after the announcement of its own destruction. By beginning the story from time immemorial, the narrator announces themselves as an authority of deep history. And after the opening frame, the narrator condenses all prior times together by talking about everything in the past tense.

To begin the story, we abruptly cut to the serpent scoring rivers into the mudflats with its enormous body and creativity, embodying the fluidity of Aboriginal time and cultural memory. Here, we are launched back to where the real story begins, which is the furthest point in time possible – the beginning of time itself, according to the Aboriginal worldview. In an awe-inspiring and very beautiful introduction to the primordial Rainbow Serpent, the river of today is embodied, it is storied, and it is related to the people. We have not yet been introduced to any human characters besides Cry-Baby Sally and her mission-breed tormentors (2). The serpent is still here; thus, a moment of time that happened billions of years ago still exists, and Dreaming and BC history bleed into the narrative present (20).

The first half of the novel is epic in scope, and is really about setting the scene: it locates the town of Desperance in space and time; it nests the Pricklebush mob and other main characters within this world; and it maps them all in relation to each other, to Uptown, and to history. At the sentence level, several layers of time are flattened and woven together. Let's consider how often the following passage changes tense while the voice comments on the interconnectedness of the events from a place of temporal omniscience:

> There was **nobody alive** who could claim to have seen this strange thing happen before, but **history was repeating itself**, because **this was the ancient story** of the prodigal coppiced tree standing there, in the middle of town. A tremendous thunderclap exploded above the tree. It came from deep inside the world of those **black serpent clouds** and even from far away, people said later on, as word filtered back, that they too had listened to the haunting echo of the thunder rolling back to the sea. Finally, when the thunder had faded away, a wind full of sand whistled over the coast from the sea bringing with it **the hardest rain ever imagined** and afterwards, **all time stopped**. (44)

We are first given chapters and chapters of historical context, both recent and far in the past, to prime the reader for the magnitude of the events in the second half of the novel, which are concerned with Norm and Will's journeys, the sagas of the mine and the cyclone. Structurally, the shape of the novel can be seen as a widely meandering river with the novel taking a long time to get to these 'main' events in the narrative present.

Wright's story design is what Kate Grenville names 'Focus' (173). The focus is Waanyi country, which contains the town of Desperance and the characters who live there – particularly the Aboriginal characters who are river people. The novel is about the people and the river, which is also the serpent, who lives in the sky and also beneath the mudflats, both now and in the past, who is continually carving songlines, which tell the history of the place. So, to tell a story about the town, Wright needed to tell the story of the river and what it is through all time.

Unlike plot-driven stories, where the shape of the novel is determined by the order of events, this story is shaped by *Carpentaria*'s narrator. Like the serpent-river scoring through the mud, the narrator's widely meandering voice carves the shape of the narrative. The narrator, like the serpent-river, winds around and around Country, deep into the earth of history and into the sky of cosmology, changing temporal zones frequently and suddenly. The narrator journeys the reader from time immemorial to the narrative present, and through all times in between. This non-linear narrative is breathtaking and dizzying, full of movement around time and place. The 'carnivalesque' narrative structure is patterned on Dreaming processes and the movement of the serpent-river, and these levels of patterning are cyclical, like Aboriginal seasonal calendars. The narrator then is serpentine *and* multidimensional in form, which to my mind describes the shape of a cyclone. This cyclonic voice sweeps and dips, swimming backward and forward through time to give this shape temporal dimension, embodying *everywhen*.

It takes a very long time to arrive at, and stay with, the events in the narrative present – this really only properly happens in chapter 6, 'Knowing fish'. This is the first chapter that is one extended scene in the narrative present, and in it we follow Will Phantom and his interactions with Mozzie and Elias, which kick off the events in the following chapters, with the story developing in a more-or-less chronological way from this point on.

The last few pages of the novel follow Norm, Hope and Bala coming onto shore from their long time at sea (516–19). (Earlier, they had lost Hope; now, Will abandons them to find Hope.) But the town of Desperance is no longer there and the landscape is unfamiliar, confusing Norm because he had tracked the place correctly. We are as close to the narrative present as we'll ever be; the story has homed in on Norm and Bala, and their trans-generational connection:

> It was a mystery, but there was so much song wafting off the watery land singing the country afresh as they walked hand in hand out of town, down the road, Westside, to home. (519)

These final lines return us to the beginning of the novel, and the serpent-river's song of creation humming off the land. In the long view of history, not much time has passed and the cyclone has blown the recent past away to resemble the primordial, or precolonial Country. These lines quietly answer the beginning of the novel that happens long before 'a nation chants', and 'church bells peal' (1).

*

Another important way *Carpentaria* performs *everywhen* is by representing two different temporal modes – Aboriginal and colonial – which Wright then plays against each other. We'll now look at how the novel presents different cultural imagery of time, and then we'll look at some of the main characters, and the specific cultural symbols of time that they are associated with, and how these are used to situate the characters within their distinct modes of temporality and relationships to time.

Critic Diane Molloy says that 'there is an underlying tension between the Western and Aboriginal view of time throughout the novel. The history of the Pricklebush people is from time immemorial, while the history of the Uptown people "is only as old as the cemetery"' (3). Uptown's cultural memory is only as long as their colonial heyday.

Wright deploys cultural symbols to situate Uptown time within the fluid vastness of *everywhen*. Recurrent imagery is used to give readers clues to understand this tension. This layering and repetition of symbols creates an emblematic resonance and reveals the deep structure of *everywhen* in the novel.

The novel uses the following Western time-keeping symbols: clocks, Gregorian calendars, town records, minutes from meetings, deadlines, writing in general, and Armageddon. The narrator figures Aboriginal ancestral memory as a massive primordial snake that runs circles around the short and recent presence of colonial history. By contrasting these lengths of time, the narrator destabilises the footholds of colonial 'scientify' and undermines their authority (123). Ancestral time, in the omnipresence of the serpent, first ridicules Australia, then also promises that it will see its own Armageddon:

> The serpent's covenant permeates everything, even the little black girls with hair combed back off their faces and bobby-pinned neatly for church, listening quietly to the nation that claims to know everything except the exact date its world will end. (11)

Dying clocks contrast Uptown's short history with Pricklebush's ancestral memory:

> The clocks, tick-a-ty tock, looked as though they might run out of time. Luckily, the ghosts in the memories of the old folk were listening, and said anyone can find hope in the stories: the big stories and the little ones in between. So ... (12)

The serpent-river interferes with Uptown time:

> Time stopped tick-tocking, because there was too much moisture in the air and it had interfered with the mechanical workings

of dozens of watches and clocks that ended up jiggered, and afterwards, were only fit to be thrown down on the rubbish dump. (44)

*

Country is the keeper of time through seasons, and blackfellas are observers of time while whitefellas attempt to measure and control time. We see this in the first few sentences with the church bells, which are traditionally used to tell the time, and specifically to remind townsfolk when they are required to attend ceremonies at the church.

Blackfella collective, communal memory locates Indigenous people in Country in all-times. Collective, communal history is embodied in *Carpentaria's* Lawmen, who are simultaneously libraries and librarians, as well as historians, genealogists, song keepers, and family commentators. They understand the relationships between seasonal calendars, astronomy, tides and the moon; these are coded in stories and songs as Aboriginal memory symbols. Mozzie Fishman and Norm Phantom both read the changing land and the star maps respectively, to locate themselves in space-time. Star maps are constantly moving, as are the moon and tides, so this is a fluid type of time.

The oral transmission of education is preferenced in Aboriginal cultures, but despite assumptions that Aboriginal cultures are purely oral and non-literate, illiterate, or pre-literate, a variety of materials are inscribed with symbols and patterns, including rocks, caves, trees, skin and clothing. This way of communicating information semiotically should also be considered a written language in that it requires a specific literacy to read and to write this way. In *Carpentaria*, information is inscribed semiotically; the origin story of contemporary Pricklebush feuding was first recorded in the land: 'The old people wrote about the history of these wars on rock' (26).

If genetics link families biologically, then similarly, members of a community are culturally linked through memetics.[2] In both cases, these links evolve unbroken through time. Connections between self and ancestors are maintained through long and ancestral memories: world-views, traditions, intergenerational traumas and strength, ghosts, hauntings, stories, songlines, are all cultural information from the past. This long view of history gives context to *Carpentaria*'s characters, and to their demons. Pricklebush feuds and cohesion are transgenerational, and attest to the passage of culture through time; *everywhen* is stacked inside them.

*

Carpentaria is very much an Aboriginal story because it features a community of characters, rather than lone or token blackfellas. The characters are drawn larger than life within the novel, befitting the way they occupy mythical proportions in their families and community. Let's look at some of the main characters and their associated symbols, and how these illustrate the characters' different relationships to time.

First, the main players from the Phantom family. Angel Day is queen of the rubbish dump. Uptown's trash is Angel Day's treasure; she is very clever and resourceful, creating a whole home for her family from scavenging perfectly good rubbish from the tip.

Angel Day's determination to possess the dump clock in chapter 2 clues us into her desire to be able to engage with Uptown and be associated with white ways. It's worth mentioning that in this context, the word 'Uptown' probably references a certain sniping slur

---

2   Not to be confused with the internet info-artefacts, memes here are a metaphor analogous to genes. Just as genes pass down biological information, memes propagate cultural information; both units can evolve and mutate through reproduction. This concept was popularised by Richard Dawkins in his 1976 book *The Selfish Gene*, but I first learnt about this framework from Susan Blackmore in her 1999 book *The Meme Machine*.

that Aboriginal people sometimes use against other blackfellas who are perceived to be above their station, or who think they're better than other mob. Sometimes it's just used against people who have transcended our generally poor socio-economic situation into middle- or upper-class comfort.

Angel Day invests time-telling with authority: she intends to use the clocks to get her kids to school on time to appear respectable to Uptown (22–3). But she also wants to tell Pricklebush mob 'what time it is'. This is another slang reference: to tell someone 'what time it is' is to have authority over a situation. Angel Day wants to tell white time to black people: she wants to be a timekeeper, someone who can judge and make decisions, who demands respect and authority. Someone like this is also known as a 'mission manager'.

Rightfully so, Angel Day is rendered as a troublemaker for her desire to tell white time to the Pricklebush mob, who have their own time. This whole situation triggers a war at the dump, and ancient grievances erupt from people's memories (24–8). This fight over traditional ownership is linked to memories, because custodial memory is linked to stake in place – a reference to how in native title claims in some communities divisions are drawn down these same lines.

It is said that Normal Phantom, Angel's husband, 'knew as much about the sky as he did about water', which is much more than most people (6). In this way, Norm is seen as a Magical Koori by Uptown, as to them, his knowledge of the river and ocean and stars *seems* quite mystical, but we know that this information is really very mathematical and scientific. His name – Normal – alongside his mystical, mythical reputation is a way to play with this trope.

Norm has mastery of *everywhen*. When he kills crocodiles, it's said that he 'ended hundreds of lives of prehistoric living fossils' (7). He has a close relationship to the gropers, too, who are just as ancient and majestic (249–50). Similarly, the Pricklebush mob say:

... that Normal Phantom could grab hold of the river in his mind and live with it as his father's fathers did before him. His ancestors were the river people, who were living with the river from before time began. Normal was like ebbing water, he came and went on the flowing waters of the river right out to the sea. (6)

The mysterious Elias Smith shows up one day walking in from the sea, completely amnesiac. In this way he could be seen as an ideal 'New Australian', as he is white, and has lost his memory and therefore his links to other places and any claims to other traditions. Try as he might he can't remember anything, so he can't locate himself or identify himself relationally.

Elias becomes good friends with Norm, and an Uncle figure to Will, as they all bond over their love of fishing. I think Elias' amnesia allows a true friendship with Norm. They see each other as equals; Elias' lack of memory equates to lack of experience, which means he is not culpable in colonisation or historical racism. Through his amnesia he is rendered harmless. So as a blank slate, devoid of Uptown's colonial mindset, he is able to engage in non-hierarchical friendship with Norm. I think that if Elias had a backstory, it would have to inform his relations with Norm, and probably interfere in their friendship.

In the Phantom family, it's not just Norm who is especially cognisant of tidal ebbs and flows, and the rhythms of the moon. Norm and Angel's son Will Phantom experiences time as 'a fleeting whisper' (164). The narrator says:

Will knew how the tides worked simply by looking at the movement of a tree, or where the moon crossed the sky, the light of day, or the appearance of the sea. He carried the tide in his body. Even way out in the desert, when he was on the Fishman's convoy, a thousand miles away from the sea, he felt its rhythms. (401)

Bala, child of Hope and Will Phantom, has a whole chapter named after him. Bala is the only blackfella with a cultural name in this book, and if we consider that the Waanyi language was classified as functionally extinct at the time of writing, and that Bala's parents and grandparents have white names, we should read this child as signifying a return to cultural traditions in more ways than one. Consider the last few pages of the book, and the transgenerational connection between Bala and his granddad Norm. Literary scholar Cornelis Martin Renes says that 'Bala's perception of the location [of Desperance] as a "big yellow snake" places the destruction wrought by the cyclone in the mythical realm of the Great Creation Being' (62).

It took me a few years to start, but reading *Carpentaria* was a big part of me wanting to write fiction. I'd always had the inkling that maybe I could write stories one day, but working to pay the bills came before the luxury of writing for pleasure. On reflection, I think what kept me away for so long is that I'd I internalised that literature was for middle-class and white people, and for serious people with mortgages and stable jobs whose biggest stories are about the minutiae of their own lives. I rarely came across any stories about characters who thought and related the way I do, who spoke the way my family and community speak – with a sense of humour and a sense of the absurd, the way of all blackfellas living on the breadline.

I was introduced to *Carpentaria* in 2008 during my BEd undergrad; I took a unit on Aboriginal Literatures with Dr Peter Minter, who set chapter 1 for a reading. I fell in love with the characters, the voice, and the place – all both familiar and fantastic. The language was meaty, chewy, magical and delicious. I didn't know writing could be like this, let alone black writing – *our* writing. *Carpentaria* showed me that a chatty, informal, blackfella voice absolutely belongs in fiction, and that stories don't have to be straightforward, linear, or realistic, because life is rarely any of these things.

This book cemented my love affair with maximalist writing, intoxicating writing, too-much-information writing, with surreal and magically real ways of telling. *Carpentaria* showed me that stories don't have to be written for the white gaze, nor to teach white Australia a lesson about itself, but are better when they are by us, for us, and about us.

In this novel, Wright has performed a deep excavation of Aboriginal Country and community. Through my own writing I explore the tensions between Aboriginal sovereignty and colonial-capitalism in human relationships, and other relationships of power, so I'm inspired by the way *Carpentaria* asserts its own sovereignty by embodying ancient, intergenerational memories of people and place.

On a deep level, this speaks back against the amnesiac assimilationist rhetoric of 'one nation' that has dominated mainstream political discourse from the time of the novel's conception through to its publication (and even up until the present day). Wright pits vast and deep Aboriginal knowledge against the short memories of Howard and Hanson and their refusal to acknowledge our old peoples' losses, which are our losses too. In this sense, *Carpentaria* weaponises our ancestral consciousness against the capitalist, colonial corporatocracy that continues to subjugate Aboriginal sovereignty today.

References

Introduction

Bennett Daylight, Tegan. 'A phone call to Helen Garner', in Debra Adelaide (ed.), *The Simple Act of Reading*. Vintage, 2015.

Jose, Nicholas, 'Rewriting Australian literature' in Brenton Doecke, Larissa McLean Davies and Philip Mead (eds). *Teaching Australian Literature: From classroom conversations to national imaginings*. Wakefield Press, 2011, 95–107.

Livesy, Margot. *The Hidden Machinery: Essays on writing*. Tin House Books, 2017.

Prose, Francine. *Reading like a Writer*. Union Books, 2012. (First published 2006.)

Kinship in fiction and the genre blur of *Swallow the Air* as novel in stories

Birch, Tony. *Shadowboxing*. Hunter Publishing, 2006.

Kennedy, Gayle. *Me, Antman and Fleabag*. University of Queensland Press, 2007.

Leane, Jeanine. *Purple Threads*. University of Queensland Press, 2011.

Noonuccal, Oodgeroo. *The Dawn is at Hand*. Jacaranda Press, 1966.

Roach, Archie. *Charcoal Lane*. Warner Music Australia, 1990.

van Neerven, Ellen. '*The Yield* by Tara June Winch.' *Australian Book Review*, August 2019, no. 413.

Watson, Samuel Wagan. *Smoke Encrypted Whispers*. University of Queensland Press, 2004.

Winch, Tara June. *Swallow the Air*. University of Queensland Press, 2012. (First published 2006.)

Rhythm and play in *That Deadman Dance* by Kim Scott

Brewster, Anne. 'Can you anchor a shimmering nation state via regional Indigenous roots? Kim Scott talks to Anne Brewster about *That Deadman Dance*.' *Cultural Studies Review* 18(1), 2012.

Brown, Stuart. *Play*. Penguin, 2009.

Mead, Philip. 'Connectivity, community and the question of universality: Reading Kim Scott's chronotope and John Kinsella's commedia.' Peter Kirkpatrick and Robert Dixon (eds), *Republics of Letters: Literary communities in Australia*. Sydney University Press, 2012.

Nolan, Maggie. 'Shedding clothes: Performing cross-cultural exchange through costume and writing in Kim Scott's *That Deadman Dance*.' *Southerly* 75(2): 2015, pp. 124–45.

—. 'Reading Kim Scott's *That Deadman Dance*: Book clubs and postcolonial literary theory.' *Journal of the Association for the Study of Australian Literature* 6(2): 2016, pp. 1–13.

Pan Macmillan Australia. '*That Deadman Dance* by Kim Scott.' YouTube, 14 September 2010, <www.youtube.com/watch?v=xqY8v1l9Pls>.

Scott, Kim. *That Deadman Dance*. Picador, 2011.
Sutton-Smith, Brian. *The Ambiguity of Play*. Harvard University Press, 2001.
Wood, Charlotte. *The Writer's Room: Conversations about writing*. Allen & Unwin, 2016.

A big sunny shack: *Cosmo Cosmolino* by Helen Garner

Brennan, Bernadette. *A Writing Life: Helen Garner and her work*. Text Publishing, 2017.
Dessaix, Robert. 'Kitchen-table candour: Robert Dessaix on Helen Garner's *The Spare Room* [Book Review].' The *Monthly*, April 2008, 58–60. <www.themonthly.com.au/issue/2008/april/1343620158/robert-dessaix/kitchen-table-candour>
Garner, Helen. *Cosmo Cosmolino*. McPhee Gribble, 1992.

Short stories ... but linked: Steven Amsterdam's *Things We Didn't See Coming*

Amis, Kingsley, and Robert Conquest. *Spectrum II*. Pan, 1965.
Amsterdam, Steven. *Things We Didn't See Coming*. Sleepers Publishing, 2009.
—. *What the Family Needed*. Sleepers Publishing, 2011.
Dunn, Maggie, and Ann Morris. *The Composite Novel: The short story cycle in transition*. Twayne, 1995.
Ingram, Forrest L. *Representative Short Story Cycles of the Twentieth Century: Studies in a literary genre*. De Gruyter, 1971.

Reading crises, writing crisis

Abbott, Sally. *Closing Down*. Hachette, 2017.
Atwood, Margaret. *The Handmaid's Tale*. McClelland & Stewart, 1985.
Baldwin, James. 'The art of fiction', *Paris Review*, No. 91, Spring 1984. <www.theparisreview.org/interviews/2994/the-art-of-fiction-no-78-james-baldwin>
Bradley, James. *Clade*. Penguin, 2015.
—. *Ghost Species*. Hamish Hamilton, 2020.
—. 'Dyschronia review.' *Australian Book Review*, March 2018. <www.australianbookreview.com.au/abr-online/archive/2018/217-march-2018-no-399/4647-james-bradley-reviews-dyschronia-by-jennifer-mills>
Chiang, Ted. 'Explains the disaster novel we all suddenly live in.' *Electric Literature*, March 21, 2020. <electricliterature.com/ted-chiang-explains-the-disaster-novel-we-all-suddenly-live-in/>
Deahl, Rachel. 'In pandemic, dystopic fiction loses its luster for editors.' *Publishers Weekly*, 15 May 2020.<www.publishersweekly.com/pw/by-topic/industry-news/publisher-news/article/83341-in-pandemic-dystopian-fiction-loses-its-luster-for-editors.html>
Doyle, Briohny. *The Island Will Sink*. Brow Books, 2017.
Findlay, Daniel. *The Year of the Orphan*. Penguin Random House, 2017.
Le Guin, Ursula K. *The Left Hand of Darkness*. Hachette, 2017. (First published 1969.)
McKay, Laura Jean. *The Animals in That Country*. Scribe, Melbourne, 2020.
—, and Jane Rawson. 'Re Dear Extinction.' *The Victorian Writer.* 13 August 2019. <writersvictoria.org.au/writing-life/on-writing/re-dear-extinction>
Michael, Rose. 'Friday essay: How speculative fiction gained literary respectability.' *The Conversation*, 2 November 2018 <theconversation.com/friday-essay-how-speculative-fiction-gained-literary-respectability-102568>

—. *The Art of Navigation*. UWA Press, 2011.

Mills, Jennifer. *Dyschronia*. Picador, 2018.

Morgan, Margaret. *The Second Cure*. Penguin Random House, 2018.

Moshfegh, Ottessa. *My Year of Rest and Relaxation*. Penguin Random House, 2018.

Mundell, Meg. *The Trespassers*. University of Queensland Press, 2019.

Newman, Sandra. *The Heavens*. Grove Atlantic, 2019.

Outka, Elizabeth. 'How pandemics seep into literature.' *Paris Review*, 8 April 2020. <www.theparisreview.org/blog/2020/04/08/how-pandemics-seep-into-literature/>

Rawson, Jane. 'One plot, at most.' *Overland* 230, Autumn 2018. <overland.org.au/previous-issues/issue-230/essay-jane-rawson/>

—. *A Wrong Turn at the Office of Unmade Lists*. Transit Lounge, 2013.

Robinson, Alice. *The Glad Shout*. Affirm, 2019.

Steinbeck, John. *The Grapes of Wrath*. Viking Press, 1939.

Treloar, Lucy. *Wolfe Island*. Picador, 2019.

The sad old flesh: How we use non-human characters to interrogate humanity

Barcz, Anna. 'Posthumanism and its animal voices in literature.' *Teksty Drugie* 1, 2015, p. 269.

Bernaerts, Lars, Marco Caracciolo, Luc Herman, and Bart Vervaeck. 'The storied lives of non-human narrators.' *Narrative* 22, 2014, pp. 68–93.

DeMello, Margo. Introduction in *Speaking for Animals: Animal autobiographical writing*. Edited by Margo DeMello. Routledge, 2013. pp. 1–14

Dovey, Ceridwen. *Only the Animals*. Hamish Hamilton, 2014.

Falconer, Delia. 'Go ape: *Only the Animals* by Ceridwen Dovey.' *Sydney Review of Books*, 25 July 2014. <sydneyreviewofbooks.com/review/only-animals-ceridwen-dovey/>

Herman, David. 'Animal autobiography; Or, narration beyond the human.' *Humanities* 5(4), 2016.

McKay, Laura Jean. *The Animals in That Country*. Scribe, Melbourne, 2020.

Nayar, Pramod K. *Posthumanism*. Polity, 2014.

Starting from place: An introduction to a different way of thinking

Bachelard, Gaston. *The Poetics of Space*. Beacon Press, 1969.

Carman, Luke. *An Elegant Young Man*. Giramondo, 2013.

de Certeau, Michel. *The Practice of Everyday Life*. New revised and augmented edition, edited by Luce Giard. University of Minnesota Press, 1994.

Molloy, Diane. 'Finding hope in the stories: Alexis Wright's *Carpentaria* and the carnivalesque search for a new order.' *Journal of the Association for the Study of Australian Literature*. (12)3, 1–8, 2012.

Ng, Lynda. *Indigenous Transnationalism: Essays on* Carpentaria. Giramondo, 2018.

Rodoreda, Geoff. 'Orality and narrative structure in Alexis Wright's *Carpentaria*.' *Journal of the Association for the Study of Australian Literature*. (16)2, 1–3, 2016.

Wood, James. *How Fiction Works*. Picador, 2008.

Wright, Alexis. *Carpentaria*. Giramondo, 2006.

—. 'A journey in writing place'. *Meanjin*. Winter, 2019. <meanjin.com.au/essays/a-journey-in-writing-place/>

Read to find yourself

Greer, Andrew Sean. *Less*. Little, Brown, & Co., 2017.

Karalis, Vrasidas. *The Glebe Point Road Blues*. Brandl & Schlesinger, 2019.

Malouf, David. *Ransom*. Knopf, 2009.

Muñoz, Jose. *Cruising Utopia: The then and there of queer futurity*. NYU Press, 2009.

Scott, Ronnie. *The Adversary*. Penguin Random House, 2020.

White, Patrick. *Voss*. Penguin, 2012. (First published 1957.)

Postcards to Charlotte Wood: Revisiting *The Natural Way of Things*

Australian Associated Press. 'Queensland woman dies from "horrific injuries" after Sunshine Coast assault.' *Guardian*, 22 August 2020.

Popova, Maria. 'Poet Jane Kenyon's advice on writing: Some of the wisest words to create and live by'. *Brainpickings*, September 2015. <www.brainpickings.org/2015/09/15/jane-kenyon-advice-on-writing/>

Sentilles, Sarah. 'We're going to need more than empathy.' *Lithub*, 6 July 2017. <lithub.com/were-going-to-need-more-than-empathy/>

Summers, Anne. 'On *The Natural Way of Things*.' Reading Australia series. *Griffith Review*, 2016. <www.griffithreview.com/reading-australia/>

Wood, Charlotte. *The Natural Way of Things*. Allen & Unwin, 2015.

—. 'Reading isn't shopping.' *Sydney Review of Books,* 14 August 2018. <sydneyreviewofbooks.com/essay/reading-isnt-shopping/>

Fearless: On Christos Tsiolkas

Day, Elizabeth. 'Christos Tsiolkas: There's a tameness to the modern novel.' *Guardian,* 30 October 2011. <www.theguardian.com/theobserver/2011/oct/30/christos-tsiolkas-slap-tv-interview>

Orwell, George. *Why I Write*. Penguin, 2005. (First published 1946.)

Tsiolkas, Christos. *Loaded*. Vintage, 1998.

—. *The Slap*. Allen & Unwin, 2008.

—. *Merciless Gods*. Allen & Unwin, 2014.

—. *On Patrick White: Writers on writers*. Black Inc., 2018.

—. *Damascus*. Allen & Unwin, 2019.

Caught in the rip: The first seven pages of Tim Winton's *Breath*

Denton, Andrew. *Enough Rope: Tim Winton, Aron Ralston*. Australian Broadcasting Corporation, 2004.

Gardner, John. *On Becoming a Novelist*. WW Norton & Co., 1999. (First published 1983.)

Winton, Tim. *The Turning*. Penguin, 2004.

—. *Breath*. Penguin, 2008.

Ending, unfurling: *The Life to Come* by Michelle de Kretser

Bishop, Stephanie. *Man Out of Time*. Sydney, Hachette, 2018.

Brewster, Anne, and Sue Kossew. *Rethinking the Victim: Gender and violence in contemporary Australian women's writing*. Routledge, 2019.

Chakraborty, Mridula Nath. '"Australian accent": Michelle de Kretser's *The Life to Come*.' *Phoenix: Sri Lanka Journal of English in the Commonwealth*, XV & XVI (2018 & 2019): 99–105

de Kretser, Michelle. *The Life to Come*. Allen & Unwin, 2017.

Duguid, Lindsay. 'A country of no importance – fiction.' *Times Literary Supplement*, 9 February 2018. <www.the-tls.co.uk/articles/a-country-of-no-importance/>

Egan, Jennifer. *A Visit from the Goon Squad*. New York, Corsair, 2010.

Ley, James. 'Fictive selves: *The Life to Come* by Michelle de Kretser.' *Sydney Review of Books*, 5 December 2017. <sydneyreviewofbooks.com/review/life-to-come-michelle-de-kretser/>

Moller, Michael. Personal interview. 31 May 2020.

Theroux, Marcel. '*The Life to Come* by Michelle de Kretser review – tales of human complexity.' *Guardian*, 3 January 2018. <www.theguardian.com/books/2018/jan/03/the-life-to-come-by-michelle-de-kretser-review>

An uneasy anticipation: Tension in MJ Hyland's novels

Elgrably, Jordan. 'James Baldwin: The art of fiction no. 78.' *The Paris Review*, 91, 1984. <www.theparisreview.org/interviews/2994/the-art-of-fiction-no-78-james-baldwin>

Hyland, MJ. *This Is How*. Text Publishing, 2009.

—. *How the Light Gets In* (2nd edn). Penguin Random House, 2010.

—. *Carry Me Down* (2nd edn). Text Publishing, 2016.

Structure in Nam Le's 'Love and honour and pity and pride and compassion and sacrifice'

Le, Nam. 'Love and honour and pity and pride and compassion and sacrifice', *The Boat*. Penguin Books, 2009.

O'Connor, Flannery. 'Writing short stories.' *Mystery and Manners*. Farrar, Straus & Giroux, 1970.

If you see the Buddha in suburbia kill him: *Anguli Ma: A gothic tale* by Chi Vu

Hanh, Thich Nhat. *The Heart of the Buddha's Teaching*. Routledge, 1998.

—. *Transformation at the Base: Fifty verses on the nature of consciousness*. Parallax Press, 2002.

Hirsch, Marianne. *Generation of Postmemory: Visual and writing culture after the Holocaust*. University of Colombia Press, 2012.

Nguyen, Viet Thanh. *Nothing Ever Dies: Vietnam and the memory of war*. Harvard University Press, 2016.

Pelaud, Isabelle. *This Is All I Choose to Tell: History and hybridity in Vietnamese American literature*. Temple University Press, 2010.

Pham, Hoa. *The Other Shore*. Seizure, 2014.

—. *Lady of the Realm*. Spinifex, 2017.

Vu, Chi. *Anguli Ma: A gothic tale*. Giramondo, 2010.

—. 'The 1.5 Vietnamese-American writer as post-colonial translator'. *Kunapipi*, 130–146, 2011.

References

Sabotage and repair: Intertextuality in Carrie Tiffany's *Exploded View*

Goldsmith, Kenneth. *The Weather*. Make Now Press, 2005.

Lethem, Jonathan. 'The ecstasy of influence.' *Harpers Magazine*, 6 June 2007, pp. 59–71.

Rich, Adrienne. 'When we dead awaken: Writing as re-vision.' *College English*, vol. 34, no. 1, 1972, pp. 18–30.

Tiffany, Carrie. *Everyman's Rules for Scientific Living*. Pan Macmillan, 2005.

—. *Mateship with Birds*. Pan Macmillan, 2012.

—. *Exploded View*. Text, 2019.

—. *On the Nature Strip: The search for an embodied Australian language in* Everyman's Rules for Scientific Living, Mateship with Birds, *and* Exploded View, PhD thesis, Deakin University, 2020.

Wright, Fiona. 'When the manuals fail us: *Exploded View* by Carrie Tiffany.' *Sydney Review of Books*, 26 April 2019, <sydneyreviewofbooks.com/review/exploded-view-carrie-tiffany/>.

Structure, serpents and Serena McGarry: Kate Jennings' *Snake*

Jennings, Kate. *Snake*. Minerva Press, 1996.

Jensen, Erik, *Writers on Writers: Kate Jennings*. Black Inc, 2017.

Lawrence, DH. 'Snake.' <www.poetryfoundation.org/poems/148471/snake-5bec57d7bfa17> 1920–21.

Lawson, Henry. *Fifteen Stories* (ed C. Roderick). Angus & Robertson, 1959.

Rawson, Hugh. *Wicked Words*. Crown Publishers, 1989.

'Not crying now, but brilliant-eyed': Epiphany in Harrower's 'The fun of the fair'

Harrower, Elizabeth. 'The fun of the fair' in *A Few Days in the Country and Other Stories*. Text Publishing, 2015.

How to build a glass church: Peter Carey's *Oscar and Lucinda*

Carey, Peter. *Oscar and Lucinda*. Faber & Faber, 1988.

—. *True History of the Kelly Gang*. University of Queensland Press, 2000.

—. *30 Days in Sydney: A wildly distorted account*. Bloomsbury, 2001.

Carter, Angela. 'Oscar for envy.' Review of *Oscar and Lucinda* in the *Guardian*, 1 April 1988. <www.theguardian.com/books/1998/apr/01/fiction.petercarey>

Falconer, Delia. *Sydney*. NewSouth, 2010.

Grenville, Kate and Sue Woolfe. *Making Stories: How ten Australian novels were written*. Allen & Unwin, 2001. (First published 1993.)

McCrum, Robert. 'Reawakening Ned', interview with Peter Carey in the *Observer*, 7 January 2001. <www.theguardian.com/books/2001/jan/07/fiction.petercarey>

Rubin, Merle. 'From Orwell's own manuscript, new light on "1984".' *Christian Science Monitor*, 28 December 1984. <www.csmonitor.com/1984/1228/122841.html>

Rushdie, Salman. *Joseph Anton*. Jonathan Cape, 2012.

Wood, James. *How Fiction Works*. Vintage, 2009.

A metaphysical meeting place: *Sixty Lights* by Gail Jones

Clayton, Barbara. *A Penelopean Poetics: Reweaving the feminine in Homer's* Odyssey. Lanham, 2004.

Costi, Angela. 'Making lace.' *Southern Sun, Aegean Light*. Ed. NN Trakakis. Arcadia, 2011.

Jones, Gail. *Sixty Lights*. Vintage, 2005.

Koval, Romana. *Books and Writing*. ABC Radio National. 27 March 2005.

Lines of sight: Living images in the short fiction of Gerald Murnane

Murnane, Gerald. *Collected Short Fiction*. Giramondo, 2018.

An obsidian mirror: David Malouf's *Ransom*

Ashcroft, Bill. 'David Malouf in conversation with Bill Ashcroft.' *UNSW Writing*, April 2010. <www.youtube.com/watch?v=QgfoPU1H3Cc>

Malouf, David. *Ransom*. Vintage, 2010. (First published 2009.)

Ten thoughts on fiction that slays: Reading Julie Koh's satire in a post-truth pandemic

An, Yueli. 'A day in quarantine.' Unpublished poem, 2020.

Atwood, Margaret. 'Margaret Atwood: the road to Ustopia.' *Guardian*, 15 October 2011. <www.theguardian.com/books/2011/oct/14/margaret-atwood-road-to-ustopia>

—. 'Margaret Atwood on science fiction, dystopias, and intestinal parasites.' *The Geek's Guide to the Galaxy*, Episode 94, 18 Sept 2013. <www.wired.com/2013/09/geeks-guide-margaret-atwood/>

Barnes, Sophia. 'The bleeding edge: New short fiction.' *Sydney Review of Books*. 21 October 2016. <sydneyreviewofbooks.com/review/after-the-carnage-peripheral-vision-portable-curiosities/>

BBC staff. 'What happens when we laugh.' *BBC Bitesize*, 2020. <www.bbc.co.uk/bitesize/articles/zjxkscw>

Boland, Michaela. 'The Australian Government has an arts problem that starts with the word itself.' *ABC News*, 11 December 2019. <www.abc.net.au/news/2019-12-11/australian-government-arts-policy-arts-funding-dirty-word/11784596>

Dierking, P. 'Post-truth named 2016 word of the year.' *Learn English*, 22 November 2016. <learningenglish.voanews.com/a/post-truth-named-2016-word-of-the-year/3603012.html>

Elliot, Robert. 'Satire.' *Britannica*. 23 August 1998. <www.britannica.com/art/satire>

Koh, Julie. *Capital Misfits*. Spineless Wonders, 2015.

—. 'The level playing field' in Lohrey, Amanda (ed.), *The Best Australian Stories 2015*. Black Inc., 2015.

—. *Portable Curiosities*. UQP, 2016.

—. Interview with Sonia Nair, *Books + Publishing*, 2016

—. 'Satirists rising: *Portable Curiosities* and the new wave.' *Kill Your Darlings*, 14 June 2017. <www.killyourdarlings.com.au/2016/06/satirists-rising-portable-curiosities-and-the-new-wave/>

—. 'The Fictional Julie Koh'. Blog:

Le Guin, Ursula. *Steering the Craft: A twenty-first-century guide to sailing the sea of story*. Mariner Books, 2015. Reprint (1998).

Nobilo, Bianca. Interview with Tom Walker. CNN. 28 November 2019. <www.youtube.
com/watch?v=E-MFQBwTNQQ&list=PL4P2d_uw3w2pBVBXtHFghsVVZMvL3-
zEj&index=7&t=0s>

Oke, Femi and Malika Bilal. Interview panel with Tom Walker. 'Can satire survive in a "post-
truth" era?' *The Stream*, Al Jazeera, 8 November 2018. <www.aljazeera.com/program/
episode/2018/11/5/can-satire-survive-in-the-post-truth-era/>

Potaka, Elise and Luke McMahon. 'Unmasking a troll: Aussie "jihadist" Australi Witness
a 20-year-old American nerd.' *Sydney Morning Herald*, 12 September 2015. <www.
smh.com.au/national/unmasking-a-troll-aussie-jihadist-australi-witness-a-20yearold-
american-nerd-20150909-gjil47.html>

Smith, Justin. 'The end of satire'. *New York Times*, 8 April 2019. <www.nytimes.
com/2019/04/08/opinion/the-end-of-satire.html>

Tumarkin, Maria. 'Not another diversity panel: Move, reader, move'. *Griffith Review 61: Who
We Are*. 30 July, 2018. 269

Van Schilt, Stephanie and Veronica Sullivan. 'Episode six: Julie Koh'. *Sisteria*, 15 May 2017.
<sisteriapodcast.com/podcast/episode-six-julie-koh/>

Wikipedia editors, '2016 in Australia'. Wikipedia. <en.wikipedia.org/wiki/2016_in_
Australia>

A manual for writers: *Elizabeth Costello*

Coetzee, JM. *Elizabeth Costello: Eight lessons*. Random House Australia, 2003.

—. 'As a woman grows older.' *New York Review of Books*, 15 January 2004.
—. 'Lies.' *New York Review of Books*, 21 December 2017. <www.nybooks.com/
articles/2017/12/21/lies/>

—. 'Australia's shame: *No Friend but the Mountains* by Behrouz Bouchani.' *New York Review
of Books*, 26 September 2019. <www.nybooks.com/articles/2019/09/26/australias-
shame/>

Kannemeyer, JC. *JM Coetzee: A life in writing*, translated by Michiel Heyms. Scribe, 2012.

Lawson, Henry. *A Camp-fire Yarn: Complete works 1885–1900* ed. Leonard Cronin.
Lansdowne, 1984.

Samuelson, Meg. 'An "international author, but in a different sense": JM Coetzee and
"Literatures of the South".' *Thesis Eleven* vol. 162 (2021).

Everywhen in everything: Reading *Carpentaria* like an Aboriginal writer

Arbon, Veronica. *Arlathirnda Ngurkarnda Ityirnda: Being-Knowing-Doing: De-colonising
Indigenous tertiary education*. Post Pressed, 2009.

Blackmore, Susan J. *The Meme Machine*. Oxford University Press, 1999.

Dawkins, Richard. *The Selfish Gene*. Oxford University Press, 1976.

Grieves, Vicki. 'Aboriginal spirituality: A baseline for Indigenous knowledges development in
Australia.' *Canadian Journal of Native Studies* 28, no. 2, 2008, pp. 363–98.

Molloy, Diane. 'Finding hope in the stories: Alexis Wright's *Carpentaria* and the carnivalesque
search for a new order.' *Journal of the Association for the Study of Australian Literature:
JASAL* 12, no. 3, 2012.

O'Brien, Kerry. 'Extended interview with Alexis Wright.' *7.30 Report.* ABC, 21 June 2007. <www.abc.net.au/7.30/extended-interview-with-alexis-wright/2679496>

Renes, Cornelis Martin. 'Sung by an Indigenous siren: Epic and epistemology in Alexis Wright's *Carpentaria.' Coolabah* 27, 2019.

Stanner, WEH. 'The Dreaming' (1953). In *White Man Got No Dreaming: Essays 1938–1973,* 23–40. Australian National University Press, 1979.

Suzuki, David. 'Aboriginal people, not environmentalists, are our best bet for protecting the planet.' *Vancouver Sun*, 2015. Published electronically June 8.

Wright, Alexis. *Carpentaria.* Giramondo Publishing, 2006.

Contributors

Debra Adelaide is the author or editor of seventeen books, including novels, short stories, essays, and academic publications. Her most recent books are the collection of short stories, *Zebra* (2019), which won the Steele Rudd Award in the Queensland Literary Awards, and *The Innocent Reader* (2019), essays on reading and writing. Until 2020 she taught creative writing at the University of Technology Sydney.

Stephanie Bishop is the author of *Man Out of Time*, *The Other Side of the World* and *The Singing*. Her work has been published in the *London Review of Books*, the *Guardian*, the *Times Literary Supplement* and elsewhere. She is currently a Senior Lecturer in Creative Writing at the University of New South Wales, Australia.

Felicity Castagna is an essayist, teacher and writer on many cross-disciplinary art projects. Her most recent novel, *No More Boats*, was a finalist in the 2018 Miles Franklin Literary Awards and is published internationally. She is also the author of *Small Indiscretions* and *The Incredible Here and Now*, which received the Prime Minister's Award for Literature. Her next book, *Girls in Boys' Cars*, will be released in 2021.

Belinda Castles is the author of four novels: *Bluebottle*, *Hannah and Emil*, *The River Baptists* and *Falling Woman*, and winner of the *Australian*/Vogel's and Asher literary awards. She teaches writing at the University of Sydney.

Tegan Bennett Daylight is a writer, teacher and critic. She is the author of three novels: *Bombora*, *What Falls Away* and *Safety*, as well as several books for children and teenagers. Her collection of short stories, *Six Bedrooms*, was published in July 2015, and shortlisted for the ALS Gold Medal, the Steele Rudd Award and the 2016 Stella Prize. Her book of essays, *The Details*, was published by Scribner in July 2020. She works as a lecturer in English and creative writing, and lives in the Blue Mountains near Sydney with her husband and two children.

Nigel Featherstone's most recent work is the war novel *Bodies of Men*, which was published by Hachette Australia in 2019 and longlisted for the 2020 ARA Historical Novel Prize, shortlisted in the 2019 Queensland Literary Awards, and received a 2019 Canberra Critics' Circle Award. His other works include short stories published in numerous literary journals, novellas, and a libretto.

Roanna Gonsalves is the award-winning author of *The Permanent Resident*, published in India as *Sunita De Souza Goes to Sydney*. Her creative and scholarly works have been published, broadcast and performed across various media internationally. She teaches creative writing in the university sector in Australia. See more at <roannagonsalves.com.au>.

Ashley Hay is the author of the novels *A Hundred Small Lessons*, *The Railwayman's Wife* and *The Body in the Clouds*, as well as four books of narrative non-fiction. Her work has won the Colin Roderick Prize and the People's Choice Award in the NSW Premier's Prize. She is the editor of *Griffith Review* and former literary editor of the *Bulletin*.

Nicholas Jose has published seven novels, including *Paper Nautilus*, *The Custodians*, *The Red Thread* and *Original Face*, and three collections of short stories. His non-fiction includes *Chinese Whispers*, *Cultural*

Essays and an acclaimed memoir, *Black Sheep: Journey to Borroloola*. He is an Adjunct Professor in the Writing and Society Research Centre, Western Sydney University and Emeritus Professor of English and Creative Writing at the University of Adelaide.

Cate Kennedy writes fiction, non-fiction and poetry and is probably best known for her short stories, which have been published internationally and are currently studied on the Victorian school syllabus (*Dark Roots*, 2006 and *Like a House on Fire*, 2012). She has edited anthologies of Australian short stories and is the recipient of several awards for her own work, including the People's Choice Award in the NSW Premier's Literary Awards for her novel *The World Beneath* (2009) and the Victorian Premier's Literary Award for Poetry for her collection *The Taste of River Water* (2011). She lives, works, gardens and writes in Castlemaine, Victoria.

Fiona McFarlane is the author of *The Night Guest* (2012) and *The High Places* (2016). She teaches creative writing at the University of California, Berkeley.

Emily Maguire is the author of three non-fiction books and six novels, including the Stella Prize and Miles Franklin Literary Award shortlisted *An Isolated Incident*. She works as a teacher and as a mentor to young and emerging writers and was the 2018/2019 Writer-in-Residence at the Charles Perkins Centre at the University of Sydney.

Angela Meyer's debut novel *A Superior Spectre* was shortlisted for an Aurealis Award, the MUD Literary Prize, an Australian Book Industry Award, and the Readings Prize for New Australian Writing. She is also the author of a novella, *Joan Smokes* (winner of the Mslexia Novella Award) and a book of flash fiction, *Captives*. She is a writing teacher, editor and former book publisher.

Rose Michael's first novel, *The Asking Game*, was a runner-up for the Vogel and received an Aurealis honourable mention. Short stories from it appeared in *Island*, *Griffith Review* and *Best Australian Stories*. Extracts from her second novel, *The Art of Navigation*, were shortlisted for a Conjure award and published in *Review of Australian Fiction*. She is a lecturer in writing and publishing at RMIT.

Ryan O'Neill is the author of *Their Brilliant Careers: The fantastic lives of sixteen extraordinary Australian writers* and *The Drover's Wives: 99 reinterpretations of Henry Lawson's Australian classic*.

A.S. Patrić is the author of three short story collections and two novels. He has won multiple prizes for his short fiction and his debut novel *Black Rock White City* won the Miles Franklin Award in 2016.

Hoa Pham is a psychologist and author of seven fiction books and one play. She holds a professional doctorate in creative writing and is the founder of *Peril*, an Asian-Australian arts and culture magazine. Her website is <www.hoapham.net>.

Peter Polites is a novelist from Western Sydney. He has written two queer noirs, *Down the Hume* and *The Pillars*, which won the 2020 NSW Premier's Multicultural Literary Award. He's also won the 2020 Woollahra Digital Literature Prize for Fiction. In 2021 he will be a writer in residence at UNSW Canberra.

Jane Rawson writes essays, stories and books, mostly about the environment and animals, and also works for a Tasmanian conservation organisation. Her most recent books are *From the Wreck* (2017) and *The Handbook: Surviving and living with climate change* (2015).

Mykaela Saunders is a Koori and Lebanese writer, teacher and community researcher, currently working on two short story collections and a novel. Her work has won the ABR Elizabeth Jolley Short Story Prize and Oodgeroo Noonuccal Indigenous Poetry Prize, among other awards and shortlistings. She has also been the recipient of several fellowships and grants. Mykaela belongs to the Tweed Goori community.

Irini Savvides is an English teacher and author. *Willow Tree and Olive* received a White Raven award (Bologna, 2002), and she was a finalist in the *Sydney Morning Herald*'s Young Writer of the Year awards. *Sky Legs* won the 2004 Peace Award. Irini has judged the Prime Minister's Literary Awards (2014–16). She was awarded her PhD in 2013 (Writing and Society, Western Sydney University).

Anna Spargo-Ryan is the author of *The Gulf* and *The Paper House*, and a winner of the Horne Prize. She is a PhD candidate in Creative Writing at Deakin University, and nonfiction editor at *ISLAND Magazine*. Her non-fiction book is *A Kind of Magic* (Picador).

Maria Takolander is the author of *The Double (and Other Stories)* (2013) and four poetry collections, including *Trigger Warning* (2021). Maria is also a reviewer and widely published scholar. She is the author of *Catching Butterflies: Bringing magical realism to ground* (2007) and co-editor of *The Limits of Life Writing* (2019). Her website is <mariatakolander.com>.

Julienne van Loon is the author of *The Thinking Woman*, which was highly commended in the Victorian Premier's Literary Awards, and three novels including the *Australian*/Vogel's-Award-winning *Road Story*. She lives in Melbourne, where she is an Associate Professor with the Writing and Publishing program at RMIT University. Her latest fiction appears in *Griffith Review 66: The Novella Project VII*.

Ellen van Neerven is an award-winning writer, editor and literary activist belonging to the Mununjali people of the Yugambeh nation. Ellen's books include *Heat and Light*, *Comfort Food* and *Throat*. Their books have been the recipients of the David Unaipon Award, the Dobbie Literary Award, the NSW Premier's Literary Award Indigenous Writers Prize and the inaugural Quentin Bryce Award.

Beth Yahp's fiction and creative non-fiction include *The Red Pearl and Other Stories*; a memoir, *Eat First, Talk Later*, which was shortlisted for the 2018 Adelaide Festival Award for Literature (Non-fiction); and a prize-winning novel, *The Crocodile Fury*. Beth currently lives in Sydney and lectures in Creative Writing at the University of Sydney.

Acknowledgments

Thank you to everyone at NewSouth Publishing. The patient generosity of Harriet McInerney, Emma Hutchinson, Joumana Awad and their team have made the complex task of co-ordinating twenty-six writers' thoughts and schedules seamless. Deep thanks to Phillipa McGuinness for immediately seeing the value in this project and working incredibly hard to make it happen. At the editorial coalface, thank you to Jocelyn Hungerford, whose steady care and intelligence has never faltered and to Anne Savage for her meticulous proofreading. Ongoing thanks to my agent, Pippa Masson. Her unique blend of insight, efficiency and glamour make her a brilliant and charming advocate. To all my students, I love to hear you talk about your reading, thank you. Thanks and solidarity to my colleagues Beth Yahp and Vanessa Berry: inspirational teachers, gentle writerly companions on this winding road.

Thank you, wholeheartedly, to the contributors to this collection. What delightful, clever colleagues you have been in this bewildering year. I could not have set myself a more sustaining task than to talk to you all about the stories you treasure. Extra thanks to Debra Adelaide, for her warm and wise counsel on how to embark on such a project. A special note to Gail Jones who, though unable to contribute, was an early and key supporter. Irini Savvides' encouragement at the outset made me brave enough to ask everyone else. Thank you, dear friend.

Thank you to the world of Australian stories, in which I have made my home; to my large family, for the love and book chat, and to my little family, Brad, Ellie and Olive, who make me happy, so I can do my work.

Index

2 Days in Paris 42

Abbey, Sue 10
Abbott, Sally 69
Aboriginal people 8–9, 15–18, 24–25, 255, 326–43; *see also* Dreaming; everywhen; stories; Indigenous
Aboriginal writers 8–12, 24–25, 325–43; *see also* Birch, Tony; Leane, Jeanine; Saunders, Mykaela; Scott, Kim; van Neerven, Ellen; Winch, Tara June; Wright, Alexis
Adelaide, Debra 1, 4, 219–32, 353
Adversary, The 107–11
AIDS 103, 108–09, 290
Amsterdam, Steven 5, 42–55
Anguli Ma 3, 193–206
animal narrators 4, 75–87
Animals in That Country, The 57, 59, 60, 64, 70, 84–86
apocalypse 62, 64–65
Arbon, Veronica 326
Atwood, Margaret 59, 114, 209, 304, 310
Aunt's Story, The 322
Austen, Jane 30, 108
Australia 319, 323–24
    Australian literature 2, 323
    Australian writing 1–2, 293
autofiction 156, 158, 309

Bachelard, Gaston 95
Baldwin, James 72, 181
Barcz, Anna 82–83
Barnes, Sophia 298
beauty 118
Bernaerts, Lars 83, 85–86
Birch, Tony 11
Bishop, Stephanie 4, 154, 272–85, 353
book covers 262–63
Bradley, James 66
Breath 5, 137–51
Brennan, Bernadette 30–31, 33
Brewster, Anne 21, 159

Brisbane 7–8, 11–12
Brooks, Geraldine 290
Brown, Stuart 19
Buddhism 193–206
bushfires 57, 67, 299, 309, 312

'C is for cockroach' 301, 302–03
Canberra 57
Capital Misfits 308
Carey, Peter 5, 244–58
Carman, Luke 5, 88–89, 97–99
Carpentaria 3, 88, 90–97, 99, 324, 325–43
Carroll, Lewis 211, 214
Carry Me Down 167, 169, 173
Carter, Angela 209, 252–53
Castagna, Felicity 5, 88–99, 353
Castles, Belinda 1–6, 244–58, 353
Chakraborty, Mridula Nath 153, 155
characters
    minor 181–82
    unlikable 226
Chiang, Ted 71–72
Clade 66
Clayton, Barbara 267–68
climate change 56–74
Closing Down 69
Coetzee, JM 4, 314–24
communitas 4, 6, 208
conjunctions 253–54
Conquest, Robert 43
contrasts 181
Corris, Peter 35–36
Cosmo Cosmolino 5, 26–41
Costi, Angela 267
COVID-19 56–74, 116, 121, 257, 287, 290, 298–99, 303, 311
creative writing classes 26–27, 36, 221
crisis 56–74, 236, 309; *see also* bushfires; climate change; plague

Damascus 132–35
Daylight, Tegan Bennett 1, 5, 26–41, 114, 354
de Certeau, Michel 90

de Kretser, Michelle 2, 3, 152–66
Deadman Dance, That 3, 13–25
defamiliarisation 86, 213, 214
DeMello, Margo 86
Dessaix, Robert 35–37, 41
Dhiravamsa, VR 196
dialogue 147–50, 175–76
Dovey, Ceridwen 77–83, 86
Doyle, Briohny 68
Dreaming 329, 331, 335–36; *see also* everywhen
Duguid, Lindsay 153
Dunn, Maggie 44
Dyschronia 65–66, 68, 69, 71
dystopian fiction 56–74; *see also* speculative fiction

Elegant Young Man, An 88–89, 95–99
Elizabeth Costello 4, 314–24
emptiness 196–98, 202; *see also* Buddhism; interbeing
endings 152–54
epiphanies 233–36, 239–43, 284–85
everywhen 326–30, 333, 335, 336–37
Exploded View 4, 207–18

Fagen, Robert 19
Falconer, Delia 81, 245
'fat girl in history, The' 301, 302–03
Featherstone, Nigel 6, 125–36, 354
fiction 19–20, 24, 41, 281, 322; *see also* literary fiction; novels; science fiction; stories; speculative fiction
Findlay, Daniel 69
Flinders, Matthew 23, 24
Ford, Clementine 114
foreshadowing 143, 178–79
Fortunes of Richard Mahony, The 322
'fun of the fair, The' 5, 233–43
Furphy, Joseph 323

Index

Gardner, John 139
Garner, Helen 1, 5, 26–41
gay literature 8, 100–11
gender 113, 116, 210–18, 318
Ghost Species 66
Glad Shout, The 69
Glebe Point Road Blues, The
  100–04
Gonsalves, Roanna 2, 3, 152–66,
  354
Great Expectations 261, 268
Grenville, Kate 256–57, 334

Handmaid's Tale, The 59, 114
Hanh, Thich Nhat 196, 201, 203
Harrower, Elizabeth 5, 233–43
Hay, Ashley 3–4, 112–24, 354
Herman, David 83
heroes 293–94
Homer 266, 291–95
How the Light Gets In 167, 169,
  170, 174, 180
Hyland, MJ 5, 167–83

Iliad, The 105–07, 286–96; *see also*
  Homer; *Ransom*
Imaginary Life, An, 293, 322–23
immediacy 142–46
Indigenous writers *see* Aboriginal
  writers
Ingram, Forrest 44
inspiration 138–39
interbeing 3, 194–95, 198,
  204, 206; *see also* Buddhism;
  emptiness
intertextuality 207–18
Island Will Sink, The 68

Jamieson, Nigel 115
Jane Eyre 209, 260–61, 264, 265,
  268
Jennings, Kate 4, 219–32
Jensen, Erik 227, 228, 231
Jones, Gail 6, 206, 259–71
Jose, Nicholas 2, 4, 92, 314–24, 354

Kafka, Franz 76, 221
Karalis, Vrasidas 100–04
Kelly, Ned 250–52, 258
Kennedy, Cate 2, 5, 137–51, 355
Kennedy, Gayle 10
Kenyon, Jane 120–21

Ker Conway, Jill 220, 222, 228
kinship 5–6, 7–12, 329
Knox, Malcolm 114
Koh, Julie 3, 297–313
Kossew, Sue 159
Koval, Ramona 270

language 13–15, 19–22, 24, 246–
  47, 317, 322; *see also* reading
Lawrence, DH 226–27
Lawson, Henry 78, 227, 323
Le, Nam 3, 184–92
Le Guin, Ursula 72, 302
Leane, Jeanine 10
Lethem, Jonathan 207–09
libraries 7–8
Life to Come, The 3, 152–66
literacy 19–20, 23, 338–39
literary awards 10, 11, 43, 77, 134,
  263; *see also* Miles Franklin
  Literary Award
literary fiction 43, 49, 59, 125, 183
literature 296, 342
Livesy, Margot 5
Loaded 100, 126–30, 131
'Love and honour and pity and
  pride and compassion and
  sacrifice' 3, 184–92

Maguire, Emily 5, 233–43, 355
Malouf, David 3, 30, 104–07,
  286–96, 322–23
maps 89–93, 100
McCracken, Elizabeth 188
McFarlane, Fiona 3, 184–92, 355
McKay, Laura Jean 57, 59, 60,
  62–64, 70, 84–86
Mead, Philip 17, 23–24
Melbourne 69, 74, 109, 126, 127,
  186, 194, 199, 264, 267
Merciless Gods 130–31
metaphor 37–38, 41, 60–62,
  140–41, 150–51, 249–51, 262,
  295
Meyer, Angela 5, 167–83, 355
Michael, Rose 3, 56–74, 356
Miles Franklin Literary Award 11,
  322, 325
Mill, John Stuart 122
Mills, Jennifer 65–66, 68, 69, 71
minor characters 181–82
miscommunication 176–77

Moller, Michael 157, 165
Molloy, Diane 336
Morgan, Margaret 60, 61, 70
Morris, Ann 44
Moshfegh, Otessa 74
Mundell, Meg 60–61
Muñoz, Jose 106
Munro, Alice 31, 36
Murnane, Gerald 4, 272–85, 323

narrative voice 76, 145, 150,
  186–87, 331–35
Natural Way of Things, The 3–4,
  112–24
Nayar, Pramod K 81–82
New South Wales 9, 222, 246,
  248–50, 323
Newman, Sandra 73
Ng, Lynda 91
Nita May Dobbie Award 10
Nolan, Maggie 19, 25
Noonuccal, Oodgeroo 12
Northern Territory Intervention
  327
novelists 13–14, 24–25, 72, 125,
  130, 139, 158, 207–08, 256–57,
  314, 319–22
novels 31, 35–37, 41, 42, 43–45,
  135–36, 319–22; *see also* fiction

O'Connor, Flannery 185
O'Neill, Ryan 5, 42–55, 227, 357
Only the Animals 77–83, 84, 86
Orwell, George 76, 125–26, 256
Oscar and Lucinda 5, 244–58
Other, the 4, 79, 81–82, 86, 120
Outka, Elizabeth 74

pace 146–47, 171, 177–78
pandemics *see* AIDS; COVID-19;
  plague
Patrić, A.S. 3, 286–96, 356
Pelaud, Isabelle Thuy 201
Perth 210
Pham, Hoa 3, 193–206, 356
photographs 269–70
place 88–99, 109–10, 249
plague 56, 58–60, 68–69, 73, 290;
  see also COVID-19
playfulness 16–19, 25
poetry 34, 99, 105, 129, 213, 221,
  226–27, 291–92, 330

point of view 49, 142–46, 148, 169–71, 224–25
Polites, Peter 6, 100–11, 356
Portable Curiosities 297–98, 307–08, 312–13
Prose, Francine 1

Queensland 7–9
queer literature 8, 100–11

Ransom 3, 104–07, 286–96
Rawson, Jane 3, 56–74, 356
reading 18, 21–23, 163, 259–71, 311
  and boredom 274
  connection to writing 1, 134–35, 265–66, 274–75
  and expectations 273
  and noticing 277–79
  pleasure of 4, 13–16, 19, 139
  as a writer 2–3, 325–43
Renes, Cornelis Martin 342
repetition 178, 179–80, 181, 270, 284–85, 337
Rhys, Jean 209
rhythm 20–22, 34, 163, 177–78, 252–54, 291–92, 330
Rich, Adrienne 209
Richardson, Henry Handel 322
Roach, Archie 11
Robinson, Alice 69
Rushdie, Salman 247

Samuelson, Meg 322
satire 297–313
'Satirist rising' 298–302, 303, 305, 307–09, 312–13
Saunders, Mykaela 3, 325–43, 357
Savvides, Irini 6, 259–71, 357
science fiction 43, 47, 66–67; *see also* speculative fiction
Scott, Kim 3, 13–25
Scott, Ronnie 107–11
Second Cure, The 60, 61, 70, 72
sentences
  length 177–78
  structure 177, 251–254
Sentilles, Sarah 119–20
September 11, 2001 287–89
setting 316
Shakespeare, William 146, 247

showing, not telling 27–29, 317
Sixty Lights 6, 259–71
Slap, The 131–32, 135–36
Smith, Justin 310
Snake 4, 219–32
Spargo-Ryan, Anna 4, 75–87, 357
speculative fiction 43, 46–49, 56–74, 304
Stanner, WEH 329
Stead, Christina 323
stories
  Indigenous 326, 329, 331–36
  short 42–55
structure (in fiction) 36, 44–46, 50, 52, 54, 102, 114, 137, 140, 150, 154, 157, 160, 168, 184–92, 195, 198, 209, 219–32, 267, 273, 302, 326, 330, 335, 337; *see also* sentences, structure
Such Is Life 323
Summers, Anne 113
Suzuki, David 328
Swallow the Air 5, 7–12
Swan Book, The 324
Swift, Jonathan 306, 308
Sydney 57, 89, 97–99, 103, 155, 222, 231, 244–46, 248–49, 251, 253–54, 302, 312

Takolander, Maria 4, 84, 207–18, 357
Tasmania 69
teaching 26–27, 299–301
technique 255–56
tense 49, 169–71, 223, 333, 334
tension 167–68, 169–75, 177–78, 181
Things We Didn't See Coming 5, 42–55
This Is How 167, 168, 170, 171, 172, 174, 176–81
thisness 247–48
'three-dimensional yellow man, The' 301–03
Tiffany, Carrie 4, 207–18
time 49–50, 153–63, 165, 187, 190–91, 196, 328, 334, 336–39; *see also* Dreaming; everywhen
Tóibín, Colm 132
'Tourists' 130–31
Treloar, Lucy 57, 59, 64, 67–68

Trespassers, The 60–61, 65
True History of the Kelly Gang, The 250–52
Tsiolkas, Christos 6, 100, 114, 125–36
Tumarkin, Maria 311

Unaipon, David 8, 10
unlikable characters 226

van Loon, Julienne 3, 13–25, 357
van Neerven, Ellen 5, 7–12, 358
Victoria 210, 250, 321
Vietnam 185–90, 193–206
voice 9, 30, 83, 88, 93, 96–99, 102, 110, 141, 144, 191, 195, 207, 211, 222, 223, 225–26, 251–53, 258, 263, 267, 316, 324, 330–35, 342–43; *see also* narrative voice
Voss 104
Vu, Chi 3, 193–206

Walker, Tom 305
Western Australia 13–25, 61
White, Patrick 104, 134–35, 322, 323
Whitman, Walt 98–99
Winch, Tara June 5, 7–12
Winton, Tim 2, 5, 31, 33, 137–51
withholding 171, 175–76
Wolfe Island 57, 59, 64, 67–68
Wood, Charlotte 3–4, 18, 21, 22, 112–24
Wood, James 89, 247
Woolfe, Sue 256–57
words 260, 263
worldbuilding 47–49, 65, 248, 258, 299–300
Wright, Alexis 3, 5, 88, 90–97, 99, 324, 325–43
Wright, Fiona 218
writing 17, 19–20, 22, 23, 54, 119, 125–26, 129, 135, 137–39, 223–25, 256–58, 302, 316–17, 318–19; *see also* fiction; language; novelists; novels; reading

Yahp, Beth 3, 297–313, 358
Yield, The 11

www.ingramcontent.com/pod-product-compliance
Lightning Source LLC
Chambersburg PA
CBHW030918050726
47498CB00003BA/794